BEAUTY, RESPONSIBILITY,
AND POWER

BEAUTY, RESPONSIBILITY, AND POWER
Ethical and Political Consequences of Pragmatist Aesthetics

Edited by

Leszek Koczanowicz and Katarzyna Liszka

Amsterdam - New York, NY 2014

The present scholarly publication was funded, in the period of 2012-2014, by a program of the Polish Ministry of Science and Higher Education under the name of "National Program for the Development of the Humanities.

 **NARODOWY PROGRAM
ROZWOJU HUMANISTYKI**

Cover illustration: *Angel of the North.* Steel sculpture by Anthony Gormley. (20 x 54 metres). Gateshead, Tyne and Wear, England. Photo by David Wilson Clarke.

Cover design: Studio Pollmann

The paper on which this book is printed meets the requirements of "ISO 9706:1994, Information and documentation - Paper for documents - Requirements for permanence".

ISBN: 978-90-420-3879-0
E-Book ISBN: 978-94-012-1162-8
© Editions Rodopi B.V., Amsterdam - New York, NY 2014
Printed in the Netherlands

CONTENTS

Introduction

BEAUTY AND ACTION
Leszek Koczanowicz and Katarzyna Liszka

As we all well know, aesthetics reaches beyond arts and beauty. In his *Art as Experience*, John Dewey shows that aesthetic experience enters all domains of human activity and is actually itself constituted by such activity. Dewey was the first thinker to propose a theoretical conceptualization of this relationship, but an idea of it had of course originated before him and has been developed in various other frameworks after him. Given this wealth and diversity, it would be presumptuous to try to outline here the intricate history of multiple models in which interconnections between aesthetics on the one hand and ethics and politics on the other have been theorized. It is perhaps worthwhile to mention only that impulses to obliterate the boundary between them have sprung both from aesthetics as well as from politics and ethics. Aesthetic theories could hardly remain indifferent toward growingly daring artistic interventions into different domains of social life. And politics, on its part, needs an aesthetic component to integrate social life, which has been increasingly fragmented by the processes of modernity. In its turn, the art of good living has engaged with aesthetics in seeking a stable foothold in the face of decomposition of codified ethical systems.

All these tendencies are expressed in the pragmatist concept of action with experience framed as a certain point in it. Art ceases to be an object of aesthetic contemplation and becomes a stimulus for an ever better understanding of our action and its meanings. What is more, aesthetic experience is not limited to and by what we call art: it permeates all layers of action, transforms it and enriches it. Dewey devoted a whole book to aesthetic experience, but similar motifs can be found in William James and even George Herbert Mead. If, as we remember, social action, which shapes our selves and minds, is crucial in pragmatism, it is clear that aesthetic experience has also its social dimension and value. It imparts a new quality to human interactions, making them fuller and deeper. From the pragmatist point of view, aestheticization of social life is thus neither a vain embellishment nor a tool of manipulation; rather, it is a necessary precondition of the development of democratic society, understood as a society of unfettered communication. Art as a vehicle of social change is central to Richard Rorty's reflection, who emphasizes that aesthetic utopias may become regulatory ideas motivating social change.

This volume contains essays which address the interrelations between aesthetics and ethics-cum-politics in the framework of pragmatist aesthetics. Most of the contributors refer thereby to the model propounded by Richard Shusterman. Following in Dewey's footsteps, Shusterman has elaborated and expanded his concept, adding new dimensions to it. The most important supplement is the idea of aesthetic experience being constituted by our bodiliness. Dewey and other pragmatists realized of course that linking action, experience, and social interaction requires a concept of the body in which all these components could be fused, but for various reasons have never put forward such a concept. In somaesthetics, pragmatism has acquired a new dimension – a fully developed, comprehensive aesthetic theory. The notion of pragmatist aesthetic, introduced into the scholarly discourse by Shusterman, has become a legitimate citizen in the polity of great aesthetic theories. Of course, pragmatist aesthetics is not limited to Dewey's and Shusterman's thought only. It enables a retrospective integration of diverse motifs of pragmatist philosophy and sheds new light on ideas proposed by Peirce, James and Mead. At the same time, pragmatist aesthetics with its essential notion of the body engages in critical dialogue with many key concepts of modernity which locate the body in social and cultural frameworks.

The articles collected in this volume illustrate the complex range of pragmatist aesthetics and its impact on the understanding of crucial issues in social and moral philosophy. Particular contributions address such matters as political dimensions of pragmatist aesthetics (Shusterman, Koczanowicz, Chmielewski), relevance of aesthetic experience to politics and ethics (Pihlström, Ryder, Schauffler), aesthetics as an inalienable dimension of humanism and social hope (Calcaterra, Liszka, Dobrowolski), and the bodily dimension of politics and pragmatism as the art of life (Višňovský, Rings, Krüger). The book offers thus a comprehensive panorama of the ways and fields in which pragmatist aesthetics ties in with vital social and ethical problems of modernity.

The book was made possible by the research grant of the Ministry of Science and Higher Education's "National Program of the Development of the Humanities." With the grant's support, an international team of researchers could explore the theme of "Practicing Pragmatist Aesthetics: Art, Politics, Society." We would like to thank all the authors for their contributions. We are also grateful to Tomasz Zaleśkiewicz, Dean of Wroclaw Faculty of the University of Social Sciences and Humanities, for the institutional support, Emil Višňovský, the editor of the series in which this book appears, and Patrycja Poniatowska for her editorial help.

Part One

POLITICS, COMMUNITY, AND THE CITY

One

SOMAESTHETICS AND POLITICS: INCORPORATING PRAGMATIST AESTHETICS FOR SOCIAL ACTION

Richard Shusterman

1.

Briefly defined as the critical study and meliorative cultivation of the experience and use of one's body as a site of sensory appreciation (*aesthesis*) and creative self-fashioning, somaesthetics emerged from two main philosophical roots. First, it built on pragmatist aesthetics, which emphasizes the active, sentient body as the necessary energetic ground and skilled medium for our capacities of artistic creation and aesthetic appreciation. Second, somaesthetics drew on the ancient idea of philosophy as a meliorative art of living in which the soma (the lived, perceptive, sentient body) must play a formative role because it is the medium for all our experience, perception, and action. The classical philosophical quest for self-knowledge and self-improvement should thus involve somatic self-cultivation.[1]

Modern philosophical ideology tends to view concern for the body as a personal or private involvement and, thus, as a retreat from the social and the political. For example, the influential Marxian theorist Fredric Jameson argues that care for the body concerns only "my individual relationship with my own body (...) and not that very different relationship between myself or my body and other people."[2] The presumption seems to be that somatic attention is inherently private and fiercely individualistic, that the body is somehow essentially hidden from social perception the way that Descartes thought the body is somehow hidden from mental perception while thought is transparent to the mind. However, as *Pragmatist Aesthetics* long ago maintained, "viewing the somatic as essentially private seems itself a problematic piece of bourgeois ideology. Not only is the body shaped by the social, but also it contributes to the social. We can share our bodies and bodily pleasures as much as we share our minds, and they can be as public as our thoughts."[3] In fact, our bodies are often more visible and transparent than our thoughts. It is easier to lie in words than to lie in body language.

Fortunately, other important contemporary social theorists, such as Michel Foucault, Pierre Bourdieu, and the gender theorists inspired by their work, have increasingly urged that seemingly private body matters have a significant social dimension, both being shaped by social factors (including social markings of class and gender) and contributing to the preservation of the society that shapes our somatic subjectivities. Somaesthetics joins these voices, but also adopts another argument linking the personal and the political. This is the ancient Confucian argument for the crucial importance of personal action in the political. The idea is that all good government requires good self-government, and that political action should start with that dimension.

Here is the argument's original and still classic statement in Confucius's *The Great Learning*, referring to the exemplary governing leaders of the past: "Their persons/bodies [*shen*] being cultivated, their families were regulated. Their families being regulated, their states were rightly governed. Their states being rightly governed, the whole kingdom was made tranquil and happy."[4] As the Chinese word *shen* 身 is the character for both the human body and the human person, so the notion of a person's self-cultivation (*xiushen* 修身) clearly includes somatic cultivation. The same idea that the macro-realm of political governance is fundamentally based on the micro-realm of self-governance is also suggested (albeit more on the conceptual level) in Plato's *Republic*, where Socrates argues that the way to understand the right order of justice in the state is by first determining the right governing order of the individual's soul.

Highlighting the political importance of individual agents' efforts is often considered and critiqued by social theorists as the product of our individualistic neoliberal ideology. But we can hardly call Confucianism (or Platonism) an individualistic or liberal political philosophy that privileges the particular person over the group, that emphasizes the self over the social. Confucianism insists rather that the individual self is essentially socially constructed. The particular self is defined by the various social relations that shape it. One is the son of M and F, the student of X, the classmate of Y, the teacher of Z, the father of A and B, the husband of W, and so on. These social roles orient one's self-cultivation and determine the direction of one's self-realization. Self-cultivation is always socially situated, and somatic self-cultivation is significantly shaped by one's social roles and duties. Consider, for example, an argument that Mencius brings for somatic self-care and self-cultivation. Recognizing the primacy of one's duty to one's parents, Mencius maintains that satisfying that duty requires fulfilling a prior trust to one's own body or self. "I have heard of those who, having kept their bodies inviolate, could serve their parents, but not of those who failing to do so, still served their parents. Whichever duty I fail to perform, it must not be my duty to my parents, for that is the duty from which all others spring. Whichever trust I fail to fulfill, it must not be that of keeping my body inviolate, for that is the trust from which others arise."[5] In other words, duties to the self are logically implicated in our duties to others, just as our relations to others essentially define the self.

These reciprocal implications suggest an important pragmatist insight and strategy: the recognition that conventional oppositions are often mere polar points connected by a complex continuity of relations. Just as with nature and culture (or body and mind, or art and life), we can, of course, distinguish the self from society, but we should not petrify this into a rigid dichotomy, because these concepts define and shape each other. As pragmatism is an American philosophy and thus associated with the American traditions of individualism, we should recognize that it is also a philosophy that emphasizes the essentially social character of thought and behavior.

Charles Sanders Peirce fiercely argued against Descartes' epistemological method of basing the criterion of truth on the clearness and distinctness of ideas in the critical consciousness of the individual's mind, insisting rather that truth and knowledge essentially depended on intersubjective, collaborative inquiry and communication. This underlies the pragmatist emphasis on the social. Community is an indispensable medium for the pursuit of better beliefs and fruitful knowledge, and even for the basic achievement of meaning through language and the arts. Social life provides the framework for the transmission and sustenance of culture and language, without which our cognitive, technological, and cultural achievements could not be preserved and advanced. Besides providing for a sharing and critique of alternative viewpoints through which the individual can correct his beliefs, society provides the very contrasts an individual needs to understand herself. Through others, we not only learn a common language to express shared ideas and values and to express our differences from others but we also acquire incentives and instruments to develop ways of thinking, speaking, and acting originally for ourselves.

Echoing Peirce's affirmation of the essential cognitive role of the social, John Dewey also made the social an ethico-political ideal. Because the self, even in its individual self-realization, is a product of social life, the kind of self shaped by rich social engagement and concern for others "will be a fuller and broader self than one which is cultivated in isolation from or in opposition" to them. Yet conversely, Dewey argues that society also benefits from individual free expression. As he puts it, if the individual is robbed of her particular individuality, "the whole social body is deprived of the potential resources that should be at its service."[6] Even William James, the most individualistic of the classical pragmatists, insists that the self is essentially formed by society, arguing that persons are "bundles of habits" and that our habits are socially shaped and are so shaped to keep society going in its established direction.[7]

Habit is thus the enormous fly-wheel of society, its most precious conservative agent. It alone is what keeps us all within the bounds of ordinance, and saves the children of fortune from the envious uprisings of the poor. It alone prevents the hardest and most repulsive walks of life from being deserted by those brought up to tread therein. It keeps the fisherman and the deck-hand at sea through the winter; it holds the miner in his darkness, and nails the countryman to his log-cabin and his lonely farm through all the months of snow; it protects us from invasion by the natives of the desert and the frozen zone. It dooms us all to fight out the battle of life upon the lines of our nurture or our early choice, and to make the best of a pursuit that disagrees, because there is no other for which we are fitted, and it is too late to begin again. It keeps different social strata from mixing. (...) It is well for the world that in most of us, by the age of thirty, the character has set like plaster, and will never soften again.[8]

This does not mean James despaired of social change. He simply realized that the mere formulation of a law or the founding of a new social institution does not entail that people's actual behavior will change, just as he realized how difficult it is for people to change their habits. He, therefore, explored the best ways to form good habits and reform our bad ones, formulating them in some pithy maxims, which he recommended to his readers.

For pragmatism and somaesthetics, it is a grave mistake to think that one must choose between efforts of personal cultivation and social action. There is no reason why a person cannot do both, focusing, alternately, sometimes more on self-improvement and at other times more on wider social reform. Moreover, one can often do both simultaneously. In preparing and giving a speech at a political meeting, one is both cultivating one's writing and oratory skills as well as engaging in meaningful social action. If we put aside the fact that oratory skills are also somaesthetic skills, we could give a more narrowly physical example, such as participating in an athletic event to raise money for some worthy social or political cause.

More generally, as I argue in *Body Consciousness*, by developing one's somatic capacities one can increase one's strength, confidence, poise, and efficacy to engage in social action. I make this argument to counter Simone de Beauvoir's fear that somaesthetic attention is dangerous for women because it distracts them from political engagement and focuses them on private, intimate matters, despite her own recognition that building bodily strength and acquiring more somatic knowledge and mastery can make women more confident and less vulnerable to exploitative manipulation.[9] I do not advocate somaesthetic cultivation as a substitute for broader social action and political engagement but rather postulate it as a means of strengthening our somatic capacities (which include our capacities for courage, endurance, empathetic social perception and nurturing care) so that we are better equipped to engage in social and political struggles.

2.

Pragmatist philosophy highlights the importance of practice, and somaesthetics defines itself as a field of practice and theory, in which two of its major branches – pragmatic and practical somaesthetics – are primarily oriented toward practice. What practical political applications does somaesthetics have? Let me focus on examples already found in the somaesthetic literature, though I expect there will be more examples as the somaesthetic field develops, for it is still a very young field.

Our ethical concepts and norms – along with the social and political institutions that both reflect and reinforce them – depend on social forms of life, including the ways we experience our bodies and the ways that others treat them. As Wittgenstein remarked in a strangely brutal passage of his *Notebooks*: "Mutilate completely a man, cut off his arms & legs, nose & ears, & then see what remains of his self-respect and his dignity, and to what point his concepts of these things are still the same. We don't suspect at all, how these concepts depend on the habitual, normal state of our bodies. What would happen to them if we were led by a leash attached to a ring through our tongues?"[10] Obviously, in such a world the political sense of human rights and the corresponding laws and political institutions governing society would be very different.

Our bodies, moreover, provide an essential medium or tool through which social norms and political power are transmitted, inscribed, and preserved in society. Ethical codes, social and political institutions, and even laws are mere abstractions until they are given life through incorporation into bodily dispositions and actions. As Michel Foucault and Pierre Bourdieu have argued, entire ideologies of domination can be covertly materialized and preserved by encoding them in somatic norms that, as bodily habits, get typically taken for granted and so escape critical consciousness. For example, in societies in which women are expected to speak very softly, walk behind the men, and meet the gaze of men only with bowed heads and lowered eyes, these implicit cultural norms both embody and reinforce such gender oppression. Domination of this subtle sort is especially hard to challenge, since the subjugated bodies have so deeply absorbed it that they themselves revolt against the challenge – as when a young secretary involuntarily blushes, trembles, flinches, or even cries when trying to raise a voice of protest toward someone she has been somatically trained to respect as her superior. Any successful challenge to oppression should thus involve somaesthetic diagnosis of the bodily habits and feelings expressing that domination so that they, along with the oppressive social conditions which generate them, can be overcome.

Somaesthetics can also explain many of our irrational political enmities. I have argued that the fanatical kind of hatred that some people have for certain foreign races, cultures, classes, and nations displays a deep visceral quality, an enmity reflecting profound concerns about the integrity and purity of the familiar body in a given culture.[11] Such anxieties can be unconsciously translated into hostility towards foreigners who challenge that familiar body and threaten to corrupt it through ethnic and cultural mixing that can alter the body in both external appearance and behavior. Rational arguments for multicultural tolerance and peace always seem to fail, because the hatred is acquired not by rational means but through discomforting somatic feelings that, though unpleasant, are often only distractedly or implicitly felt.

Wittgenstein, for example, explains the often rabid anti-Semitism of highly rational European countries in terms of a somatic metaphor and a corresponding somaesthetic feeling. The Jews are felt as a diseased tumor (*Beule*) in Europe. "'Look on this tumor as a perfectly normal part of your body!' Can one do that, to order? Do I have the power to decide at will to have, or not to have, an ideal conception of my body?" he asks, then continues: "Within the history of the peoples of Europe (…) the Jews (…) are experienced as a sort of disease, and anomaly, and no one wants to put a disease on the same level as normal life (…). We may say: people can only regard this tumor as a natural part of the body if their whole feeling for the body changes (or if the whole national feeling for the body changes). Otherwise, the best they can do is *put up with* it." In Wittgenstein's view, "You can expect an individual man to display this sort of tolerance, or else to disregard such things; but you cannot expect this of a nation, because it is precisely not disregarding such things that make it a nation. I.e. there is a contradiction in expecting someone *both* to retain his former aesthetic feeling for his body [*aesthetische Gefühl für seinen Körper*] and *also* to make the tumor welcome."[12]

Even if it is incongruous to expect a person to welcome a tumor while retaining his former aesthetic feeling for the body, this does not mean that the tumor (or the foreign population) must be exterminated. An alternative would be to modify that person's aesthetic feeling for the body and the body politic. Here, somaesthetics' discipline of body consciousness can provide a pragmatic remedy. If racial and ethnic enmity resists resolution through logical means of verbal persuasion because it has a visceral basis of discomforting unfamiliarity, then as long as we do not consciously attend to these deep visceral feelings, we can overcome neither them nor the enmity they generate and foster. Improved body consciousness can help us identify these disturbing somatic sensations so that we can better control, neutralize, or overcome them. Moreover, it can help us transform them through somaesthetic training because they are already a product of training. Such feelings of discomfort from foreign bodies are almost entirely the results of learning or habit rather than an innate instinct; as such they are malleable to efforts of reformation. This is a commonplace of gastronomy, athletics, and somatic therapies; but modern philosophical ethics and political theory have not given it enough attention.

Somaesthetics is helping to initiate a change here, suggesting how sensitizing, consciousness-raising somatic training can deal with issues of racism, sexism, homophobia, and violence.[13] Such somaesthetic consciousness-raising, it has been argued, should not be limited to the awareness of momentary bodily feelings but can include the aesthetics of compelling somatic-oriented genealogical narrative.[14] Because there is an underlying somatic communication in every face-to-face political meeting that pervades and partly shapes the general atmosphere of the meeting and the momentary energies, attitudes, and feelings of the participants, it is important to be able to sense that unarticulated atmosphere somaesthetically and regulate one's bodily behavior accordingly to improve the atmosphere in the desired direction. Negotiations often go much more smoothly and successfully, for example, in pleasurable contexts of dining together, where the atmosphere is friendly, pleasant, and more relaxed, where trust is shared through shared pleasure.[15]

3.

Wittgenstein's analogizing of the Jews to a tumor on the body of Europe recalls the deeply entrenched notion of the body politic as a metaphor for the corporate identity of the nation state (and note how the word "corporate" is likewise a term suggesting embodiment). The metaphor, which also exists in French as *corps-d'état*, is typically extended to view the governing ruler as the head of state, an image concretely rendered in the famous cover of Thomas Hobbes' *Leviathan* showing a body formed of a multitude of citizens on top of which rests the head of a king.[16] The body politic metaphor is likewise extended to frame political dysfunction, disorder, corruption, and conflict in terms of somatic problems, e.g., physical weakness, disease, or disability. Wittgenstein's tumor metaphor is an example of this tradition. Sometimes the body politic metaphor is also read back the other way to render various body parts as hierarchically arranged, depending on their more "aristocratic" status or governing function.[17]

The centrality of this metaphor suggests another way that somaesthetics might be useful for political thinking. Of course, analogizing the nation state to the body carries the evident risks of excusing intolerance for the sake of policing purity on the model of old-fashioned eugenics, but a closer contemporary scientific view of the body reveals that the human body cannot thrive in self-sufficient somatic purity. Most of the cells in the human body are not human at all; foreign bacterial cells in our bodies outnumber our human cells ten to one and provide vital help with basic physiological processes, such as digestion, growth, and self-defense. The body can be likened to a complex ecosystem made up of various subsystems containing trillions of bacteria and other microorganisms inhabiting our skin, genital areas, mouth, and especially intestines.

This image of the body as a system of systems is useful for providing an answer to a dilemma of political critique that has become prominent since postmodernism. The critical attitude has long been thought to require critical distance, and such distance is presumed to require a perspective outside of the object being criticized. Yet in our postmodern globalized world, there seems to be no truly external, autonomous vantage point outside of and detached from the globalized world of politics. But somaesthetics helps challenge this presumption by showing how we can critically examine aspects of our somatic experience without going outside our bodies to some putative detached, disembodied mind. We use a finger to probe a small bump on our face; we use our tongue to discover and remove the traces of food on our upper lip or on our teeth. We discriminate or assess our pain within the painful experience, not only after it has passed and we are, in that sense, beyond or outside it. Beyond these ordinary practices of somatic consciousness, a variety of meditative disciplines are engaged with heightening the soma's conscious critical self-examination. Moreover, even beneath the level of explicit conscious awareness, the soma critically monitors and corrects itself unreflectively through entrenched motor schemas.

In short, somatic self-examination provides a model of immanent critique in which one's critical perspective does not necessitate being entirely outside the situation critically examined but merely requires a reflective perspective on it that is not wholly absorbed in the immediacy of what is experienced; a perspective better described as positionally eccentric (or decentered) rather than as external. Such perspectives can be achieved by efforts of disciplined deliberate attention but also often arise spontaneously through experiences of *somatic dissonance*, in which a disruption in unreflective coordination stimulates a decentered, reflective critical attention to what is going on. Critical somatic consciousness involves some aspects of the soma's complex array of systems examining other aspects of that complexity. In the same way we can explain how individuals pervasively shaped by sociopolitical forces can develop critical social consciousness through internal tensions or coordination breakdowns between diverse ideals embedded in the state's social traditions and actual political practices. Like the individual human body, the political body of a society presents a comprehensive, cohesive, relatively stable system that integrates smaller systems, which cohere but also can function to some degree independently such that its different functioning can sometimes fail to integrate harmoniously and its experienced dissonance can then stimulate critical consciousness. Some of that political dissonance can be experienced in distinctly somatic terms.

4.

A good example of this somatic reaction can be found in the experience of oppressive colonization described so powerfully by Frantz Fanon in *The Wretched of the Earth*, which also exemplifies how even extremely astute thinkers who recognize the somatic dimension of political experience nonetheless fail to theorize it properly so as to articulate a way of thoughtfully using this dimension to advance one's political ends.[18] Fanon repeatedly characterizes the suffering, colonized "native" subject in terms of perpetual muscle tension that comes from colonialism's repressing of the native's freedom and movement and from the native's self-repression in conforming to colonial dictates and stifling his anger and desire to strike out against the colonizing oppressors.

"The native's muscles are always tensed," writes Fanon, because he "is a being hemmed in; apartheid is simply one form of the division into compartments of the colonial world. The first thing which the native learns is to stay in his place, and not to go beyond certain limits. This is why the dreams of the native are always of muscular prowess; his dreams are of action and of aggression (…) he finds he is in a state of permanent tension."[19] This intensified "tonicity of muscles the whole time" disturbs the thought processes and behavior of the colonized subjects, Fanon argues, and indeed generates in a variety of psychosomatic ailments that he (as a trained psychiatrist) outlines at the end of the book. This chronic somatic reaction affects even the intellectual native's thinking and listening powers so that whenever "Western values are mentioned they produce in the native a sort of stiffening or muscular lockjaw."[20]

Rather than having the somaesthetic capacity to reflect on their problems in a relaxed state of body-mind, the natives are overwhelmed by heightened tension, which desperately seeks relief through some sort of explosive bodily experience whether in the outbursts of bloody violence or in the ecstasy of frenzied dance. As Fanon describes it,

> The native's muscular tension finds outlet regularly in bloodthirsty explosions – in tribal warfare, in feuds between sects, and in quarrels between individuals. (…) Tribal feuds only serve to perpetuate old grudges buried deep in the memory. By throwing himself with all his force into the vendetta, the native tries to persuade himself that colonialism does not exist, that everything is going on as before, that history continues. Here on the level of communal organizations we clearly discern the well-known behavior patterns of avoidance. It is as if plunging into a fraternal bloodbath allowed them to ignore the obstacle, and to put off till later the choice, nevertheless inevitable, which opens up the question of armed resistance to colonialism. Thus collective autodestruction in a very concrete form is one of the ways in which the native's muscular tension is set free. All these patterns of conduct are those of the death reflex when faced with danger, a suicidal behavior which proves to the settler (whose existence and domination is by them all the more justified) that these men are not reasonable human beings.[21]

Besides its expression in such pernicious "fratricidal combats," the pent-up muscular tension of the native finds relief in "the emotional outlets of dance and possession by spirits."[22] But these do not help promote the rational search for promising political solutions to the natives' plight. The oppressed natives must develop and deploy a more acute and rational consciousness in order to achieve a better understanding of their political situation and possibilities so that they can unite and channel their energies of violence in a more productive way. Fanon's text suggests a sort of mind-body dualism in which the natives' consciousness lags behind their bodily power and their sense of "the strength of their own muscles," so that their actions are too often governed by "biological decision."[23] Fanon, therefore, regards with suspicion any focus on sports as a tool of confidence building and national pride: "The youth of Africa ought not to be sent to sports stadiums but into the fields and into the schools," so they can learn the productive values of agricultural and intellectual work. "The African politician should not be preoccupied with turning out sportsmen, but with turning out fully conscious men, who play games as well."[24]

Although Fanon's views are extremely insightful, somaesthetics would suggest a corrective here that could be helpful. Sports are wrongly contrasted with consciousness, since surely success in sports requires a conscious knowledge of various rules, strategies, and tactics that govern the playing of games while also developing important rational skills of discipline and order in one's training as well as the rational and volitional skills of channeling one's energy and regulating one's emotions. More generally, a somaesthetic approach would not pit soma against consciousness, since all our perception and thought (as well as all action) is done through the soma which is also our site and medium of consciousness. A somaesthetic approach to the troubled somatic consciousness of colonized subjects would involve developing their reflective, critical awareness of their muscular tensions so that such tensions could be rationally released when they hamper important thought or social processes but also, conversely, intensified and channeled for more effective use when their explosive energy is needed in violent, national struggles. Developing critical mastery over one's muscular tensions and other somatic habits does not mean turning oneself into a purely docile subject with no powerful emotions. We need emotions as well as rationality for good political solutions; solidarity, for example, so important for political action (including political resistance) is not only enhanced by bonds of feeling but is also, in large part, constituted by them.

Solidarity expresses the ideal of fraternal harmony, which in turn suggests the Chinese notion of governing the polis harmoniously by drawing on more basic ideas of family and personal harmony. In Confucian thought, the aesthetic value of harmony and grace is essential both to self-government and broader social government. One governs better through the aesthetics of harmony and attraction than through rigid rules, harsh commandments, and cruel punishments. The Confucian *Analects* underline this point. "The exemplary person (*junzi*) attracts friends through refinement (*wen*), and thereby promotes virtuous conduct (*ren*)."[25] Admirable persons of authority spread virtue by attracting others to emulate their virtuous acts so as to become similarly attractive and admirable. Virtue thus includes an essential aesthetic dimension. Appearances are essential for expressing the proper feelings of virtue – hence the Confucian emphasis that virtuous conduct must include "the proper countenance" or "demeanor," and that aesthetic practices like ritual and music (including the recitation of the classic *Songs*) are crucial for cultivating this proper demeanor of virtue.[26] Another ancient Chinese text likewise insists on the aesthetic value of harmonious unity for a good political state, where the state's unity ultimately derives from the attractively harmonious unity of virtue radiating from its noblest citizens and ultimately from its king. "Where sageness, wisdom, ritual, and music are born is the harmonious combination (...). Being unified you are musical. If there is music there is virtue and a state and its families can arise. King Wen's appearance was like this."[27]

The ancient Chinese idea that somaesthetic attractiveness is important for leadership might seem quaintly outmoded and foreign to Western political thinking. But is it really? Think of how much money and effort is spent on selecting political candidates for their physical attractiveness and personability, and then how much more is further spent on finding ways to make them still more attractive to the voting public. It is foolish for academic political theorists to dismiss these considerations as trivial when their pragmatic effects are so significantly real. It is also wrong to condemn attractiveness as irrelevant to good leadership, even if it is certainly not sufficient for being an effective leader. We surely should condemn the worship of superficial beauty as the key criterion for choosing political leaders, but that does not mean that an attractive style is not beneficial to good governing. Attractiveness (including the attractiveness of somatic style) is more than a matter of visual appearance; it includes habits of action and styles of attractive conduct, which in turn imply behavior that embodies admirable virtues. There is a substantial overlap of ethics and aesthetics that our compartmentalizing modernist logic often obscures, but that the Greek notion of *kalon-kai-agathon* (like the ancient Confucian notion of the five virtues as five beauties) usefully highlights. We speak morally of things being "right," "just," "fair," "fitting," or "appropriate," but all of these terms have clear aesthetic connotations.

Harmony is another word with tonalities that extend from aesthetics to ethics to politics. It is an important value for pragmatist aesthetics and somaesthetics, but it should not be erected as the only or always overriding value. Some harmonies may be experienced as forced and unhappily stifling, as something that suppresses or neutralizes difference and dissent. (Contemporary Chinese Internet slang indeed uses the expression "to be harmonized" in order to indicate being neutralized or forced into conformity). Sometimes a dose of dissonance can usefully add a tonic note of freedom, openness, and change that is both aesthetically and politically positive and promising. One reason my 1992 book *Pragmatist Aesthetics* took "knowledge rap" as its exemplar for an embodied, progressive, and politically engaged popular art was that genre's astute recovery of the positive aesthetic and political values of dissonance – reflected both in its aggressive musical style deploying various techniques of fragmentation and in its belligerent political attitude. The choice was also partly intended to distance my contemporary pragmatist aesthetics sufficiently from Dewey's wonderfully inspiring aesthetics, whose celebration of unity seemed to me too one-sided and not sufficiently nuanced. His praise of art as "a remaking of the experience of the community in the direction of greater order and unity" and his celebration of "the power of music in particular to merge different individualities in a common surrender, loyalty and inspiration" could easily suggest the aesthetic designs of the fascist state, though Dewey wrote the book before the dangerous effects of such surrenders to order and unity were unmistakably visible.[28] Amidst our aesthetic appreciation of social and political harmonies, we should always be sensitive to discordant voices that are being muffled or excluded from expression.

We have seen from Fanon that somaesthetic dissonance or disharmony as expressed in muscle tension can be useful if it is channeled toward political resistance to oppression rather than wasted on "fratricidal combat." Such tension or feelings of disharmony can be better managed and channeled when we have a more perspicuous and critically reflective awareness of them; practical somaesthetic disciplines of body consciousness can provide us that superior awareness and control (where control does not mean suppression). In my practical somaesthetic workshops, I make a point of introducing feelings of disharmony (usually by disrupting – in a safely gentle way, for a brief period, and in a protected environment – our normal sense of bilateral equilibrium) for such aims of heightening somatic awareness. Introducing such disharmonies is cognitively useful for developing a person's perceptual discriminations of differences in his/her body feelings and equilibrium. It is also useful in making us appreciate the lost harmony of equilibrium and the creative challenge of finding a new, perhaps better harmonious balance. There may be a lesson here for politics outside the workshop world. But I cannot explore that idea in this paper; nor can I embark upon the intriguing questions concerning the ethical norms and political values that structure my somaesthetics workshops which create a miniature, temporary social world. I close by at least acknowledging the importance of such issues.

NOTES

1. For an explanation of these roots of somaesthetics, see Richard Shusterman, *Body Consciousness: A Philosophy of Mindfulness and Somaesthetics* (Cambridge: Cambridge University Press, 2008), chap. 1 and "Introduction," *Thinking through the Body: Essays in Somaesthetics* (Cambridge: Cambridge University Press, 2012).
2. Fredric Jameson, "Pleasure: A Political Issue," *The Ideologies of Theory: Essays 1971–1986*, vol. 2. (Minneapolis: University of Minnesota Press, 1988), p. 70.

3. Richard Shusterman, *Pragmatist Aesthetics: Living Beauty, Rethinking Art* (Oxford: Blackwell, 1992), p. 260.
4. James Legge (ed. and trans.), *Confucian Analects, The Great Learning, and The Doctrine of the Mean* (Oxford: Clarendon Press, 1893), p. 266.
5. W.A.C.H. Dobson (ed. and trans.), *Mencius: A New Translation* (Toronto: Toronto University Press, 1969), p. 138, para. 4A20.
6. John Dewey, *Ethics* (Carbondale: Southern Illinois University Press, 1985), p. 302; *The Later Works of John Dewey*, vol. 11, ed. Jo Ann Boyston (Carbondale: Southern Illinois University Press, 1981), p. 219.
7. William James, *The Principles of Psychology* (Cambridge: Harvard University Press, 1983), p. 130.
8. *Ibid.*, p. 125.
9. See the chapter on de Beauvoir in *Body Consciousness*.
10. Ludwig Wittgenstein, *Denkebewegung: Tagebücher 1930–1932, 1936–1937* (Innsbruck: Haymon, 1997), pp. 139–40
11. See Shusterman, *Body Consciousness*, chap. 4.
12. Ludwig Wittgenstein, *Culture and Value*, trans. Peter Winch (Oxford: Blackwell 1980), pp 20–1
13. See David Granger, "Somaesthetics and Racism: Toward an Embodied Pedagogy of Difference," *Journal of Aesthetic Education*, 44 (2010), pp. 69–81; Andrew Fitzgibbon, "Somaesthetics: Body Consciousness and Nonviolence," *Social Philosophy Today*, 23 (2012), pp. 85–9; and my own discussions of these matters in *Body Consciousness* and *Thinking through the Body*.
14. Marjorie Jolles, "Between Embodied Subjects and Objects: Narrative Somaesthetics," *Hypatia*, 27 (2012), pp. 301–18.
15. This is suggested from narratives of some of the more successful Middle-East political negotiations, and we can also find experimental evidence in a recent study on business negotiations, http://blogs.hbr.org/cs/2013/01/should_you_eat_while_you_negot.html.
16. The English indeed distinguished between the king's two bodies — that of his mortal flesh and another of a more abstract and divine character.
17. Friedrich Nietzsche, *Will to Power*, trans. Walter Kauffman and Reginald J. Hollingdale (New York: Random House, 1968), para. 660.
18. Frantz Fanon, *The Wretched of the Earth*, trans. Constance Farrington (New York: Grove Press, 1963).
19. *Ibid.*, p. 52.
20. *Ibid.*, p. 43.
21. *Ibid.*, p. 54.
22. *Ibid.*, p. 58.
23. *Ibid.*, pp. 127, 130.
24. *Ibid.*, p. 196.
25. Roger T. Ames and Henry Rosemont (eds. and trans.), *The Analects of Confucius: A Philosophical Translation* (New York: Ballantine, 1998), p. 12, para. 24.
26. *Ibid.*, p. 1, para. 12; p. 2, para. 8; p. 4, para. 1; p. 4, para. 17; p. 8, para 4; p. 12, para. 24; p. 13, para. 6.
27. I cite from the ancient "Five Aspects of Conduct" as translated in Kenneth W. Holloway, *Guodian: The Newly Discovered Seeds of Chinese Religious and Political Philosophy* (Oxford: Oxford University Press, 2009), p. 136.
28. John Dewey, *Art as Experience*, in *The Later Works of John Dewey*, vol. 10, ed. Jo Ann Boydston (Carbondale: Southern Illinois University Press, 1987), pp. 87,

338. For my criticism of Dewey's one-sided emphasis on unity (including its political dangers), see Richard Shusterman, "Pragmatism and East-Asian Thought," *The Range of Pragmatism and the Limits of Philosophy*, ed. Richard Shusterman (Oxford: Blackwell, 2004), pp. 13–42. Dewey seems more sensitive to the dangers of totalitarianism in his later work of 1939, *Freedom and Culture* reprinted in *The Later Works of John Dewey*, vol. 13, ed. Jo Ann Boydston (Carbondale: Southern Illinois University Press, 1988, pp. 69–72), where he is critical of totalitarianism as expressed both in Nazi Germany and Stalinist Russia.

Two

EMBODIED COMMUNITIES

Leszek Koczanowicz

"We commune with bodies only to encounter specters," as someone intimated, trying to define the ends of philosophy. The maxim undeniably conveys a certain truth. Social and political philosophy, and also political sciences, tend to look into politics as if they were analyzing a game of chess, in which the shape of the pieces were entirely irrelevant both to the course and to the final outcome of the game. Instead, what really matters to them is a sequence of disembodied moves which might as well be unfolding in the observer's mind. In this way, politics is reduced to an intricate game of shadows, to a reflection in "a wilderness of mirrors," to use T. S. Eliot's phrasing, in which all references to the actual, physical realities of the social are slowly, but surely, vanishing. Whatever it is that the really existing society creates disappears and, together with it, the bodily investment that has its part both in the construction and in the destruction of social life is dissolved.

To explore the various reasons behind this disembodied thinking about society is unfeasible here, be it because their genealogy reaches far back into a very distant past. Yet we should at least point out some factors which have contributed to such a purely spiritual account of the social. Prominent among them is Western culture's pervasive dualism, which has dominated reflection on man and society for the last two thousand years. As the bodily became subordinated to the ideal, political discourses focused on the idea, ousting the tangibilities of the body from their field of inquiry. If they feature the body at all, they usually relegate it to the symbolic or mythical realm. When in his seminal doctrine of "the King's two bodies" Ernst Kantorowicz describes the complicated network of relationships between the monarchs's real, live body and his immortal, legal body, it is clear that the symbolic, immortal body prevails over the physical, mortal one. Evidently, even if the idea of sovereignty is embodied, as was the case in the political doctrine of feudalism, embodiment as such mutates into doctrinal symbolism. "The individual king may die; but the King who represents sovereign Justice and was represented by the supreme judges, was not dead; he continued his jurisdiction ceaselessly through the agency of his officers even though his natural body had passed away."[1]

After the theological justifications of sovereignty were discarded, or at least undercut, bodiliness still lingered at the backstage of politics. In Thomas Hobbes's *Leviathan*, undoubtedly one of the founding texts of modern political thought, the realities of human existence are largely consigned to an artificial construct of "the state of nature." In famous passages depicting the nature of man and a resultant war of all against all, Hobbes sketches a very palpable image of human behaviors: "Nature hath made men so equal in the faculties of body and mind, as that, though there be found one man sometimes manifestly stronger in body, or of quicker mind than another, yet when all is reckoned together, the difference between man, and man is not so considerable, as that one man can thereupon claim to himself any benefit, to which another may not pretend, as well as he. For as to the strength of body, the weakest has strength enough to kill the strongest, either by secret machination or by confederacy with others that are in the same danger with himself."[2] In this perspective, the social contract, which leads to the creation of the state, seems to be another victory of the soul over the body. While not entirely amenable to reason, human nature can certainly be harnessed by it, and the reasoned power of the state makes people feel secure even though it breaches their freedom. The body submits thus to the soul, and the social contract produces "a community of fear."

Blaise Pascal seems to have been Hobbes's only near contemporary to realize how powerful the bodily habits are and how deeply they affect the formation of society. "How few things are demonstrated! (...) Custom provides our strongest and most firmly believed proofs. It inclines the automaton, which drags the mind unconsciously with it. Who has demonstrated that it will dawn tomorrow and that we shall die? And what is more believed? It is, then, custom that persuades us, that makes so many Christians; it is custom that makes them Turks, heathens, professions, soldiers, etc."[3] Pascal grasps what so many political theorists have failed to recognize, that is, that our attitudes and pronouncements are shaped beyond our reason, and that our decisions are made before we become aware of them. He can demonstrate both how we are fashioned, but also how we can fashion ourselves. On the one hand, society influences us by regulating our bodies-automata through customs, while on the other, our will enables us to perform the same operations on ourselves that custom performs on us. Our bodies and the ways in which we act upon them – that is, practices and *technologies of the self*, to use Michel Foucault's coinage – are *loci* of the forces that affect the mind. The Pascalian vision of politics, and social life as such, represents these domains as a site of whimsical and contingent choices which are dictated by a habit and external coincidental conjunctures ("My friend, you were born on this side of the mountain; it is therefore right that your older brother should have everything.")[4] If so, it is highly doubtful whether "practicing politics" as a conscious engagement is at all viable. With the contingent nature of politics impossible to resist or oppose, man can only pursue spiritual self-development and seek liberation from randomness in other realms. Also, attainment of truth is precluded in social life; it can be found only through inner search for certainty. Mystical though it may sound, Pascal differs from the mystics in that he appreciates, as mentioned above, the impact of habit on the perpetuation of certainty arrived at by reasoning or by heart. What is it then that possibly remains in the social except the chaos of habits? A kind of "habit management," perhaps, making sure that politics opens up a space in which an individual transformation can take place.

Nevertheless, "the community of customs," implied in Pascal's considerations, seems to be an idea capable of re-directing thinking about politics and its identitary dimension. The community's identity, namely, is here posited as rooted in bodily habits and not in abstract ideas. Unfortunately, we can see in retrospect that Pascal's voice has not resonated effectively in social philosophy.

On the contrary, with the onset of the dominant Enlightenment thought, when community became both a theoretical and a practical issue, the theme immediately turned into a battlefield of Enlightenment's slogans of equality, freedom, and fraternity, on the one hand, vying against the counter-Enlightenment reflection with its idea of collective and group identities being anchored in a nation's culture, on the other. The counter-Enlightenment thought posits community as constituted by cultural values shared by all its members and translated into the sense of identity by means of language. The national language is ascribed a special role as an expression of cultural instances. Originating in Hamann and Herder, the idea was elaborated on by Wilhelm von Humboldt. The contemporary philosopher Charles Taylor, who clearly builds on this tradition, encapsulates the concept of language developed by Hamann, Herder, and Humboldt as "the locus of different kinds of disclosure. It makes us aware of the expressive dimension and its importance. And it allows us to identify a constitutive dimension, a way in which language does not only represent, but enters into some of the realities it is 'about.'"[5] Obviously, identification with the nation has its bodily manifestations, customs, and rituals, which ever since Herder have been meticulously studied by ethnographers. Yet, these bodily dimensions of communality are supposed to gesture toward its originary conditions to be found in language as a vehicle of and for values.

Toward the end of the 19th century, the community of values expressed in language was gradually being supplanted by the community of "blood and soil" (*Blut und Boden*). The gruesome effects of the ideology of a nation as a biological community have effectively undone thinking in terms of an embodied community. As if naturally, an embodied community was pitted against a cultural community, and the very concept of community came to be seen as an opposite of society in a liberal democracy founded upon the primacy of free, autonomous individuals over any kind of collective identity forms.

Of course, when we examine these issues historically, we are bound to come across multiple cases in which the two community types intersect or overlap. The adherents of the biological notion have discerned analogies between liberal politics and a decomposition of hereditary traits in individuals. For example, Francis Galton, in one of his programmatic texts, explained a dispersal of hereditary traits in siblings in the following way:

The great dissimilarity frequently observed between brothers or sisters is to be accounted for and easily illustrated by a political metaphor. We have to recognise, on the one hand, that the stirps of the brothers and sisters must have been nearly alike, because the germs are simple organisms, and all such organisms breed true to their kind, and on the other hand, that very different structures have been developed out of those stirps. A strict analogy and explanation of all this is afforded by the well-known conditions and uncertainties of political elections. We have abundant experience that when a constituency is very varied, trifling circumstances are sufficient to change the balance of parties, and therefore, although there may be little real variation in the electoral body, the change in the character of its political choice at successive elections may be abrupt. A uniform constituency will always elect representatives of a uniform type; and this result precisely corresponds to what is found to occur in animals of pure breed, whose stirp contains only one or a very few varieties of each species of germ, and whose offspring always resemble their parents and one another. The more mongrel the breed, the greater is the variety of the offspring.[6]

Although such remarks, scattered across Galton's writings, shed light on his specific engagement with social issues, they do not determine to what extent the concept of eugenics, which he invented and promoted, is to be blamed for all the crimes perpetrated in his name. Similar motifs, namely, emerged also in entirely different ideological contexts.[7] Undoubtedly, however, the ideologies of national or racial purity, which had ensued from interpretations of findings of biological sciences, validated radical exclusion from the national community of individuals who, by the standards of these ideologies, did not deserve to belong to the community on the grounds, precisely, of their biological attributes. In her poem about the Holocaust in Poland titled "Still," Wisława Szymborska captures this conjunction in a most dramatically condensed form:

Let your son have a Slavic name,
for here they count hairs on the head,
for here they tell good from evil
by names and by eyelids' shape[8]

In this light, it is hardly surprising that the body as a vehicle of community has long been shunned by social theorists. A dread of an embodied idea converged with and was reinforced by the prevalence of structuralist frameworks in the humanities and social sciences. Ferdinand de Saussure's linguistic concepts, in which language is perceived as a structure of binary opposites, have been triumphantly transplanted onto the thinking about society. The political sphere, in turn, is suffused with injunctions to champion liberalism with its concept of an autonomous, free individual as the groundwork of society's political organization. The body as a theoretically developed category is not a piece which would fit into this jigsaw puzzle. This, of course, does not mean that the issues of bodiliness are absent from the discourse on society. Bodiliness appears at the heart of Maurice Merleau-Ponty's phenomenology and in cultural psychoanalysis, features prominently in Herbert Marcuse's thought, and is central to Helmuth Plessner's philosophical anthropology. Each of these concepts deserves a thorough discussion, which is however beyond the scope of this paper. All these very different theories seem to share a focus on the concrete and an attempt to expose the bodily core of all ideologies and, thus, to reveal their true content. A contemporary social theorist would in all probability be highly inspired by Helmuth Plessner's concepts. In his early study *The Limits of Community*, Plessner emphasizes that "one can love only something individual that stands before one in concrete form and, reaching through it, then grasp hold of something general. What does it mean when I love my people, land, humanity, the world? It means to have an intention to love that does not need to be cooler than a sincere erotic impulse."[9] However, his commentators show that community understood in this way is inevitably doomed to a perpetual inner conflict between the concrete and real, on the one hand, and the general and, in a way, illusory, on the other.[10]

The potential of conflict inherent in society is highlighted also by Herbert Marcuse. In his reading, Freud's analysis is intrinsically political since "the psychoanalytic categories do not have to be 'related' to social and political conditions – they are themselves social and political categories. Psychoanalysis could become an effective social and political instrument, positive as well as negative, in an administrative as well as critical function, because Freud had discovered the mechanisms of social and political control in the depth dimension of instinctual drives and satisfactions."[11] Of course, psychoanalysis conceives of bodiliness in a very particular way which does not offer much opportunity of developing an embodied community. Psychoanalysis posits rather a highly intricate relationship in which an individual is a "site" onto which society inscribes its rules. In his analysis of the Freudian concept of mass and crowd, Stefan Jonsson stresses that "in psychoanalytic theory, society is present within the subject from the outset, and it is society that enables the subject to become a conscious individual."[12] Given the complicated history of psychoanalysis, we should rather conclude that the body becomes in it a sign, or a symbol, rather than a real object which affects the physical and social world. A psychoanalytical community is founded upon repression mechanisms, which control and curb the primal bodily drives. Drawing on psychoanalysis, Herbert Marcuse formulated his concept of libidinal revolution that strives to create a utopian community free from repression. However, contemporary social theory has been far more affected by Jacques Lacan, who locates the body in the imaginary represented by the mirror stage and insists on its utter symbolization in the successive stages.

Many of the doubts and queries that haunt the concepts of the body referred to above are inspiringly responded to by pragmatism. Always foregrounding the body and its habits, the pragmatist tradition offers a fertile ground for theorizing bodiliness. And there are several reasons for that. First, pragmatism has been part of the anti-dualist, anti-Cartesian movement. William James, for example, attempted to overcome Cartesian dualism in his work. He put the sentient body at the center of his thought although he was not able to show convincingly that ways in which the body influences mental activity. This residual dualism, which plagued his psychology, can be accounted for partly by underdeveloped neuroscience and partly by the dominance of introspectionism, which held him in its thrall even though he mutinied against it somehow.

Second, the next generation of pragmatists, including John Dewey and George Herbert Mead, argued that the self emerges from interactions among cooperating individuals. Hence, they stressed that our ethical obligations arise from bodily cooperation, and we are able to take ever broader groups into our selves. George Herbert Mead's concept of taking the role of the other and embracing the standpoint of the increasingly generalized other is the most impressive elaboration on bodily cooperation as a cornerstone of the social bond to be found in contemporary philosophy.

Third, they (especially John Dewey) developed the concept of the experiential body as the core notion of their philosophy. This concept has two dimensions. On the one hand, Mead and Dewey showed the impact of our biological endowment on the development of mental faculties. In his famous lectures published as *Mind, Self, and Society*, Mead argues that our human selves have evolved from a biologically grounded exchange of gestures. On a specifically human level, communication is carried out by means of meaningful gestures, that is, through significant symbols. Gestures acquire meaning when an individual who performs them reacts in the same way as an individual to whom they are addressed. This allows both the co-ordination of actions among individuals and behavioral self-control.[13] The pragmatists' appreciation of the body, however, is hardly limited to the genetic aspects of the human self and mind. Dewey devotes a lot of attention to the body as a vehicle of experience. Since experience is for him the most important factor in the construction of knowledge, Dewey, by the same token, assumes that the body is of paramount importance in acquiring knowledge of the external world.

In the pragmatist tradition, it is Richard Shusterman who has developed a consistent concept of the body as a vehicle of human emancipation. He draws on classical pragmatism and, in particular, on Dewey's work. In his essay on Dewey's concept of the body, "Redeeming Somatic Reflection: John Dewey's Philosophy of Body-Mind," Shusterman traces the roots and defines the contemporary significance of Dewey's thought. He emphasizes that Dewey developed his theory of the body not only through philosophical speculation but also through a close scrutiny of scientific findings and personal engagement with Alexander's technique for improving the functioning of the body.[14] Shusterman recognizes flaws inherent in Dewey's concept of the body and, consequently, the expediency of correction. I am not going to examine in detail Shusterman's account of Dewey's philosophy of the body here, noting only that he discerns a troubling dilemma in Dewey's thought:

> Here then is the core practical dilemma of body consciousness: We must rely on unreflective feelings and habits – because we can't reflect on everything and because such unreflective feelings and habits always ground our very efforts of reflection. But we also cannot entirely rely on them and the judgments they generate, because some of them are considerably flawed and inaccurate. Moreover, how can we discern their flaws and inadequacy when they are concealed by their unreflective, immediate, habitual status; and how can we correct them when our conscious, reflective efforts of correction spontaneously rely on the same inaccurate, habitual mechanisms of perception and action that we are trying to correct?[15]

In the quoted text, Shusterman does not provide a definitive answer to this query, but he hints that despite technological developments we are still heavily dependent on our bodies, which are in turn enmeshed in our social and cultural practices.

> Despite our evolutionary progress of rational transcendence (including the technological advancements that some regard as rendering us posthuman cyborgs), we still essentially and dependently belong to a much wider natural and social world that continues to shape the individuals we are (including our reasoning consciousness) in ways beyond the control of our will and consciousness. As oxygen is necessary for the functioning of consciousness in the brain, so the practices, norms, and language of society are necessary materials for our processes of reasoning and evaluation. It is not moral perfectionism but blind arrogance to think otherwise.[16]

Seeking inspiration for his research, Shusterman resorts to the Eastern philosophies of Confucius and Mencius, showing that they vividly depict the close interdependence between the progress of our mental faculties and the state of our bodies. All these diverse sources share one important conviction, namely that the more we focus on the body, the more we realize that the body cannot be considered in separation from the environmental contexts, both natural and social, in which it develops and progresses. Therefore, the training aimed to perfect our bodies can both improve our relationship with the outer world and enhance our self-understanding. Shusterman concludes that:

By enabling us to feel more of our universe with greater acuity, awareness, and appreciation, such a vision of somaesthetic cultivation promises the richest and deepest palate of experiential fulfillments because it can draw on the profusion of cosmic resources, including an uplifting sense of cosmic unity. Enchanting intensities of experience can thus be achieved in everyday living without requiring violent measures of sensory intensification that threaten ourselves and others. And if we still prefer more dangerous psychosomatic experiments of extreme intensity, our somaesthetically cultivated sensory awareness should render us more alert to the imminent risks and also more skilled in avoiding or diminishing the damage.[17]

In his subsequent books and papers, Shusterman repeatedly shows how various practices of the body can contribute to the amelioration of our lives. In recent years, he has developed the concept of a new discipline which he calls "somaesthetics." In the "Introduction" to his latest book *Thinking through the Body*, Shusterman writes:

Beyond reorienting aesthetic inquiry, somaesthetics seeks to transform philosophy in a more general way. By integrating theory and practice through disciplined somatic training, it takes philosophy in a pragmatic meliorist direction, reviving the ancient idea of philosophy as an embodied way of life rather that a mere discursive field of abstract theory.[18]

Therein he shows that throughout the history of Western philosophy, starting from antiquity through Christianity to most contemporary philosophies, the body has been neglected and denied validity as a subject of philosophical reflection. It serves primarily as a contrasting backdrop against which the mind – the real locus of specifically human personhood, consciousness, creativity, and the like – is considered. Shusterman acknowledges the iconic status of the body in contemporary culture, but admonishes at the same time that in this context it is pervasively treated an object to be displayed to others. He counteracts such approach to the body, advocating the idea of the body as a vehicle of melioristic human emancipation:

Somatic self-consciousness in our culture is excessively directed toward a consciousness of how one's body appears to others in terms of entrenched societal norms of attractive appearance and how one's appearance can be rendered more attractive in terms of these conventional models. (And these same conformist standards likewise impoverish our appreciation of the richly aesthetic diversity of other bodies than our own.) Virtually no attention is directed toward examining and sharpening the consciousness of one's actual bodily feelings and actions so that we can deploy such somatic reflection to know ourselves better and achieve a more perceptive somatic self-consciousness to guide us toward better self-use.[19]

Developing Shusterman's concept will allow us to outline, at least in broad lines, a framework of embodied communities – of what they are and how they function. Their most salient feature is, perhaps, their concreteness. The body abhors abstraction, it is always immersed in the physical reality and, therefore, it always refers to the material. Hence, as Plessner notices, embodied communities are rather small, medium-sized at best. They bind us to those closely familiar to us, both the loved and the loathed ones, with the emotions they evoke ensuing from immediate experiences rather than from abstract, ideological speculations.

Such a model of an immediate embodied community definitely needs a supplement. That could be provided by anthropologically, sociologically or even neurophysiologically grounded accounts which indicate that the body is a site onto which society inscribes its norms and rules. In his habitus theory, Pierre Bourdieu underscores that "the habitus is necessity internalized and converted into a disposition that generates meaningful practices and meaning-giving perceptions; it is a general, transposable disposition which carries out a systematic, universal application – beyond the limits of what has been directly learnt – of the necessity inherent in the learning conditions. That is why an agent's whole set of practices (or those of a whole set of agents produced by similar conditions) are both systematic, inasmuch as they are the product of the application of identical (or interchangeable) schemes, and systematically distinct from the practices constituting another life-style."[20] We could imagine a community of habitus or a community of somatic styles, to use Shusterman's category, as a community whose members are more unified by particular ways in which they use their bodies than by values and norms which their language expresses. And we could still argue that such a community would anyway be based on values, values which are engraved in and enacted by bodies.

I believe, nonetheless, that specific bodily practices are something more than a simple reflection of acknowledged values expressed in language. There are good reasons to think so. As bodily experiences often cannot be conveyed in language, embodied communities do not necessarily overlap with linguistically constituted communities. Feminist thinkers have employed this argument to undercut the communitarian concept of a community, pointing out that differences in women's experiences depending on their distinct cultural contexts do not preclude the formation of women's community. A similarly conspicuous example is provided by sexual minorities. However, these are by no means the only instances of the solidarity of bodily experiences we could refer to. Suggestive examples of embodied communities produced by mechanisms of oppression are analyzed by Michel Foucault in his *Discipline and Punish*, which focuses on how repression and subjugation shape bodies and make them docile.

It is by no means coincidental that such groups develop their own cultures which rely on bodily practices rather than on the language of values for articulation of their fundamental mechanisms. The gamut of these practices tends to be very comprehensive, starting from particular modes of using the body and ending with unique ways of modifying it by self-mutilation and/or tattooing. Foucault distinguished a special group of body-focused practices which "permit individuals to effect by their own means or with the help of others a certain number of operations on their own bodies and souls, thoughts, conduct, and way of being, so as to transform themselves in order to attain a certain state of happiness, purity, wisdom, perfection, or immortality."[21] He dubbed them as *technologies of the self*. Technologies of the self enable individuals to resist and oppose the pressures exerted by power by reversing the forces that affect them and deploying them in and for self-creation. The emancipatory dimension inherent in technologies of the self is curbed, however, because the body still remains a site of fixture between the subject and power. While not entirely vulnerable to pressures from outside, individuals and their actions are still constrained by external conditions.

In his polemic with Foucault, Shusterman insists that bodily practices can indeed have an emancipatory potential: engaging in them, people improve their lives and acquire skills which allow them to expand their perception and knowledge. If we build on Shusterman's conception, we can speak of emancipatory embodied communities in which shared bodily practices serve such meliorist ends. But saying this, we must at the same time inquire if it is legitimate to call a group of people who share bodily practices a community.

The bonds among the members of embodied communities may indeed be fleeting and linguistically ungraspable. Consequently, embodied communities of experience are not necessarily enduring or long-lasting. They arise by a confluence of particular emotions or sensations. The crowd is a classical illustration of such a community. In his pioneering work, Gustave Le Bon describes the crowd as a collection of individuals such that: "under certain given circumstances, and only under those circumstances, an agglomeration of men presents new characteristics very different from those of the individuals composing it. The sentiments and ideas of all the persons in the gathering take one and the same direction, and their conscious personality vanishes. A collective mind is formed, doubtless transitory, but presenting very clearly defined characteristics."[22] Much of what has traditionally been described in categories of crowd or mass could effectively be rendered in terms of the body. A helpful framework for such an enterprise is to be found in the James-Lange theory of the origin of emotions, which explains them in terms of realization that certain processes have taken place in our bodies. Interpreted in such terms, the crowd becomes a *temporary* community of emotion. Such a community, admittedly, can rapidly disperse into individuals, but it may also initiate a more permanent social movement in which a community aware of its values and norms comes into being.

NOTES

1. Ernst Kantorowicz, *The King's Two Bodies: A Study in Mediaeval Political Theology* (Princeton: Princeton University Press, 1997), p. 418.
2. Thomas Hobbes, *Leviathan, Parts I and II, Revised Edition*, eds. Aloysius P. Martinich and Brian Battiste (Peterborouhg: Broadview Press, 2010), p. 121.
3. Blaise Pascal, *Pensées*, trans. and ed. Roger Ariew (Indianapolis: Hacket Publishing, 2005), p. 202.
4. *Ibid.*, p. 8.
5. Charles Taylor, "Theories of Meaning," *Philosophical Papers: Human Agency and Language*, vol. 1 (Cambridge: Cambridge University Press, 1985), p. 273.
6. Francis Galton, "A Theory of Heredity," *The Journal of the Anthropological Institute of Great Britain and Ireland*, 5 (1876), pp. 329–48.
7. Patrick Parrinder, "Eugenics and Utopia: Sexual Selection from Galton to Morris," *Utopian Studies*, 8:2 (1997), pp. 1–12.
8. Wislawa Szymborska, "Still," *Sounds, Feelings, Thoughts*, trans. and eds. Magnus J. Krynsky and Robert A. Maguire (Princeton: Princeton University Press, 1981), p. 23.
9. Helmuth Plessner, *The Limits of Community: A Critique of Social Radicalism*, trans. Andrew Wallace (New York: Humanity, 1999), p. 88.
10. Andreas Hess, "Against Unspoilt Authenticity: A Re-appraisal of Helmuth Plessner's *The Limits of Community*," *Irish Journal of Sociology*, 16:2 (2007), pp. 11–26
11. Herbert Marcuse, *Five Lectures: Psychoanalysis, Politics, and Utopia,* trans. Jeremy J. Shapiro and Shierry M. Weber (Boston: Beacon Press, 1970), p. 44.
12. Stefan Jonsson, *Crowds and Democracy: The Idea and Image of the Masses from Revolution to Fascism* (New York: Columbia University Press, 2013), p. 123.
13. Cf. George Herbert Mead, *Mind, Self and Society: From the Standpoint of a Social Behaviorist*, ed. Charles W. Morris (Chicago: Chicago University Press 1959), p. 69.
14. Cf. Richard Shusterman, *Body Consciousness: A Philosophy of Mindfulness and Somaesthetics* (Cambridge: Cambridge University Press, 2008), pp. 180–216.
15. *Ibid.*, p. 212.
16. *Ibid.*, p. 214.
17. *Ibid.*, p. 216.
18. Richard Shusterman, *Thinking through the Body: Essays in Somaesthetics* (Cambridge: Cambridge University Press, 2012), p. 3.
19. Shusterman, *Body Consciousness*, p. 6.
20. Pierre Bourdieu, *Distinction: A Social Critique of the Judgment of Taste,* trans. Richard Nice (Cambridge: Harvard University Press, 1984), p. 186.
21. Michel Foucault, "Technologies of the Self," *Technologies of the Self: A Seminar with Michel Foucault*, eds. Luther H. Martin, Huck Gutman and Patrick H. Hutton (Amherst, MA: University of Massachusetts Press, 1988), p. 17.
22. Gustave Le Bon, *The Crowd: A Study of the Popular Mind* (The Floating Press, 2009), p. 26.

Three

OSTENTATION AND AGORAPHOBIA IN THE CITY

Adam Chmielewski

The purpose of this paper is to sketch out a conception of urban political aesthetics aimed to demonstrate a continuing relevance of philosophy to understanding the city. I shall attempt to show in particular that the political aesthetics outlined here may shed some new light on the problem of urban aesthetics of absence, the concept introduced to urban studies by Richard Shusterman. I argue that the tendency of individuals to withdraw from the present urban spaces, constituting a form of public agoraphobia, is encouraged by the processes of commodification which fuel rapid transformations of the city. I also stress that increasing the levels of sophistication, required of individuals in order to participate in contemporary urban life, generates a phenomenon of interpassivity which adversely affects the civic agency of urban citizens.

1. Philosophy and the City

Plato's *Phaedrus* is his only dialogue set outside the city walls. Socrates is taken for a walk to the countryside by young Phaedrus, who hopes to discuss the matters of love with him. On their way, Phaedrus notices that Socrates, though knowledgeable about mythical events which are said to have happened in various locations around the city of Athens, is rather unfamiliar with its actual vicinity. He comments: "anyone would take you (...) for a stranger being shown the country (...) never leaving town to cross the frontier nor even, I believe, so much as setting foot outside the walls."[1] Begging for forgiveness, Socrates famously responds: "I am a lover of learning, and the trees and open country won't teach me anything, whereas men in the town do,"[2] adding that the reason he agreed to a countryside walk instead of strolling the city streets is the wisdom he hopes to learn from the speeches which Phaedrus promised to present to him. This passage signifies the humanistic turn in philosophy, which in fact had been effected earlier through the Sophistic opposition between *physis* and *nomos*, the laws of nature and the laws established by human communities. In this Platonic dialogue, the opposition between natural and civilized forms of life is employed in order to endorse the values which may only be cultivated in a city.

As a matter of historical fact, philosophy rarely left the city, also in the sense that it rarely left the city outside the scope of its interest. Plato devoted himself to designing a perfect city-state; Aristotle saw in the city the highest form of political organization.[3] Protagoras, a leading figure of the pragmatically oriented Sophistic movement, drafted a constitution for the city of Thurii. The significance of philosophy for understanding the city may also be seen from the vast philosophical utopian literature aimed at formulating idealized visions of the perfect and just urban life.[4] Philosophers have also expressed negative opinions about the city; a critical approach towards the existing forms of urbanism, formulated by Rousseau, has inspired numerous dystopian visions of urban life and the establishment of an outspoken movement of the intellectual and political anti-urbanism.[5]

The general aim of this paper is to outline a conception of urban political aesthetics which demonstrates a continuing relevance of philosophy to understanding the city. More specifically, I shall attempt to show that the political aesthetics in question may shed some new light upon the problem of the urban aesthetics of absence, i.e. a theme developed by the pragmatist philosopher Richard Shusterman[6] in his criticism of Georg Simmel's seminal paper on mental life in the metropolis,[7] and inspired by Richard Sennet's[8] urban studies as well as Walter Benjamin's[9] aesthetic writings. In particular, I shall argue that mental and political withdrawal of individuals from the active participation in urban life, which I interpret as a form of public agoraphobia, is engendered, among others, by the processes of commodification which encroach upon ever new spheres of human life, and by the phenomenon of interpassivity, which increasingly supplants the traditional, direct relationships among individuals and encourages vicarious modes of relationships among them. I also argue that these processes and phenomena are both results and causes of rapid transformations of contemporary city, while these transformations find expressions in, and are identified by, aesthetic characteristics specific to them.

2. The Urban Dynamics

As a form of organization of social life and satisfaction of human needs, the city consistently demonstrates its remarkable effectiveness and resilience. Despite many negative aspects of urban life, cities remain compellingly attractive as a form of human cooperation. This is evidenced by the rapidity of the urbanization processes which have been particularly intense during the past two centuries. In 1800, only two cities in the world were inhabited by one million of people or more; in 1900, there were 17 such cities; in 1950 – 86; whereas in 2000 – 387. In 1800, the average size of the largest one hundred cities was 187 thousand people; in 1900 – 725 thousand; in 1950 – 2.2 million; whereas in 2000 it reached 6.3 million people.[10] In 1900, only 13 per cent of the world population lived in the cities; over the 20th century the number of cities-dwellers increased tenfold: in 2007 the urban population exceeded the population living in rural areas. The urban population now exceeds 3 billion and is equal to the whole world population in 1960.

The global urbanization process is an effect of the concentration of the production of goods and services in urban centers, which turns cities into economic powers on their own.[11] To illustrate this point one should observe that in the 20th century the GNP produced in cities exceeded the GNP of the rural territories; the volume of the urban GNP accounts now for 80 per cent of the global product, while in the developed countries it amounts to 85 per cent of GNP. The forecasts for the decades to come suggest that the urban dynamics will be even more intensive.[12]

In most general terms, the urban success may be explained by cities' ability to generate knowledge and resources necessary for the satisfaction of human needs, as well as creation of new ones. The growth of knowledge in urban centers has helped them to develop in innovative ways which have been variously exemplified throughout millennia of urban history, most overwhelmingly in the industrialization of cities in the 19th and 20th centuries, as well as in the current processes of their de-industrialization, associated with the dematerialization of production. Cities as economic, cultural and intellectual centers have now become the genuine agents of globalization, some of them becoming megacities or global cities.[13] Globalization has resulted in a decline of the political, economic and cultural role of the states and in an increase of the significance of cities. Technological developments in transportation and related urban infrastructure have enabled the mobility of populations on a mass scale. Though motivated mainly by economic reasons, the mobility is also driven by aspiration for attractive leisure, now available to ever increasing masses of people. All forms of human mobility carry with themselves a great economic potential, but also grave and intricate problems in managing the fast-growing urban human traffic, whereas attempts to tap the potential and to solve those problems deeply affect the ongoing transformation of contemporary cities.

3. The City as a Work of Art

In the 19th century cities became centers of industrial capitalist production. The accompanying urbanist, demographic and cultural transformations have become a subject of sociology, which has to a large extent superseded philosophy in its attempts to understand the city. The latest developments in the character of capitalist production, and in the nature of the goods produced, have tremendously affected the development of cities and transformed them from the industrial into post-industrial centers. This transformation has re-directed the attention of urban scholars toward the role of knowledge, culture and arts, i.e. symbolic goods, in the functioning and development of cities, as well as toward the rise of creative classes responsible for the creation of symbolic capital. It has also led to the establishment of urban studies as a discipline in its own right, which evolved from interdisciplinary research into the intense contemporary urbanization processes. However, even if the present-day urban scholars focus on cities as the centers of production, exchange, and consumption of symbolic capital and cultural goods, they tend to perceive these goods in an instrumental way, i.e. as means of solving practical problems generated by the very form of urban life.[14] Despite their focus upon practical aspects of urban life, urban studies are unavoidably underpinned by philosophical and anthropological visions of individual and social life; and since human beings are inherently moral, aesthetic, and artistic creatures,[15] ethical and aesthetic preconceptions constitute a natural and integral part of these visions. More often than not, however, within urban studies those preconceptions are taken for granted rather than critically appraised and debated. Since a critical discussion of these assumptions and preconception is a truly philosophical task, it seems to validate philosophy's bid for reclaiming its original role in understanding the contemporary urban life.

Another argument for the import of the philosophical approach in understanding the city is based upon a rather uncontroversial observation that the city itself and each aspect of urban life are cultural formations. The city is a complex embodiment of human excellence in various arts: planning, designing, engineering, construction, but also in the political arts of managing the social and moral life. In this sense the city is a work of art.[16] At the same time, the city was the birthplace of arts and of their growth. Moreover arts, in an almost self-referential gesture, often turn their attention to the city itself in order to reflect upon it, depict it, and explain it in their own poetic manner. This dialectic relationship of the city and arts as means of understanding, description, and formation of the city should be perceived as an essential characteristic of cities, for the city cannot be fully understood without reference to arts, but also arts cannot be understood without reference to the city, the milieu which made them possible.

In other words, cities are sites of production, distribution, and consumption not only of material goods, but also of symbolic ones. Various symbolic values and goods play a number of instrumental roles in the city; but they are also endowed with an autotelic status and as such cannot be reduced to their instrumental usefulness only. For they play not only the role of external values within urban practices, but also the role of internal ones, and as such they must be perceived as constitutive of these practices.[17] The city, as a specific cultural formation, is thus a place of creation, accumulation, transmission, distribution, and consumption of cultural goods and symbolic values. I believe that these phenomena and processes may be understood most effectively from the perspective of urban political aesthetics, a philosophical discipline whose task is to explicate them and demonstrate their constitutive role for the practices of contemporary urban life. Such an approach seems especially justified in view of the intense growth of cities and their present role not only as economic and political, but also leading cultural agents.

4. The City as a Space

The predominance of the sense of sight in human cognition, memorably remarked upon by Aristotle,[18] indelibly and crucially affects the development of all human cultures. It thus seems that the proper point of departure for urban political aesthetics should be the fact that human cultures develop in a way which reflects the fundamental role played in human life by the perceptual, visual, and spectacular. In order to make this point, one may take advantage of the Berkeleyan principle *esse est percipi*, which served to express his epistemological subjectivism. A reinterpretation of this principle may be employed to explain contemporary cities as dominated by the culture of visibility. Many forms of urban developments, achievements and human behaviors are performed in order to be noticed by others. Vying for attention is, on the one hand, among chief reasons for emergence of a specific urban human way of life, but also, on the other, turns cities into exposition places and sites of ceaseless rivalry for attention. One may thus say that in order to be in the urban spaces one must be perceived within them. Accordingly, urban spaces may be understood as areas of agonistic rivalry for recognition in the Hegelian sense, which is entered into by individual and collective subjects alike. From this point of view, cities as cultural formations are manifestations of people's attempts to create and recreate spaces they inhabit in accordance with their desire for being seen, which is satisfied in accordance with, or – ever more often today – in violation of, various and continuously changing customs and requirements of their cultures, determining the temporarily acceptable modes of public conduct.

The city is then a unique space which itself consists of many sub-spaces, created and recreated by people in order to live their lives in them. Spaces of human life should be understood as products of historically changing social practices and as *loci* of continuous transformation of human life. The spatial nature of the city implies, in yet another way, that if the city is to be understood, it needs to be approached from an aesthetic point of view. Thus the categories of space and its production, the conditions of its transformations, and the subjects taking part in, and affected by, these processes constitute basic concepts of political aesthetics.[19]

The philosophical-anthropological understanding of space departs from common intuitions about it, which inform the view of the public space as an agora in which individuals gather in order to develop and exercise their agency. Through an analogy to contemporary physics, in which space exists in so far as there are particles which fill it with their kinetic energy, one should rather understand spaces of human life as existing in so far as there are social particles which fill them with their political, moral, and aesthetic energy. The spaces are constituted by, and change according to, the energy generated by the individuals and communities moving in them.[20]

Spaces of human life, while they incessantly intersect and mutually blur each other's borderlines, are nevertheless distinct from each other: the social aspects of human life are not identical with the public ones, and both are distinguishable from the private and intimate spheres. The intimate space is part of the private sphere, but cannot be fully identified with it, for it is created by needs which cannot be satisfied by activities in any of the remaining spaces. Individuals function in these spaces as formed by nature and culture. They enter them as individuals and as members of communities. The evolution of forms of social life has generated norms which regulate the conduct of individuals within each of these spaces, as well as at their intersections. Each of these spheres has its own history and is governed by its own rules which require compliance with them. Actions performed in each of them have moral and political consequences, and are subject to an aesthetic assessment, for aesthetic categories constitute an integral part of human orientation in the spaces of human life.

Cities are dynamic social, political, and cultural formations. Their dynamics is a result of deep-seated conflicts within them, which are contained, with varying success, by continuous attempts to impose some order upon them, while forms and shapes of those imposed orderings are in themselves an object of agonistic urban rivalry. This necessarily means that functioning in urban spaces involves a sustained effort; to be in them is to be prepared for a struggle for a place in them. This feature of urban spaces may be illustrated by saying that a place once assumed by an individual in such spaces cannot be claimed as her permanent property, for upon returning to it, she will often find it occupied, no less legitimately, by another person. For this reason urban spaces are continuously partitioned, while these partitions form the basic mode of the distribution of social goods. Urban spaces are constituted by objective conflicts and oppositions, which account for their incessant dynamics. It is this facet of the spheres of human life that turns them into places of ceaseless rivalries, while their rules constitute the rudimentary forms of the social distribution of goods.

5. The City as a Spectacle

The above-outlined perspective suggests that urban spaces are *loci* of continuous and wholesale transformations of human life which both reflect and rebound on the on-going transformations of the modes of production and consumption. Material production is now increasingly superseded by the production of immaterial goods; as a result, the productive and symbolic aspects of social life undergo processes of an unprecedented spectacularization.[21] Through privileging the culture of visibility, the ubiquitous media of mass communication additionally boost the spectacularization and aesthetization of social relations. Due to the increasing spectacularization of human life, the visual aspect of the city has become much more pronounced and stimulates now efforts to turn the cities themselves into spectacles.[22] The contemporary city functions today both as an aesthetic object and as a venue for the display and marketing of cultural goods and symbolic values.

Contemporary cities, both as exposition places and as spectacles, attract new inhabitants, thus increasingly becoming cosmopolitan centers. There are several forms of contemporary urban cosmopolitanism, each of them accompanied by a characteristic aesthetics of its own.

One of them, a quotidian cosmopolitanism, is a result of the mixing of various ethnic and cultural groups which migrate to the cities in search of livelihood. This kind of cosmopolitanism is usually characterized by an aesthetics of variety, and it engenders urban areas of great diversity which, though inclusive, may also become arenas of major internal conflicts. Due to their specificity, such areas are usually remarkably distinct from the neighboring districts. Their distinctiveness leads sometimes to their ghettoization; they are also subject to political and aesthetic actions aimed at transforming them into "theme parks," which is often perceived by their inhabitants as segregatory, divisive and unjust treatment.

The second kind of cosmopolitanism is also quotidian in character; it is a result of expansive forms of the production of space and of their commodification; these transformations have engendered the phenomenon of the horizontal urban sprawl. It was made possible by the growth of motorization, and has been followed by a specific suburban culture and aesthetics of uniformity, often represented in arts; it is also accompanied by the culture and aesthetics of mobility.[23] These transformations in many urban areas, characterized by the absence of any strong communal relationships, have been aptly captured by the slogan *Anywhere City*. It is worth remarking that cities in Central and Eastern Europe are an interesting variation of this development. After World War Two, their spaces have been filled with stereotypical apartment blocks serving to produce and concentrate the working classes, necessary for the modernization of the backward states. Construction of such housing facilities allowed those classes to enjoy comforts of a more civilized life, and contributed to the growth of the urban population. At the same time, however, this model of housing architecture has deeply affected their social relations by breaking up the traditional family ties and leading to the privatization of their life. The relative weakness of the economies of post-socialist cities makes it impossible for them to replace these buildings with more socially functional ones. As a result, in the foreseeable future, they will remain part of the social and urban landscape in this region. The recent housing boom in these countries has been shaped, in case of individual home builders, by an aesthetics of ostentation typical of the *nouveau riche*; it has also encouraged the construction of new urban areas whose chaos defies any aesthetical categorization. The social harm resulting from the desire to possess a house or an apartment without respect for the quality of social relations, their harmoniousness with the existing urban and natural landscape, and their aesthetic features, has been great and will be irreversible in the near future.

The third cosmopolitanism, an elite one, is exclusive and is accountable for the emergence of a specific urban aesthetics which organizes the servicing of the mobile elite whose expectations of state-of-the-art urban comforts affect significant, usually crucial elements of the urban structure.[24] An aesthetics of uniformity, accompanying this kind of cosmopolitanism, induces the production of identical and conventional spaces irrespective of their geographical location. The elite urban cosmopolitanism promotes also an aesthetics of ostentation aimed to offset the boredom of the aesthetics of uniformity and in this way to attract global attention to cities. It finds an expression especially in the spectacular "signature" architecture, as in the widely discussed reconstruction of Paris by Georges Haussmann, or in the more recent example of Bilbao, now emulated with various success by other cities. This kind of urban aesthetics of ostentation has received an additional boost from the latest technological innovations, which have made possible novel and often striking forms of the urban vertical sprawl, as in the case of spectacular architectural constructions in Shanghai, Dubai, and numerous other cities vying for global recognition.

6. The Urban Aesthetic Politics

The transformation of ever new urban spaces into exposition places and venues of ostentation is also an incentive for the consumption of the symbolic and prestigious goods, and is a driving force behind the emergence of the urban creative classes, consisting of the workers of the sectors of knowledge, education, culture, arts, and business management.[25] This also propels the innovative development of arts and their instrumental use in enhancing the attractiveness of the cities. Contemporary cities, themselves works of various arts, are increasingly shedding their character of industrial centers and are becoming chiefly venues of production of symbolic goods. As such, they are even more prone to the processes of spectacularization mentioned above.

The de-industrialization of contemporary cities is accompanied by wide-ranging changes in the socio-economic structure of urban centers, especially the structure of the working classes. This change leads to claims about the demise and dispersal of the working class, which, in the industrial period, was concentrated in the cities. In view of the unprecedented growth of the world population, and the correlated demand for all sorts of goods, both material and non-material ones, such claims seem *prima facie* contestable. They appear to be sustained by an obsolete, yet persistent, political aesthetics in the understanding of both a worker and the goods produced. It is remarkable that the worker continues to be perceived as a man "with a hammer in his hand and coal dust in his pores,"[26] dressed in overalls with rolled-up sleeves, while the product continues to be envisaged as a locomotive, an internal combustion engine, or a brick.[27] It thus seems that this antiquated political aesthetics, which lags behind the realities of continuously changing capitalist modes of production, is a major obstacle in addressing properly the present dynamics of urban populations. Together with the de-materialization of production, a corresponding change should take place in the political aesthetics of the working classes, while obsolete stereotypes haunting the analyses of changes in the urban social stratification need to be questioned.

In virtue of their nature, symbolic goods are less amenable to measurement than other kinds of goods. It does not prevent them, however, from becoming marketable commodities, as it never has. The production of spectacles in itself has become a subject of an intense commodification. In the culture of visibility, spectacularization has become a precondition of the commodification of symbolic goods, which has now reached an unprecedented scale. Commodification and spectacularisation are thus obviously correlated: the culture of visibility makes the spectacles a much sought commodity, while the mass media make them easily marketable. As a result, spectacles are now becoming the chief commodity of contemporary culture, and their production is the most rapidly growing industry. Consequently, access to them is increasingly regulated by the market mechanisms. Because of the unrelenting commodification of public spaces, which in Western societies increasingly determines the forms of participation in them, gaining access to these spaces, and functioning in them, involves an ever-increasing effort. Commodification generates the sense alienation of individuals in cities, and affects the presence and perception of symbolic values in urban spaces.

The perception of the city both as a work of art and as a cradle of arts has already received more than ample attention in various conceptions of political aesthetics. Some of them stress the fact that cities are places of a variety of forms of inequality which affect also the extent to which their citizens participate in cultural goods. The level of participation of individuals and groups, or classes, in cultural productions, embodied in education, arts and artistic culture, may be taken as a measure of the social access to symbolic values and of the degree of involvement in the creation of symbolic capital.[28] Yet there is something to be added to this, for these issues have also a direct political dimension. The unequal access to cultural goods is as a rule additionally aggravated by the mechanisms of municipal subsidies for cultural productions. Their beneficiaries tend to be members of the local elites who, in virtue of their education and material status, do not need any additional economic incentives to enjoy arts, whereas the majority of the citizenry, especially the economically disadvantaged or otherwise deprived, are not among their beneficiaries. In effect, a lion's share of the taxes, which for the most part come from contributions of the lowest income groups, is being redirected in order to provide a sophisticated entertainment for the elites at the cost of the excluded groups. This widespread mechanism increases the severity of exclusions and significantly contributes to iniquities in many cities. These consequences of the urban aesthetic politics are yet another way to justify the claim that political aesthetic considerations should be an important element in understanding many aspects of urban life.

7. Absence as Agoraphobia

One of many non-economic factors stimulating the growth of cities is a relative anonymity of life in urban spaces, which offer a greater scope of freedom from repressive means of social control still persisting in traditional, more tightly-knit non-urban communities. Cities are thus not only opportunities to establish relationships with others. They also enable individuals to select them at will, avoid them while continuously enjoying the tantalizing possibility, real or virtual, of re-entering them, or shun them altogether. That is why cities are also places of privacy and seclusion, isolation and solitude. The specific nature of social relations made possible by the urban settings turns them also into objects of aesthetic enjoyment and voyeuristic consumption epitomized in the Baudelairesque *flâneur* attitude.[29]

The intensity of interaction and the level of sophistication – prerequisites of successful functioning in contemporary society, resulting from technological advancements and the increased level of rivalries in the spaces of human life – generate an attitude which may be described as public agoraphobia. Public agoraphobia is, on the one hand, enforced by economic and social exclusions, and, on the other, is self-induced as a form of self-exclusion from the public life. These phenomena, as effects of the commodification and the agonistic character of the spaces of human life, tend to amplify each other. Public agoraphobia adversely affects the political and social agency of individuals, engendering attitudes of civic passivity in them.

Public agoraphobia is also fuelled, yet at the same time partly alleviated, by a phenomenon which may be described as interpassivity. In simplest terms: in order to be inter*active*, one is supposed to be personally involved in a social relationship; in order to be inter*passive*, one is supposed to substitute one's own activity with an object, or another person, within such a relationship. Cities are a particularly fertile ground for the development of interpassive attitudes. This is due to the growth of the division of labor, as well as creation, professionalization, and specialization of services which are, obviously, available to a greater extent within urban forms of collective life than within rural ones. As a result, in the urban environment individuals feel positively discouraged from performing many duties, tasks, and chores which they would otherwise perform themselves, were it not for the easy availability of professionals ready to perform them instead of them. Through these processes, mutual meaningful relations among individuals are increasingly mediated by expedient third parties. One has to emphasize that an essential part in this expediency lies in the fact that those intermediaries are themselves easily replaceable and conveniently disposable. Contemporary urban societies increasingly approximate the ideal type of "abstract societies," in which "men practically never meet face to face (...), in which all business is conducted by individuals in isolation who communicate by typed letters or by telegrams, and who go about in closed motor-cars."[30] The interpassive attitude together with public agoraphobia and commodification enhance each other and affect adversely both relationships among the individuals as well as their civic agency.

8. Politics and Ostentation

In conclusion, it has to be observed that the aesthetics of ostentation, some forms of which were mentioned above, grows also on a fertile soil of local urban politics which, for the most part, has not been immune to the overwhelming processes of spectacularization. Much to the contrary. It is an outcome of decisions of the city managers, who quite often treat their jobs as ego-rides and occasions to realize their ambitions by involving the cities they manage into spectacular but often miscalculated, ill-designed, excessively costly, and sometimes ruinous undertakings. Such ventures in ostentation adversely affect the stability of a growing number of cities across the globe. As a matter of fact, the greatest current danger to the stability of the Chinese economy, and thus to the world economy as a whole, comes now from a huge debt incurred by innumerable Chinese municipalities, large and small, which, restrained only by the limits of their ambitions and imagination, have become involved in misguided development schemes. Rather curiously, in some cases it took the form of constructing large scale or even identical replicas of some European cities. As a result, Chinese municipalities are now responsible for 25 per cent of their country's overall debt.[31] In view of this, a recent claim that mayors may be able to solve problems of the world economy better than nation states[32] seems grossly flawed, for it is evident that mayors, instead of solving the world's economic problems, are now actually busy creating new ones, even greater and less solvable than those actually at hand.

This kind of urban governance, which is by no means confined to the Chinese territories, is accompanied by various pathologies. One of them is rampant urban cronyism and clientelism of groups that stand behind the privatization of the urban public sphere and make up the core of the new urban patriciate. It is worth noticing that the class of new patricians is easily identified by an aesthetics of ostentation of its own.

More serious among these pathologies, however, is insufficient control of the municipal management by the urban democratic systems. For urban ostentation goes hand in hand with urban agoraphobia, the latter being a precondition of the former. Civic passivity of urban citizens, who forfeit their right to participation in the management of their cities, is no less damaging than adventurousness of their mayors. For through their withdrawal, they are becoming invisible and, thus, politically insignificant; through their public absence, they condone the transformation of urban forms of self-government into local despotisms; through their silence, they encourage the privatization of the traditional urban agora, contributing in this way to the atrophy of the public sphere in contemporary cities. Thus, if urban governance today resembles a set of crowd-management techniques rather than a joint democratic effort for the common good of the city inhabitants, it is due not only to the despotic leanings of the city managers, but also, to a greater extent, to the public desertion of the urban citizens.

These developments, which are both a cause and a consequence of prevalent public agoraphobia, are a reason why Socratic perambulations through the city streets in search of people to learn from, being now confined to shrinking urban enclaves, have been all but replaced by a detached *flaneurish* consumption of their appearances.

NOTES

1. Plato, "Phaedrus," *The Collected Dialogues of Plato*, trans. Reginald Hackforth, eds., Edith Hamilton and Huntington Caims (Princeton: Princeton University Press, 1985), para. 230c.
2. *Ibid.*, para. 230d.
3. Aristotle, *Politics*, trans. Benjamin Jowett (New York: Dover Publication, Inc., 2000), para. 1252a1–7.
4. Thomas More, *Utopia*, eds. George M. Logan and Robert M. Adams (Cambridge: Cambridge University Press, 2002); Tomasso Campanella, *The City of the Sun: A Poetical Dialogue*, trans. and ed. Daniel J. Donno (Berkeley: University of California Press, 1981); Francis Bacon, *New Atlantis* (Los Angeles: Philosophical Research Society, 1985).
5. Jean-Jacques Rousseau, *Emile, or on Education*, trans. and ed. Allan Bloom (New York: Basic Books, 1979).
6. Richard Shusterman, "Urban Scenes and Unseens," *Filozofski Vestnik*, XVII (2/1996), pp. 171–9; also, in an expanded form: "The Urban Aesthetics of Absence," *New Literary History*, 28 (1997), pp. 739–55.
7. Georg Simmel, "The Metropolis and Mental Life," *The Sociology of Georg Simmel*, trans. Kurt Wolff (New York: Free Press, 1950), pp. 409–24.
8. Richard Sennett, *The Conscience of the Eye: The Design and Social Life of Cities* (New York: Knopf, 1990).
9. Walter Benjamin, "On Some Motifs in Baudelaire," *Illuminations*, trans. Harry Zohn (New York: Schocken, 1988).
10. David Satterthwaite, *The Scale of Urban Change Worldwide 1950–2000* (London: International Institute for Environment and Development, 2006).
11. Jane Jacobs, *The Economy of Cities* (New York: Random House, 1969).
12. *Urban World*, MacKinsey Report 2011.

13. Saskia Sassen, *Cities in a Word Economy* (London-Delhi: Pine Forge Press, 2000); *Global Networks, Linked Cities* (London: Routledge, 2002); *The Global City: New York, London and Tokyo* (Princeton: Princeton University Press, 2000).

14. Cf. e.g. Dorota Ilczuk, *Ekonomika kultury* (Warszawa: PWN, 2012).

15. Ellen Dissanayake, *Homo Aestheticus* (Washington D.C.: University of Washington Press, 1995); Denis Dutton, *Art Instinct* (New York: Bloomsbury Press, 2009).

16. Jane Jacobs claims that "there is a basic aesthetic limitation on what can be done with cities: a city cannot be a work of art." See Jacobs, *The Death and Life of Great American Cities: The Failure of Town Planning* (Harmondsworth: Penguin, 1965), p. 386, after: Hedley Smyth, *Marketing the City. The Role of Flagship Developments in Urban Regeneration* (London: E & FN Spon, 1994), p. 225. Despite that, I believe that cities may be considered as works of arts in the sense delineated above. This is because Jacobs's claim is based upon a unduly sharp distinction between "arts" and "life." Jacobs's remark remains valid, however, in relation to attempts to endow cities with the status of the works of art in the narrow sense of this concept, especially by means of their spectacularization, referred to below.

17. Cf. Alasdair MacIntyre, "After Virtue and Marxism: A Response to Wartofsky," *Inquiry*, 27: 2–3 (1984), pp. 253–4.

18. Aristotle, *Metaphysics*, trans. and ed. David E. Luscombe (Oxford: Clarendom Press, 1971), para. 980a.

19. Susanne Langer, *Philosophy in a New Key: A Study in the Symbolism of Reason, Rite, and Art* (Cambridge: Harvard University Press, 1942); Henri Lefebvre, *The Production of Space* (Oxford: Blackwell, 1991); *Writings on Cities* (Oxford: Blackwell, 1996); *The Urban Revolution* (London: Routledge, 2003). See also Łukasz Stanek, *Henri Lefebvre on Space: Architecture, Urban Research, and the Production of Theory* (Minneapolis: University of Minnesota Press, 2011), and David Harvey, *Rebel Cities: From the Right to the City to the Urban Revolution* (London: Verso, 2012).

20. Cf. Adam Chmielewski, "The Gaze and Touch in the Public Space: Toward a Political Aesthetics," *Wrocław Non Stop: Urban Space* (Wrocław, Galeria Design, 2008), pp. 84–92.

21. Guy Debord, *Society of the Spectacle* (Detroit: Black & Red, 1983).

22. Marsha Meskimmon, *Engendering the City: Women Artists and Urban Spaces* (London: Scarlet Press, 1997); Doreen Massey, *Space, Place and Gender* (Cambridge: Polity Press, 1994).

23. Francine Houben, "From Centre to Periphery: The Aesthetics of Mobility," *City Edge: Case Studies in Contemporary Urbanism*, ed. Esther Charlesworth (Oxford: Architectural Press, 2005), pp. 100–117.

24. Jon Binnie, Julian Holloway, Steve Millington, and Craig Young (eds.), *Cosmopolitan Urbanism* (Oxford: Routledge, 2006).

25. Richard L. Florida, *Cities and the Creative Class* (London: Routledge, 2005); *The Rise of the Creative Class: And How It's Transforming Work, Leisure, Community and Everyday Life* (New York: Basic Books, 2002).

26. Naomi Klein, *The Shock Doctrine: The Rise of Disaster Capitalism* (London: Allen Lane, 2007), p. 173.

27. Cf. Adam Chmielewski, "Postmodernizm i jego wrogowie," *Odra*, 6 (2013).

28. Pierre Bourdieu, *Distinction: A Social Critique of the Judgment of Taste* (Cambridge: Harvard University Press, 1984).

29. These phenomena may be interpreted as forms of a more general category of urban absence as discussed by Richard Shusterman in his critical reading of Simmel's view of on the mental life in metropolis, cf. Shusterman, "Urbans Scenes and Unseens," p. 177.

30. Karl Popper, *The Open Society and its Enemies*, vol. 1 (London: Routledge and Kegan Paul, 1962), p.174.

31. The debt of Chinese municipalities is estimated at 13 trillion yuan (ca US$ 2,22 trillion).

32. Cf. Benjamin Barber, *If Mayors Ruled the World: Dysfunctional Nations, Rising Cities* (New Haven and London: Yale University Press, 2013). Barber writes: "Cities are increasingly networked into webs of culture, commerce and communication that encircle the globe. These networks and the cooperative complexes they embody can be helped to do formally what they now do informally: govern through voluntary cooperation and shared consensus. If mayors ruled the world, the more than 3,5 billion people (over half of the world's population) who are urban dwellers and many more in the exurban neighborhoods beyond could participate locally and globally at the same time — a miracle of civil 'glocality' promising pragmatism instead of politics, innovation rather than ideology, and solutions in place of sovereignty" (p. 5).

.

Part Two

AESTHETIC EXPERIENCE

Four

"ANYTHING GOES" VS. "WHO TOUCHES THIS BOOK TOUCHES A MAN": WILLIAM JAMES AND PAUL FEYERABEND ON METAPHYSICAL, ETHICAL, AND AESTHETIC "ABUNDANCE"

Sami Pihlström

> Hearing mere fairytales may not be your cup of tea – you may want to hear THE TRUTH. Well, if that's what you want, then you are better off elsewhere – only for the life of me, I can't tell you exactly where that would be.
> — Paul Feyerabend

1. Introduction

Pragmatist aesthetics should not, in my view, be understood as a self-contained or isolated field of inquiry but ought to be regarded as closely connected with other pragmatist inquiries – especially those into metaphysics, epistemology, ethics, and even philosophy of science. Moreover, pragmatism itself, more generally, should not be understood as disconnected from other philosophical approaches and methodologies. It can even be suggested that pragmatist philosophy is at its most original and creative when it considers ideas and thinkers that are "at the limits" or even outside of pragmatism – or lie somewhere between pragmatism and other philosophical orientations.[1]

It is from the point of view of these guiding thoughts that I will present the following reflections on pragmatist aesthetics, ethics, and metaphysics. This essay, thus, offers a somewhat unusual comparison between William James's pragmatism and Paul Feyerabend's philosophy (which I hesitate to encapsulate in any single "ism," because the one most often associated with him, "anarchism," is profoundly misleading). The topic is unusual in more than one way. Firstly, James and Feyerabend have only very seldom been brought together, and, secondly, pragmatist aesthetics, ethics, and metaphysics have also very seldom been integrated in the manner I propose they should be through my James–Feyerabend comparison.

The key idea to be developed in the following is an ethico-aesthetic emphasis on the importance of what we may call (following Feyerabend) a certain kind of *"abundance" or "richness" (variety) of both nature and the human cultural world*. Both James and Feyerabend argue that we should let a wide variety of human voices be heard, and a plurality of pragmatically embedded perspectives open, in our individual and social attempts to know, and to cope with, the world we inhabit. Culturally and politically, this stance is opposed to what both James and Feyerabend found an intellectually and ethically narrow-minded *scientism*; we can also see these two philosophers as defending a deeply *democratic* view of experience against scientific "imperialism." Richness here means *diversity* and *irreducibility*, which can be understood as ethical and aesthetic, but also metaphysical ideas (or, better perhaps, ideals). However, this does not presuppose the doctrine Feyerabend is notorious for, that is, the "epistemologically anarchist" thesis that "anything goes" – not, at least, in its received and often ridiculed formulations. One can develop a pragmatist appreciation of the metaphysico-ethico-aesthetic abundance of irreducibly different perspectives in a much more tenable and responsible way.

More generally, my treatment of the hitherto underappreciated James–Feyerabend connection should be understood as a defense of *the ethical functions and ethical significance of aesthetic experience in pragmatism*. Aesthetics, as pragmatist aestheticians (most famously Shusterman)[2] have argued, is not self-sustained or independent of other practices we engage in (as "aestheticism" would presuppose) but deeply experiential and linked with various human practices and habits of action. Therefore, aesthetics, just like metaphysics[3], must also continuously be evaluated ethically. Both aesthetics and metaphysics should, arguably, even be grounded in ethics as a general examination of the conditions of good life. We may ask, for instance, what kind of ethical "outcomes" aesthetic works of art or aesthetically valuable natural structures, or our aesthetic experiences and appreciations of such works and structures, produce or may produce. Posing such questions does not entail a moralizing attitude to art and artists but encourages the continuous application of art, and of aesthetic perspectives more generally, to the pragmatist inquiry into and reflection on the kind of moral (and political) problems that inevitably concern us all. (As philosophers associated with the Wittgensteinian tradition in moral philosophy have argued, fictional literature, by reflecting on, say, evil, guilt, and death, can often deal with moral problems much more profoundly than theoretical philosophical argumentation. This is also a key topic in, e.g., Iris Murdoch's ethical thought.)[4] Thus, instead of lying beyond the moral sphere, art can and should (a moral "should"!) be deeply ethical, and our appreciation of art may, and should, have an irreducibly ethical dimension, while avoiding moralizing. Conversely, our ethical life may include profound aesthetic aspects. This *reciprocal inclusion of ethics and aesthetics* is, in my view, something we can learn from pragmatism in general and from the Jamesian-Feyerabendian position to be outlined here in particular.

As the paper unfolds, I will also try to connect these ideas with the theme of abundance through a brief discussion of the human – and therefore ethical and political – significance of *libraries*. First, however, we need to (re-) examine Feyerabend's and James's basic views and explore the possibilities of a critical synthesis.

2. Feyerabend's "Anarchism"

In order to set the record straight, I will start by reviewing the notorious "anarchist" thesis. Paul Feyerabend is usually portrayed as a radical epistemological relativist and anarchist, according to whom "anything goes." There is no such thing as *the* scientific method; instead, science, according to Feyerabend, cannot be normatively distinguished from other human practices and discourses, in principle even from fairy tales and other clearly non- or pseudo-scientific discourses or practices.[5] Thus, Feyerabend has even come to play the role of an *enemy* of science and reason – a paradigm case of irresponsibly relativist thinking. His reputation was not particularly helped by his infamous defense of creationists in the 1980s.

For this reason, it has been important for pragmatists, as well as many other serious thinkers committed to normatively governed inquiry, to carefully distinguish their views from Feyerabend's. For example, philosophers sympathetic to William James's pragmatism[6] have insisted that Jamesian pragmatism, despite its pluralism and anti-reductionism, is *not* a Feyerabendian-styled "anything-goes" doctrine, even though it has occasionally been mischaracterized as such. It is, thus, not a species of relativism or subjectivism. Indeed, already in his lifetime – before Feyerabend was even born – James had to confront misinterpretations (spread by George Edward Moore and Bertrand Russell, in particular) of himself as a radical relativist or subjectivist.

In fact, in my own survey of pragmatist philosophy of science and its history (or, rather, a reflection on what it would mean, and what it wouldn't, to write such a history), I maintained the following:

> The pragmatist does not hold, with Paul Feyerabend, that 'anything goes,' or that a pluralist proliferation of scientific practices and methods is a good thing as it stands, because scientific practices have their own in-built normativity, and normative distinctions between good and bad science are internal to those practices themselves, hence something that the pragmatist ought to take seriously. However, this does not mean that the norms of scientific methodology would be handed down to us from above; to the contrary, science is a continuing critical process, in which not only theories but the methods used to justify them are constantly open for reevaluation. Instead of celebrating pluralism and anarchy as such, the pragmatist follows Dewey in emphasizing the *critical* function

of philosophy, its role as 'the critical method for developing methods of criticism.'[7]

On the other hand, in the same essay I also posed the following question: "If, as I suggest, we approach [Thomas] Kuhn as a pragmatist (or pragmatic realist), should we also acknowledge Feyerabend[8] – the anarchist and arch-relativist – as a pragmatist, in some sense?"[9] My answer was positive, at least "inasmuch as we also acknowledge [Richard] Rorty's entitlement to the word 'pragmatism.'" This is because, while Feyerabend avoids committing himself to the pragmatist (or any other) tradition, he does speak about "pragmatic philosophy" when referring to people or groups "participating in the interaction of traditions." Such pragmatic philosophy is required for an "open exchange" between people and traditions, which is, in turn, needed to transcend simple relativism.[10] Therefore, I concluded, "Feyerabend's pluralism, antiessentialism, and antifoundationalism are clearly close to pragmatism, especially James's pragmatism."[11] This is the line of thought I now want to continue in more detail. Even if we have – as we do – good reasons, including pragmatic reasons, to oppose the unacceptably relativist consequences of the "anything goes" thesis, we may find valuable insights in Feyerabend's position.

3. Feyerabend and James

It must be noted that Feyerabend's radical views (like James's in their own way) are often radical primarily, or at least partly, because of his flamboyant rhetorical style. His defense of creationism does go too far by any reasonable standards, but it is, I think, obvious that he held no creationist beliefs himself (nor any other clearly anti-scientific ones for that matter). What he is opposed to is a certain philosophical understanding of science and a certain philosophical picture of science as part of culture. In his campaign *against dogmatic and, as we may say, "imperialist" views of science*, he clearly joins William James. His views are in many important respects very close to Jamesian pragmatism, although he rarely, if ever, directly refers to James (nor has his philosophy of science been usually discussed in the context of pragmatism scholarship – with the possible exception of Rorty's neopragmatism).

Feyerabend's interface with James – or, better, philosophical views that can be developed by synthesizing some of their key ideas – includes at least the following overlapping proposals, which I here offer not as detailed accounts of Feyerabend's thought but as openings hopefully inducing intensified discussions of these matters:

– Theoretical and methodological *pluralism* (but not radical relativism or anarchism – keeping in mind that it is not easy to separate clearly these allegedly different positions): there should be a plurality of rival theories to be tested not only against reality but also against each other.[12]

– Saving *human beings* and their natural social and cultural *practices* from the "tyranny of science" and the "dehumanizing" effects of Western science (cf. James's slogan, "the trail of the human serpent is over everything"; cf. section 4). This idea(l) incorporates both metaphysical and ethical dimensions, emphasizing the need critically to examine the scientific worldview and its historical development from a broader ethical and cultural perspective. This entails an anti-reductionist celebration of *abundance*, the richness of the world, and the *disunity* of science, in contrast to a reductionist picture of unity and harmony (metaphysical, ethical, or aesthetic).

– Saving *particularity* by avoiding sweeping generalizations (i.e., what James called "vicious intellectualism"): individual perspectives and experiences are crucial for our world-categorization and - engagement, both ethically and aesthetically as well as metaphysically (and even religiously or theologically).

– Grounding truth – scientific truth, in particular – ultimately in *ethics*: an ethical attitude to both the richness of the natural world and the history of human traditions and culture.

– Taking *disharmony* seriously: *against "theodicies"* of all kinds (religious, non-religious, secular, scientific). The world-order is not neat and harmonious; there is real evil, misery, and suffering; furthermore, there is also genuine "otherness" not reducible to a single totality.

For these positions – insofar as they can be articulated as philosophical positions – we may find textual evidence in Feyerabend's posthumously published writings.[13] In *Conquest of Abundance* (1999), Feyerabend begins by rejecting any "grand dichotomy" between "a solid, trustworthy, genuine reality on one side and deceiving appearances on the other."[14] Dichotomies between the real and the apparent, between knowledge and (mere) opinion, and (in religious traditions) between righteousness and sin have been introduced throughout our history in order to "conquer abundance."[15] In this historical process, "views that reduce abundance and devalue human existence" have become very powerful, and Feyerabend wants to explain why.[16] Scientific realism, in particular, has ideologically and dogmatically sought to reduce away the variety of ontologies, the richness of what is "real."[17] James would have readily agreed with Feyerabend that "science certainly is not the only source of reliable ontological information,"[18] and he would have equally readily agreed to join Feyerabend in denouncing the mistake of identifying some particular "manifest reality" developed within science with "Ultimate Reality,"[19] the mistake equivalent – in Kantian terms –

to the mistake of identifying the empirical world with things as they are in themselves.

We cannot discuss the details of Feyerabend's complicated historical narrative beginning with the Greeks (nor can we deal with John Dewey's versions of an in many ways similar historically informed critique of misleading dichotomies), but we should note its striking analogies to the vision that James arrives at through his pragmatist critique of problematic dualisms and dichotomies. Just like James (and, arguably, Wittgenstein), Feyerabend interweaves philosophical and scientific argumentation intimately in the texture of human life-practices: "Arguments about reality have an 'existential' component: *we regard those things as real which play an important role in the kind of life we prefer.*"[20] Arguments, that is, have power only insofar as they conform to "nonargumentative pressures."[21] This is one reason why there cannot be any "clear and lasting line between the 'objective' and the allegedly 'subjective' ingredients in the process of knowledge acquisition and of knowledge itself."[22] This position can easily be compared to James's account of "philosophical temperaments."[23] In viewing the history of philosophy as a history of clashes of philosophical temperaments, James also appreciated both "subjective" and "objective" dimensions in our knowledge-seeking and argumentation. Our objective epistemic projects are inevitably rooted in our subjective attempts to make sense of our existence, and there is no principled dichotomy to be drawn between these aspects of our ethical, aesthetic, and epistemic lives. We can see Feyerabend's work as offering a recent variation on this Jamesian theme.

An "ontological (epistemological) pluralism," Feyerabend further argues, is "closer to the facts and to human nature" than any "unitarian realism" about "Ultimate Reality."[24] Science itself is inherently pluralistic and full of conflicts;[25] as early as in the 1960s, Feyerabend argued in his famous papers that scientific progress "comes through *'theoretical pluralism'*, allowing a plurality of incompatible theories, each of which will contribute by competition to maintaining and enhancing testability, and thus the empirical content, of others."[26] Feyerabend's later defense of the richness of scientific and non-scientific perspectives on the world – arguably employing a version of the "pragmatic method" – is perfectly exemplified in the following:

> Now if science is indeed a collection of different approaches, some successful, others wildly speculative, then there is no reason why I should disregard what happens outside of it. Many traditions and cultures, some of them wildly 'unscientific' (...) succeed in the sense that they enable their members to live a moderately rich and fulfilling life. Using this extended criterion of success I conclude that non-scientific notions, too, receive a response from Nature, that Nature is more complex than a belief in the uniformity and unique excellence of science would suggest (...).[27]

Furthermore, just like James[28] suggested in a *constructivist* vein that real things are those that serve our interests and needs in pragmatically efficacious ways, and are hence "made" more than just found by us, Feyerabend argues that scientists are "sculptors of reality," not merely acting causally upon the world but also "*creat[ing] semantic conditions* engendering strong inferences from known effects to novel projections and, conversely, from the projections to testable effects."[29] Our "entire universe," he tells us in his characteristically exaggerating tone, "from the mythical Big Bang via the emergence of hydrogen and helium, galaxies, fixed stars, planetary systems, viruses, bacteria, fleas, dogs to the Glorious Arrival of Western Man is an *artifact.*"[30]

The metaphoric – and apparently deliberately aesthetic – reference to "sculptors" should be taken seriously. Feyerabend not only rejects standard dichotomies between the subjective and the objective, or between the real and the apparent; he also questions the absoluteness of the lines we draw between art, science, and nature. In his 1994 essay, "Art as a Product of Nature as a Work of Art" (published as chapter 8 of *Conquest of Abundance*), he suggests that "works of art are a product of nature, no less than rocks and flowers," while conversely "nature itself is an artefact, constructed by scientists and artisans, throughout centuries, from a partly yielding, partly resisting material of unknown properties."[31] Our "intellectual generalizations" around notions such as art, nature, and science are to be pragmatically understood as "simplifying devices that can help us order the abundance that surrounds us," as "opportunistic tools, not final statements on the objective reality of the world."[32] Again, James would have agreed. Insofar as "we inquirers construct the world in the course of our inquiries" – as Preston[33] summarizes Feyerabend's late view – Dewey presumably could have agreed as well, given his view that the objects of inquiry are constructed through, or arise from, inquiry, instead of existing "ready-made" prior to inquiry.[34]

I am not claiming that Feyerabend's (or James's) view, which clearly is intended as politically pertinent, is easy to accept. On the contrary, the challenge common to all forms of *pragmatic realism* as a middle path between radical relativism and metaphysical realism threatens to frustrate every attempt to maintain the "sculptor" metaphor while also saying that "Nature is not something formless that can be turned into any shape; it resists and by its resistance reveals its properties and laws."[35] So, the world (or Nature) has "its" ("its own"?) properties and laws, after all? As Preston[36] observes, Feyerabend occasionally endorses views that no one would deny, but that are not relativist, while occasionally subscribing to genuine relativism but failing to show why it ought to be accepted. The pragmatists' (including James's) trouble with maintaining a compromise between realism and relativism is similarly structured.

Be that as it may, both James and Feyerabend underscore the fundamental role that ethics plays in relation to both ontology and science. In my *Pragmatist Metaphysics*, I examined James's use of the pragmatic method as a method of tracing out the pragmatic core of metaphysical disputes (concerning, e.g., substance, the free will, theism, or monism vs. pluralism) in terms of their ethical dimensions. Unfortunately, I overlooked the fact that, already in his 1992 paper, "Ethics as a Measure of Scientific Truth,"[37] Feyerabend had observed that "ethics (in the general sense of a discipline that guides our choices between forms of life) affects ontology."[38] This is exactly the point that James makes and one that a true pragmatist, in my view, should make, because "real" is, for us pragmatists, *"what plays an important role in the kind of life one wants to live."*[39] Therefore, we should, Feyerabend proposes, argue not from allegedly objective scientific facts to norms (e.g., human rights) but the other way around "from the 'subjective,' 'irrational,' idiosyncratic kind of life we are in sympathy with, to what is to be regarded as real."[40] This is somewhat extreme, but it does recapitulate James's point about the ethico-metaphysical significance of philosophical temperaments – or, to put this in a more Wittgensteinian terminology, the dependence of ontological commitments on forms of life, which may also embody aesthetic ways of being in the world.

In those of Feyerabend's late ideas that are available in the 2011 volume, *The Tyranny of Science*, based on a series of lectures delivered in 1992, it is again interesting to observe that when Feyerabend considers the relation (and potential conflict) between the great discoveries of modern science and the negative features of modernity – "war, murder, cruelty" – he is in a way asking the same questions that James struggled with in his attempt to accommodate philosophically both the scientific worldview and the human need to make ethical (and aesthetic) sense of the world. The philosopher's task is an *emancipatory* one: human beings need to be freed from the "tyranny of science," that is, the tyranny of the dogmatic picture according to which there is but one way things objectively are. In particular, the idea of a "harmonious world" – whether scientifically or theologically elaborated – cannot be an ethically sound postulation.[41] Similarly, James asked why there should be any eternal harmony and worried that postulating such a harmony is tantamount to a theodicist fallacy as we may call it.[42] Now, Feyerabend perceptively shows that science can take the role of a theodicy. What he opposes – and what James opposes as well – is the dichotomous picture of reality according to which there is a "perfect but inhuman order" (either scientific or theological) over and above the "stupidity and disorder" of human life and reality.[43] And what he is concerned with, just like James, is the scientistic and materialist view that the scientific world-picture offers us a "world without purpose," a "frozen universe of solitude."[44] Such a conception of science can, however, be democratically criticized,[45] because scientists themselves are not the final authority on "the use of their products," including the interpretation of science itself.[46] In short, "questions of reality are too important to be left to scientists."[47] Now, instead of unity, what we truly experience is diversity and difference; and if, as good empiricists (and again like James), "we take experience as our only guide," then "we must say that there is diversity, not unity."[48] Feyerabend offers an updated version of the "piecemeal pluralism" James subscribed to in *A Pluralistic Universe* (1909). He also revisits the worry that the advancement of science might have a "de-anthropomorphized" and "de-humanized" nature, "until humans themselves were no longer viewed in a humane way," and argues strongly against the idea of "value-free" science, insisting that "values play an important role in the constitution of scientific facts."[49] James, once again, would have readily agreed.

One way of summarizing the issues concerning eternal harmony versus conflict that both thinkers were preoccupied with is, as Feyerabend explains, in terms of the choice between Sophocles and Plato. Whereas Plato wanted "tragedy to be replaced by a view of good and bad which permits an escape from the bad and which doesn't have [a] tragic conflict in it," Sophoclean tragedies find the world "inherently contradictory" and, thereby, having a "tragic dimension."[50] Feyerabend, in a Jamesian manner, admits that any judgment on this issue is largely a matter of individual philosophical temperament. As to whether to follow Plato or Sophocles, he says, "it's up to whoever considers the question."[51] As human beings, we face the fundamental issue of living with our philosophical views individually. For individuals like James and Feyerabend, Sophocles is clearly the winner in this dispute.

4. From "Anything Goes" to "Who Touches this Book"

It should be investigated in further detail why, and how, these commitments that I have claimed are largely common to James and Feyerabend do *not* lead to radical relativism. That is, as the Feyerabendian formulations quoted above sound more like pragmatism (and even pragmatic realism) or non-reductive naturalism than any kind of anarchism or relativism, a Jamesian-Feyerabendian anti-theodicist pragmatist believer in disunity and disbeliever in ("theodicist") eventual harmony must also be able to replace the kind of anarchism voiced in the infamous "anything goes" slogan with more responsible philosophical commitments that preserve the possibility of drawing normative distinctions between the good and the bad, or the acceptable and the unacceptable, in science and ethics (as well as aesthetics). I suggest that this is best done by appealing to some well-known Jamesian maxims instead of the one for which Feyerabend is most famous (even though, admittedly, James himself, in the first lecture of *Pragmatism*, describes the pragmatist as an "anarchist," "happy-go-lucky" kind of creature).

Let us focus, then, on the following Jamesian one-liners that offer themselves as loose analogies of the Feyerabendian themes outlined in the previous section:

- "Don't be deaf to the cries of the wounded!" The cries of the wounded – the (unintended) victims of our pragmatic attempts to experimentally develop our practices and habits of action – are among the (abundant, rich) "voices" of reality that we must hear, and learn to hear better, instead of reducing them away from the eventual harmony. There is a sense in which these voices challenge us to action, not letting us rest. The theodicist, on the contrary, *is* deaf to the cries of the wounded, reducing evil and suffering away.[52]

– "Our science is a drop, our ignorance a sea."[53] We should always take seriously the *finitude* of our scientific and other intellectual endeavors. The more our scientific knowledge grows, the more there is for us to ask further questions about. Science produces not only knowledge but also further questions and problems, further ignorance. It should, therefore, produce humility instead of hubris (as it often does).

– "The trail of the human serpent is (…) over everything."[54] This is James's appeal for the ultimately human character of all world-categorizations, readily comparable to Feyerabend's suggestions to the same effect quoted above. There is no final ontological categorization of the world as it is in itself. The world we live in is a human world, and we are *responsible* not only for what we do in the world but also for how we categorize it.

– Consider, finally, the phrase James (mis)quotes from Walt Whitman's poem "So Long!" in *Pragmatism*: "who touches this book touches a man." This line appears in the context of James's discussion of individual philosophical temperaments that "with their cravings and refusals do determine men in their philosophies, and always will."[55] The correct Whitman quote, as the editors of the volume explain,[56] is this: "Camerado! This is no book; Who touches this, touches a man." The fundamental idea, common to James and Feyerabend, seems to be here that our "books" – whatever philosophical, scientific, ethical, political, aesthetic, or any other perspectives on the world we produce – are not just neutral descriptions of reality but expressions of our individuality, among the abundant "voices" that need to be heard by human beings, whether they engage themselves with science, art, or any other pursuit.[57]

That is, we must take seriously both *our human finitude*, the fact that we are radically limited beings, and the insight that any perspective on the world (including any book produced and/or read by us) is a human achievement, rather than a privileged representation of a perspective-independent reality. This also entails taking seriously our *fallibility*, which is part of our finitude. The world cannot be known by finite beings like us in its totality from a God's-Eye-View but can be experientially approached in its historically unfolding abundance. Such experiences of abundance and of the extreme diversity of our possible human perspectives on the world are of paramount importance, ethically as well as aesthetically, for us. Moreover, they are also, partly because of their ethico-aesthetic significance, metaphysically (and possibly even theologically or religiously) significant.

In addition, then, it must be observed that Feyerabend, especially in his late period, insisted on the "openness of cultures" and contrasted this idea with the relativistic view that cultures or conceptual systems are "closed" and isolated.[58] In fact, relativism and its key rival – (scientific) realism – share the assumption that "traditions" are "well defined and clearly separated."[59] Instead, Feyerabend urges, cultures and traditions are open to each other – to the world they are embedded in: *"potentially every culture is all cultures."*[60] Pragmatist insistence on finitude and human fallibility, on the one hand, and Feyerabend's anti-relativistic (yet also non-realist) "openness" view, on the other, go very well together.

Without being open to otherness – to other cultures or traditions as well as to other individuals' philosophical temperaments – and without genuinely seeking to hear what they have to tell us, we cannot fully realize our own finitude, which is something we need to realize in order to adequately understand the richness of the world around us. It is only through appreciating our own finitude and fallibility that we can learn to appreciate the significance of the abundance of other perspectives on the world.

5. Libraries as "Nests of Abundance"

I want to briefly illustrate these thoughts with an example that neither James nor Feyerabend (as far as I know or remember) explicitly discusses in any detail. It may be suggested that *libraries* are a humanistic equivalent of the abundance of nature. They contain extreme richness and variety of unique points of view on the world; each book stored in a library is like a human being[61]: unique and different. And so is each scholar's individual point of view on the world. The challenge for any serious library, especially any serious academic library, is to maintain this diversity and to celebrate it, offering individual scholars and other library users opportunities to partake of the abundance in their work. This means, among many other things, creating spaces where one can encounter such abundance, both physically and virtually. Furthermore, libraries also serve to remind us of our finitude and even mortality, while also giving us a touch of immortality. No one can ever read more than a tiny portion of what is contained in a library, be it even a modest one (let alone major national or university libraries). Wandering in libraries, "killing time" in them (to quote the title of Feyerabend's autobiography), we learn to appreciate and acknowledge our finitude and insignificance, yet also, hopefully, to appreciate even the tiniest contribution to learning that may be preserved in the library (optimistically, beyond a nuclear catastrophe that our civilization's scientific "rationality" could precipitate). There is always a possibility of an unexpected discovery, a chance for chance. This may be as close to immortality – or eternity, infinity – as we can get.

Gottfried Wilhelm Leibniz, Jorge Luis Borges, and Paul Auster, different as they are, can serve here as philosophical and literary examples illuminating, hopefully, in both aesthetic and metaphysical sense. All three of them have explicitly or implicitly used the metaphor of a library as an expression of the immense richness of the (human) world. I have in mind Leibniz's *Monadology*[62] in particular, which describes the key characteristic of monads: the generality in individuality, and Borges's "The Book of Sand,"[63] which depicts the awe-inspiring eponymous book with an infinite number of pages, which the protagonist eventually hides into a shelf in the National Library of Argentina.

Consider, finally, Auster's *Invisible*, which is a recent example of Auster's skill in thematizing writing, books, literature, and human beings engaged with them. The novel's protagonist works at Butler Library, Columbia University, and a curious incident is related in the novel: his superior notices that he has put two books at each other's places on the shelf, albeit only "about twelve inches" from each other. The superior is angry: "Please, (…) don't ever do it again. If a book is put in the wrong place, it can be lost for twenty years or more, maybe forever." The narrator then reflects (note the unusual second-person narration here): "It is a small matter, perhaps, but you feel humiliated by your negligence. Not that the two books in question could have been lost (they were on the same shelf, after all, just inches away from each other), but you understand the point (…). You think: Twenty years! Forever! You are astounded by the idea. Put something in the wrong place, and even though it is still there – quite possibly smack under your nose – it can vanish for the rest of time."[64]

As is often the case in Auster's work, an everyday incident opens the perspective of eternity. Accordingly, we might say that a *tension or dialectics between mortality and immortality* is profoundly characteristic of the operations of a good library – and of any serious human pursuit, including science or art, the "artisan" practices that, as Feyerabend claims, we engage in to construct the "artifact of nature." A single book almost disappears like a drop of water in the sea, possibly vanishing "for the rest of time"; still, it never completely disappears in fact, but – together with an immense number of other books around it – it contributes to the preservation of our civilization. In this sense, mortality and finitude, and the yearning for immortality emerging from them, are a key to a proper "philosophy of the library" (just as they may be a key to the philosophy of science conscious of the "disunity" Feyerabend insists on) – and this, surprisingly, may be something we can learn from Feyerabend's reflections on science and culture. Again, these reflections have, quite explicitly, both aesthetic and ethical, as well as metaphysical and even theological, significance. Our sense of finitude in a vast library can come quite close to our experience of insignificance – and yet fundamental significance of each insignificant item of reality – in moments of religious awe and wonder.

6. Conclusion

Concluding, we may suggest that the "tyranny of science," which both Feyerabend and James worried about, can and should be avoided by steering clear of scientistic reductionism and ideological dogmatism – not by renouncing science or by endorsing anti- or pseudo-scientific ideas – and by affirming fallibilism (and, more generally, finitude) in a pragmatist spirit. Jamesian pragmatism can thus be (re)connected not merely with major twentieth-century figures, such as Willard V. Quine and Thomas Kuhn, whose ideas, though controversial, have always been more acceptable within mainstream philosophy of science than Feyerabend's,[65] but with Feyerabend the arch-anarchist as well. This might hopefully lead to an increased understanding of a deep pragmatic dimension in twentieth-century philosophy of science, with an equally increased awareness of its interrelatedness with aesthetics and ethics. In none of these fields of inquiry can we, as pragmatists, afford to forfeit the possibility of making normative distinctions that can be employed to evaluate our thought and action; this possibility is a crucial ethical and political precondition of reasonable thought and practice that we cannot give up, while simultaneously maintaining at least rudimentary forms of our science, morality, or aesthetic practices. Yet those distinctions and their employment cannot, on the other hand, be based on "imperialist" scientism but should emerge from the richness of our practices themselves. This is an insight we can come to appreciate by elaborating on Feyerabend's "Jamesian" pragmatism.

NOTES

I am grateful to Professor Leszek Koczanowicz and Dr. Wojciech Malecki for the kind invitation to join their project, *Practicing Pragmatist Aesthetics*, and for the opportunity to present an early version of this paper at the conference *Rethinking Pragmatist Aesthetics*, in Wrocław, Poland (August–September, 2012). Thanks are also due to Patrycja Poniatowska for excellent editorial help.

1. Cf. also Sami Pihlström (ed.), *The Continuum Companion to Pragmatism* (London and New York: Continuum, 2011).
2. Richard Shusterman, *Pragmatist Aesthetics: Living Beauty, Rethinking Art* (Oxford: Blackwell, 1992).
3. Cf. Sami Pihlström, *Pragmatist Metaphysics: An Essay on the Ethical Grounds of Ontology* (London and New York: Continuum, 2009).
4. Cf. Iris Murdoch, *Existentialists and Mystics: Writings on Philosophy and Literature*, ed. Peter Conradi (Harmondsworth: Penguin, 1997); Sami Pihlström, *Pragmatic Moral Realism: A Transcendental Defense* (Amsterdam: Rodopi, 2005).
5. See the overview of Feyerabend's views in Eric Oberheim, "Feyerabend, Paul K. (1924-1994)," *Dictionary of Modern American Philosophers*, ed. John R. Shook (Bristol: Thoemmes Press, 2005) and John Preston, "Paul Feyerabend," *Stanford*

Encyclopedia   of   Philosophy   (2009)   available   online:
http://plato.stanford.edu/entries/feyerabend/; cf. e.g., Ilkka Niiniluoto's fierce
criticism of Feyerabend in Niiniluoto, *Is Science Progressive?* (Dordrecht: Reidel,
1984) and *Critical Scientific Realism* (Oxford: Oxford University Press, 1999).

6. Including, e.g., Hilary Putnam, *Reason, Truth and History* (Cambridge: Cambridge
   University Press, 1981), but also the present author: cf. Sami Pihlström,
   "Structuring the World: The Issue of Realism and the Nature of Ontological
   Problems in Classical and Contemporary Pragmatism," *Acta Philosophica
   Fennica*, 59 (1996); *Pragmatism and Philosophical Anthropology:
   Understanding Our Human Life in a Human World* (New York: Peter Lang,
   1998); *"The Trail of the Human Serpent Is over Everything": Jamesian
   Perspectives on Mind, World, and Religion* (Lanham: University Press of
   America, 2008); "How (Not) to Write the History of Pragmatist Philosophy of
   Science?" *Perspectives on Science*, 16 (2008).

7. Pihlström, "How (Not) to Write the History of Pragmatist Philosophy of Science?"
   p. 43. See Paul Feyerabend, *Against Method: An Outline of an Anarchistic
   Theory of Method*, (London: Verso, 1993), chap. 1 and John Dewey, *The Quest
   for Certainty: A Study on the Relation between Knowledge and Action* (Boston:
   G.P. Putnam's Sons, 1960).

8. Feyerabend, *Against Method*.

9. Pihlström, "How (Not) to Write the History of Pragmatist Philosophy of Science?" p. 52.

10. Cf. Feyerabend, *Against Method*, pp. 217–18, 226–28.

11. Pihlström, "How (Not) to Write the History of Pragmatist Philosophy of Science?" p. 52.

12. On pluralism cf. also Hilary Putnam, *Philosophy in an Age of Science*, eds. Mario
    de Caro and David Macarthur (Cambridge: Harvard University Press, 2012);
    Russell B. Goodman, "Some Sources of Putnam's Pluralism," in *Reading Putnam*,
    ed. Maria Baghramian (London and New York: Routledge, 2012), pp. 205–18.

13. Cf. in particular Paul Feyerabend, *Conquest of Abundance: A Tale of Abstraction
    versus the Richness of Being*, ed. Bert Terpstra (Chicago: The University of
    Chicago Press, 1999) and *The Tyranny of Science*, ed. Eric Oberheim
    (Cambridge: Polity Press, 2011).

14. Feyerabend, *Conquest of Abundance*, p. 9.

15. *Ibid.*, p. 13.

16. *Ibid.*, p. 16.

17. *Ibid.*, p. 122.

18. *Ibid.*, p. 145.

19. *Ibid.*, p. 214.

20. *Ibid.*, p. 71.

21. *Ibid.*, p. 79.

22. *Ibid.*, p. 78.

23. William James, *Pragmatism: A New Name for Some Old Ways of Thinking*, eds.
    Frederick H. Burkhardt, Fredson Bowers, and Ignas K. Skrupskelis (Cambridge:
    Harvard University Press, 1975), chap. 1.

24. Feyerabend, *Conquest of Abundance*, p. 215.

25. *Ibid.*, p. 239.

26. Preston, "Paul Feyerabend," para. 2.10.

27. Feyerabend, *Conquest of Abundance*, p. 195.

28. James, *Pragmatism*, chap. 7.

29. Feyerabend, *Conquest of Abundance*, p. 144.

30. *Ibid.*, p. 224; cf. p. 240.
31. *Ibid.*, p. 223.
32. *Ibid.*
33. Preston, "Paul Feyerabend," para. 2.16.
34. Cf. e.g., Dewey, *The Quest for Certainty.*
35. Feyerabend, *Conquest of Abundance*, p. 238.
36. Preston, "Paul Feyerabend," para. 2.15.
37. See Feyerabend, *Conquest of Abundance*, chap. 9.
38. *Ibid.*, p. 247.
39. *Ibid.*, p. 248; original emphasis.
40. *Ibid.*, p. 251.
41. Feyerabend, *The Tyranny of Science*, p. 11.
42. Cf. Sami Pihlström, *Pragmatic Pluralism and the Problem of God* (New York: Fordham University Press, 2013).
43. Feyerabend, *The Tyranny of Science*, p. 25.
44. *Ibid.*, p. 35.
45. *Ibid.*, pp. 35–6.
46. *Ibid.*, p. 51.
47. *Ibid.*
48. *Ibid.*, p. 38.
49. *Ibid.*, pp. 94–5.
50. *Ibid.*, pp. 61–2.
51. *Ibid.*, p. 62.
52. My forthcoming book, *Taking Evil Seriously* (Basingstoke: Palgrave Pivot, forthcoming 2014), deals with this issue in more detail from a Jamesian point of view.
53. William James, *The Will to Believe and Other Essays in Popular Philosophy*, eds. Frederick H. Burkhardt, Fredson Bowers, and Ignas K. Skrupskelis (Cambridge: Harvard University Press, 1979).
54. James, *Pragmatism*, p. 37.
55. *Ibid.*, p. 24.
56. *Ibid.*, p. 151.
57. Cf. also section 5 below.
58. Feyerabend, *Conquest of Abundance*, p. 78.
59. *Ibid.*, pp. 122 23, 215.
60. *Ibid.*, pp. 215–16; original emphasis; see also p. 240.
61. Cf. Whitman and James again.
62. Gottfried W. Leibniz, *Monadology* (1714), available online: http://www.earlymoderntexts.com/pdf/leibmona.pdf, para. 61.
63. Jorge Luis Borges, "The Book of Sand" (1975), available online: http://bookofsand.net/hypertext/.
64. Paul Auster, *Invisible* (New York: Simon & Schuster, 2009), p. 102.
65. Cf. Pihlström, "How (Not) to Write the History of Pragmatist Philosophy of Science?".

Five

EXPERIENCE AND JUDGEMENT: POLITICAL AND AESTHETIC

John Ryder

For those of us who do philosophy in the pragmatic vein, it is common to draw inspiration from classical pragmatist philosophers, most commonly Peirce, James, Dewey, and Mead.[1] One of the defining traits of pragmatism in the hands of these forebears is a distinctive conception of experience. In fact, it is in their approach to experience that the classical pragmatists differ most from neo-pragmatists. The latter, especially Rorty, had no use either for experience as a philosophical concept or for any articulated theory of experience. For the classical figures, their pragmatism is incomprehensible outside of an explicit and distinctive conception of experience.

Though James and Mead made much of experience, as did Peirce in his own way, it was Dewey for whom the concept of experience was a touchstone for most of the rest of his ideas across a range of topics. His approaches to education, democratic theory, aesthetics, religion, ethics, logic, indeed nature itself, are all rooted in, or at least inextricably related to, his broader understanding of experience as the constitutively relational interaction of individuals with their environments. And not by accident, the Columbia University environment, in which Dewey was working from the early years of the 20th century, also saw the development of the other major American philosophic tradition of the first half of the century, generally referred to as Columbia Naturalism. Through the 1960s, and beyond at other universities, American naturalism intersected with classical pragmatism to form a philosophic tradition that remains rich in conceptual resources.

For the purposes of this paper, I would like once again to draw inspiration from Dewey and his approach to experience to explore how we might understand the close relation between political and aesthetic experience. In this effort, we will complement other contemporary pragmatist philosophers who also understand the close relation among the political and the aesthetic, most significant among them being Richard Shusterman and Krzysztof Skowroński, and, to some extent, Richard Rorty.[2] And we will, as I have suggested above, draw on the related work of naturalist philosophers, specifically Justus Buchler, to couch the interactionist understanding of experience in a broader conception of judgment. The pragmatic naturalist theory of judgment will provide the categories that will allow us to develop an understanding of aesthetic and political theory and experience as related processes.[3]

1. Experience and Judgment

Because there may be readers who are not familiar with the pragmatic naturalist approach to experience, it is worthwhile to begin with a brief overview. This is important not simply by way of introduction and to set the stage, but more because there is a danger of assuming an understanding of experience, still common among philosophers, that has its roots in the empiricist tradition. If one makes such an assumption, it is almost certain that one will fail to understand our conception of experience and everything that follows from or is conceptually related to it, in which case we will be talking past rather than with one another. In an effort to avoid such an outcome, it is wise to dwell for a short time on how we wish to understand both experience and judgment.

The term "experience" is used in many ways, as we are all aware. We may speak about experience "of" an object, for example, in which case we probably mean something like the more traditional empiricist conception of having a sensory impression of it. But we may also speak in different ways, for example about the "human experience," or "religious experience," or about being "experienced" in this or that respect. These uses of the term do not suggest simply sensory impressions, but rather a cumulative outcome of innumerable related events. Some languages have available different words for different such phenomena, but in English we use the word "experience" for all of them. This is sometimes a disadvantage, especially when translating from English into other languages, but philosophically it has turned out to be fortuitous because it has inclined us to develop a rich conception of experience that encompasses its many forms, types, and expressions.

In Dewey's hands these and many other meanings of "experience" come together to form a single, coherent picture of the human interaction with our environment. Experience in this sense is the constitutively relational interaction of a person with the environment in its full scope that makes us all human beings and makes us each the specific human individuals that we are. The emphasis in this general understanding of experience is on the fact that our relations with our environing conditions are both active and passive; they involve both doing and undergoing, manipulation and assimilation. This is one of the more important differences between our conception of experience and the traditional empiricist notion, which posits experience as a far more passively understood process. Experience in our sense is a process in which we are actively and passively involved, in which we both manipulate our environment and absorb it.

We will, however, place our understanding of experience in a broader conception of judgment. In the sense in which we are here using the term "judgment," which we have taken from Buchler, it is not meant to refer to a mental process, though certainly sometimes judgments of various kinds are mental processes. However, not all of them are. Judgments are, rather, the ways in which we manipulate our environments on the countless occasions in which something results or is produced. Not all of our judgments are mental events, though some are; not all of our judgments are conscious, though some are; not all of our judgments are methodic or systematic, though some are; not all of our judgments are instrumental, though some are; not all of our judgments are momentous or even noticed, though some are; not all of our judgments are relevant to our experience, though some are, with the degree of relevance depending on the specific circumstances of the case.

Each of these kinds of judgment represents a human activity or process that has been identified in our various intellectual traditions as constituting our lives. We frequently make the distinction between conscious and unconscious activity, for example, though the products of both are human judgments even if they function differently in our experience. When we judge methodically or systematically, we are engaging in some sort of sustained, directed process. Dewey might have called it "inquiry," but he would have made a category mistake in doing so. Some of our methodic and systematic judging is inquiry, but some does not so much inquire as demonstrate or depict. We may say, again following Buchler, that all methodic and systematic judging is a form of query, of which inquiry is a species. Sometimes our activities result in completed processes, culminations, or fulfillments. Dewey might have called such a judgment "an experience," and he more than anyone has helped us understand the significance of such moments in our experience. However, much of our quotidian experience has a more fluid, tentative character, perhaps never achieving a fulfillment of any kind before transforming into something else. The products of both kinds of processes are equally judgments.

As a category of analysis, "judgment" is more generic than many of the other concepts we are more accustomed to using. It refers to any product of our interaction with the rest of nature, of any kind. Why, we may ask, do we need to introduce a concept of this generality into our understanding of experience? This is an important question, one that deserves a far more developed response than we can provide here. The most directly relevant answer for the purposes of this discussion is that the concept of judgment will help us articulate and clarify our considerations of political and aesthetic experience, as we will see. More generally, though, the concept of judgment allows us to sustain a more adequate conception of experience than we are able to manage without it.

Experience prevails in a broader natural context. This fact has proven to be a difficult one for philosophers to accommodate. Much of nature is not of our own making, and most of it, one may safely assume, lies permanently beyond the direct or even indirect experience of any one of us in our individual lifetimes. That is not to say that there are aspects of nature that are in principle beyond any possible experience, a view that is almost certainly false, and in any case pointless to hold. There is indeed good reason to hold the view that nature is so constituted relationally that in principle any of it is accessible in experience. That is to say, the idea of a "natural surd" is an oxymoron. But still, experience is not co-extensive with nature, a point to which our own experience regularly attests.

If nature is a broader category than experience, then one may say that experience is couched in nature, or that experience is a natural process. The relation between the two has, however, proven to be a troublesome one to understand. The Platonist traditions, both religious and secular, tend to render nature, in so far as we experience it, in some way an illusion relative to something "greater" or "more real" beyond, behind, or underneath it. The Kantian tradition erects a more or less impermeable barrier between nature itself and nature as it is experienced, given the way it understands how experience happens. And most of our currently prevailing philosophical and scientific frameworks readily relegate nature experienced to the realm of "appearance," despite the fact that such experiences as train tracks converging in the distance and the sun revolving around us through the day are ubiquitous and consistent.

We may say that nature is "whatever there is," and that our experience prevails in and through, or consists of, a subset of "whatever there is." We may say further that some aspects, or more technically complexes, of nature are related to us as human beings and serve as the natural conditions that distinguish us from other beings. Such complexes, we may say, largely define that to which we refer when we speak of the "human experience." Some complexes are related uniquely to a subset of individuals, for example Americans, and are what enable us to speak of the "American experience," or to women, thus enabling us to speak meaningfully of "women's experience." Some complexes are related uniquely to each of us, and constitute what we mean by your or my experience.

So far, however, we are still speaking too imprecisely. In the end, it is not sufficient to speak of experience in this or that sense as consisting of a "subset" of complexes. The reason it is insufficient is that this way of speaking continues to suggest, or at least allow, the idea that there is some sort of break or barrier between a given subset of complexes and the rest. Our normal experience belies this idea, however, in that we rarely if ever in normal daily activity have to wonder how our experience relates to reality, other than in specific situations in which the veracity of our perceptions or suspicions is under question. Our experience, we may say, bleeds across the boundaries of these various subsets of natural complexes, a fact made possible by the relational constitution of all the complexes of nature. The boundaries of the various "subsets" of complexes are highly porous, and so defining the different "realms" of experience in terms of them is misleading.

The details of the concept of judgment help us correct this insufficiency in our understanding of experience. One of the features of experience that has received inadequate appreciation is the fact that in experience we produce. We do not produce all the time, and not everything related to us is a product merely by being related to us. But we produce a great deal, and all of those products in experience are judgments. They are the ways we interact individually and collectively with nature that taken together create nature as experience. By attending to judgment within our experience, we can bring into focus aspects of a good deal of what we do and what we create in ways that are more clear and effective than by talking simply about experience.

At the most general level, there are three forms or modes of judgment: assertive, exhibitive, and active. Every dimension of our experience may be characterized by products, by judgments, in one or more of these three modes. This in the end is the reason that such seemingly disparate aspects of our experience as political and aesthetic activity have much more in common than we might at first think. Both political and aesthetic experience will include, even in large measure consist of, judgments that assert something, for example specific goods or goals; that exhibit something, perhaps that arrange formal components of a picture or a piece of music, or of a national tradition; and that perform something, perhaps a political process or a dramatic encounter. Political experience and aesthetic experience, we may say, have shared forms of judgment; they participate in or consist of activities and processes that overlap in character, meaning, and force.

This is so because experience involves judgment in one or more of the three modes. Some judgments are assertive in that they make a claim about something. They say something, generally something that has a truth-value in a traditional sense. Much, though not all, of our ordinary speech is assertive in this sense, as is for the most part both journalism and academic writing. Assertive judgments are most obviously associated with linguistic utterance, but there is no necessary connection between them. Language, as is well known, may be used for performative utterance, and it may also be used in exhibitive judgment, as is the case for poetry and literature as a whole. That literature and poetry are not assertive judgments for the most part is the reason that philosophical discussions of them that describe propositions in a fictional work as "false" are misguided. Except in special circumstances, the statements made in a fictional context do not have a truth-value in the sense appropriate to assertive judgments because they are not assertive judgments. There are senses of truth that may be applied in exhibitive judgment, but they are truth in different senses than typically meant in assertive judgments.

So exhibitive judgments differ from assertive judgments in significant ways. As we have suggested, exhibitive judgments do not assert anything; they do not consist of propositions. Rather, exhibitive judgments show something; they arrange materials, that is materials of any kind, in such ways that something is revealed to us. In powerful works of art (and art is the paradigmatic case of exhibitive judgment), the materials appropriate to a given medium are skillfully arranged such that something new is shown, demonstrated, exhibited. Sometimes we are struck by it immediately; at other times, repeated viewings or hearings are necessary before we grasp the fuller import of what has been exhibited. Exhibitive judgments are not necessarily matters of art, however, because meaning and even truth may be displayed throughout the range of our experience. Because our overall concern here is with the relation between political and aesthetic experience, it is worthwhile to point out that political meaning can be, and often is, expressed in and through exhibitive judgment. A propaganda poster, or a political billboard, or sometimes simply a photo can have a powerful political resonance. Some readers, especially those old enough to remember the Vietnam War, are familiar with the famous photo of a young Vietnamese girl running naked down a road in the aftermath of a napalm attack, an image and exhibitive judgment that conveyed a powerful message and that served to support political opposition to the war. The photo did not describe terror and pain or assert propositions about it; rather, it demonstrated terror and pain, and it did so in this case with considerable political import.

The third mode of judgment is the active, because in some cases it is in our actions themselves that we judge. When we move something from here to there, or chop wood, or clean the house, or in countless other kinds of actions, we are judging. And in some cases, the kinds of actions that typically function in one mode of judgment are central to another. We mentioned above that sometimes speech acts are performative, in which case a linguistic utterance does not assert something but performs an action, and the meaning of the utterance is in the action itself; sometimes actions can be exhibitive, as in performance art. Furthermore, any given judgment may, depending on the circumstances and context, function in more than one mode simultaneously. A dance is a good example, in which movement is as much exhibitive as active judgment.

This conception of judgment helps to fill out an understanding of experience by elucidating the ways our productive experience generates meaning and is related to knowledge, truth, beauty, and a host of other dimensions of our lives. Experience can be described not simply as the interaction with our environment in which we manipulate and assimilate, but also as the interaction with our environment in which we undertake the significantly human functions of asserting, exhibiting, and acting.

2. The Political and the Aesthetic

We are making a number of assumptions in this discussion. One of them is that it is reasonable to speak philosophically about experience, and in our case judgment as well. As we pointed out earlier, this assumption is not universally shared and has been challenged by Rorty and others. Another assumption we make is that it is reasonable to speak of something we refer to as aesthetic experience, and also in our case political experience. Political experience has been less of a contested issue, probably because people simply have not made much use of it as a philosophical concept. When the term "political experience" is used, it tends to refer to the extent of familiarity with political processes, or the length of time one has been around politics, rather than a specific form of experience. But the idea of aesthetic experience has been widely contested. When we speak of aesthetic experience, we do not mean the extent of one's familiarity with aesthetic objects or situations, or the length of time we have been around aesthetic objects; rather we mean either experience with certain characteristics or we mean, following Dewey, certain aspects of experience generally, and more than a few philosophers have claimed that we cannot give coherent and consistent sense to aesthetic experience in either version. At the risk of begging important questions, I would like to stipulate that both political experience and aesthetic experience are concepts to which we can ascribe significant meaning and about which we can speak to some worthwhile effect. The subsequent discussion will go some modest way toward making a pragmatic argument in support of that stipulation.

The literature on aesthetic experience is considerable, and there is little value in rehearsing it here. It is worthwhile, though, to point to several salient aspects of aesthetic experience because doing so will help us make some sense of political experience and the relation between the two. To be clear, this is not a thorough or systematic account or description of the various characteristics that have been assigned to aesthetic experience. Nonetheless, the following traits have often enough been said to characterize aesthetic experience: unity, continuity, integration, consummation, feeling, value for its own sake, harmony, direct engagement, and content of a certain kind. Let us consider these briefly to give a flavor of what aesthetic experience may amount to.

In the pragmatist literature, the traits most definitive of aesthetic experience have been unity, harmony, continuity, and of course consummation in the understanding of "an experience." These concepts were put to work by Dewey to such great effect and have been developed by others in the pragmatist tradition, most prominently John McDermott and Richard Shusterman.[4] For those not familiar with the idea, there are many good sources to look at for descriptions and discussions.[5] Briefly, though, the idea is that all of our experience, that it to say experience in the sense of the ongoing interactive and mutually constitutive relation of individuals and their environments, is imbued with traits that we may properly describe as aesthetic. Specifically, they are the harmony, unity, and integrity that give our experience explicit content, integrity as individual moments in experience, and ultimately meaning. These are aesthetic insofar as they are those traits that experience in general shares with our creative production of and engagement with art. Experience in general has an aesthetic dimension because all of it participates, we may say, in those characteristics that are especially applicable to works of art and to the experience of producing and engaging with art. The traits are more explicitly and intensely available in our interaction with art, which is how we may say that though all experience has an aesthetic dimension, not all experience and not all products of judgment are art. So though we do not want to say that all experience is art, we do want to say that all experience has an aesthetic dimension, and we further wish to say that in a nutshell the aesthetic dimension is the harmony, unity, and integrity we find in experience.

Sometimes in the ongoing flow of experience we find ourselves engaged with and in unusually distinct, intense, and meaningful experiences. These can be of many different kinds in the sense that they can be interactions with other people, with wilderness, with a city street, with a work of art, with a moment in a basketball game, or with anything else. They are experiences that stand out particularly intensely; they are not simply finished, but complete, or consummated, to a degree that most moments in experience, even those we may explicitly identify, are not; they are in a sense fulfillments, and they are unusually meaningful and significant. These moments are what Dewey and others call "an experience," and they are relevant to an understanding of the aesthetic in experience because they are the occasions in which the aesthetic traits of experience are the most explicit and fully expressed.

Dewey thought that the idea of the aesthetic dimension of experience is necessary for a fuller understanding of experience generally. This idea has been worked out by many other philosophers in the decades since Dewey developed it, and as a result there is no shortage of good reasons to understand experience more or less in this way. Furthermore, when we insert the conception of judgment as we have developed it, we add another layer of good sense to the pragmatist idea of aesthetic experience because we can speak in analogous ways of the reach of the exhibitive mode of judgment and its intersection with the aesthetic in experience. Just as one may say that all experience expresses in various ways and to varying degrees aesthetic traits, so we may say that our judgment generally expresses exhibitive dimensions that form much of what enables us to communicate meaningfully.

The questions we have set for ourselves are whether we may also speak profitably about a political dimension of experience, analogous to the aesthetic dimension; what the political dimension of experience may consist in; and how the political may relate to the aesthetic. We may now turn to these questions.

Some scholars have been exploring, if not the idea of political experience as we are proposing it here, then at least the close relation between the aesthetic and the political in experience. Michael Eldridge, for example, has pointed out that "for Dewey there was a single phenomenon – experience – that could be understood metaphysically, aesthetically, politically, or epistemically." Eldridge takes this observation not so much in the direction of a political experience or political dimension of experience, but he develops what he calls a Deweyan "political technology," by which he means an instrumentalist approach to social action and to the resolution of social problems.[6] Larry Hickman has spoken about "technological activity," by which he means the kind of activity that cognitively makes use of tools, a concept that overlaps to a considerable extent with the theory of judgment, and may have implications for what we mean by political experience or the political in experience.[7] And James Campbell has made the point that Dewey's entire understanding of experience is political.[8]

In a sense, it may seem to become unnecessary to make a point of political experience if experience is such a central category for Dewey, and if, as Campbell suggests, social reconstruction is equally central. It is more than worthwhile to notice that Campbell's idea of community reconstruction, Hickman's technology, and Eldridge's political technology are valuable ideas, and I would say good interpretations of Dewey, though they are not what we mean by "political experience." When we talk about the political, we do not mean the cognitively inferential in experience, as Hickman does by "technology," nor do we mean, like Eldridge, social action, and nor do we mean Campbell's community reconstruction, important though all of them were to Dewey and important though they are as dimensions of the political in our lives, entirely independent of Dewey.

When we talk about the political, we do not have in mind the political in these senses. Nor do we refer to partisan politics, or the "political" in the sense of the competition among political parties. That process, as well as partisan politics in general, is certainly one possible dimension of political life and activity, but it is a fairly narrow slice of it. That in some contexts the "political" is equated with partisan competition is an example of how distorted the understanding of the political aspects of our lives can become. When we talk about the political, we mean rather the entire dimension of individual and social lives that has to do with the systematic exercise of public authority. In this sense, the political is to be distinguished from experience that bears only on individual matters, or issues that concern only a slightly larger circle of people, such as families or neighbors, but that are nonetheless private. It is also to be distinguished from activity and experience that concern a wider range of people, or we may say social groups and organizations, but that do not have to do with authority and its exercise. Civil society generally falls into this category, as do NGOs, religious organizations in so far as they deal exclusively with spiritual concerns, arts organizations, groups of people with single interests, for example families whose children all attend a specific school, and other groups of people with a social function but without access to public authority. Economic activity is yet another category, as are the structures and organizations, either private or public, through and in which economic activity is carried out. Such organizations can have extensive social reach, and they can concentrate a good deal of power over individuals and social organizations, but as this does not necessarily entail public authority, they are not inherently political.

All such organizations may become political, or at least intersect with the political, when in their activity they engage public authority. Groups of parents and teachers may constitute a school board, in which case their activity pertains to public policy and authority; NGOs may find themselves needing to negotiate with public authority in order to function; arts organizations may need public support, and whatever *quid pro quo* arrangements such support requires, in order to prosper or even to survive;

people living in the same neighborhood may think it prudent to constitute themselves a neighborhood watch committee and, thereby, collaborate with the local police and other organs of public authority; and corporations or groups of small businesses generally find it necessary to engage public authority in the interest of policy making that they find acceptable. No individual or social group that partakes of the structures of contemporary organized life can avoid the political, at least not for long, but they are not therefore identical with the political. This is a significant point because we need to be able to distinguish political from other forms of social experience if we are to say anything significant about it.

Also by way of definition, it is important to notice that we are speaking here of public authority rather than state power to identify political experience. There are several reasons for this. The first is that the "political" ought not to be limited to that which concerns the state, if only for the obvious reason that political activity also occurs on much smaller or local levels than state concerns. When the American Congressman Tip O'Neil famously said "all politics is local," he was exaggerating for effect, but he had a point. Political activity is at least local as well as national.

A second reason to distinguish public authority from state power is that authority and power are not the same thing. All power is a form of authority when exercised legally, particularly within an area in which it has the legal right to function, but not all authority is power, or at least not power in the same sense. The state's control over legally exercised violence is certainly a form of power, as is its ability to persuade through other more peaceful means. The distinction between hard and soft power is now a familiar and in some respects a useful one, but for our purposes one should notice that power in either sense is not authority. No state has authority over another, though it may have the means to exercise hard and soft power in relation to it. Moreover, public bodies, local or national, may exercise authority without exercising power. For example, the state body that has the responsibility for taxation may exercise in a variety of ways its authority over the taxes I pay and the processes through which I pay them without calling into play the power it may also have to enforce that authority. The point is simply that power and authority are not the same thing, and that we wish to identify the political as that activity that concerns itself not necessarily with power, but necessarily with public authority.

Is there, we may now ask, a form of experience that may usefully be identified as political experience? Our answer, as we have already suggested, is that just as there is an aesthetic dimension that permeates experience, there is also a political dimension, and just as we can speak of aesthetic experience, we can equally meaningfully speak of political experience. One strong candidate for a trait of our activity that is a constituent of political experience is interests. We all act to some extent to achieve interests. We may do so instinctively or reflectively; we may so act haphazardly or systematically; we may pursue interests intelligently or not; we may advance our interests through our actions or we may damage our interests because we have misidentified them. Whatever the detailed description of how and why we pursue interests in any specific case, we act in general to achieve or advance our perceived interests, and not knowingly against them. Of course, our interests are involved in one way or another in many forms of our activity and experience. We pursue our economic interests in our commercial and market relations; we pursue interests of other kinds in supporting a favorite team or in playing for our own; we engage our aesthetic interests when we visit a museum and our spiritual interests when we attend religious services. So the pursuit of interests is not exclusive to political experience; it is, however, definitive of it because when we are engaged in activity that concerns public authority, we are invariably looking to secure our interests. That we also do so in other forms of activity and experience indicates, as we will see below, that there are indeed aspects of political experience that pervade experience generally, much as there are aspects of aesthetic experience that pervade experience generally.

In fact, we need to back up a bit and place interests in a proper perspective, because as an element in political experience they are related to others: to be specific, there are three traits of the political dimension of experience: individual, community, and interests. More needs to be said about each to clarify the idea.

"Individual" conveys the integrity of experience and experiences, i.e. the fact that we may speak of experiences as a plurality and not simply a mass term. Nature in general, including experience, is constituted by complexes rather than simples. Ours is a relational rather than an atomistic nature. Nonetheless, it is a nature in which there are individuals in relation, even as we insist that those individuals are themselves relational. And this general description applies to experience and experiences no less than to nature as a whole.

"Community" conveys the complexity and relationality in experience, the fact that in experience we continually deal with many factors, most generally described as the ongoing interaction of organism and environment, and the many distinct elements of those two moments in experience. If "individual" captures the plurality and multiplicity within experience, then "community" captures the relations among the multiple constituents. In this sense, "community" is an expression of the even more general trait of relationality. The term "community" applies here because, for the most part and despite the occasional bumpy ride, our experience hangs together; it is not simply a collection of events and processes, but a collection with an integrity of its own, and in some senses even a trajectory of its own.[9]

"Interests" are, we may say, the force of experience; they play the role that Hegel or Marx would have assigned to contradictions. It is in the pursuit of our interests of any kind – individual, social, economic, aesthetic, bodily, and all these and others in various combinations – through which experience "grows," as James and Dewey both said. At this general level, we do not yet need to distinguish various forms of interests or the kinds of relations that may prevail among differing sets of interests. Those considerations come, as we will see, when we unfold the general traits of political experience into some of its varieties and versions. At this point, we simply need to indicate that the three general traits of individual, community, and interests are traits of experience generally, and definitive traits of political experience.

I confess that the Hegelian sound of this is a bit unnerving, even to me: there are two general traits, individual and community, more or less opposite or contrasting traits, that frame the context in which our pursuit in experience of the third element, interests, provides the motor that energizes our experiential process. This may have a somewhat forced or artificial ring to it, but it nevertheless seems to me to make sense. So rather than applaud or condemn ourselves for this Hegelian moment, let us play it out and see where it goes.

So these are characteristics of experience in general, and they describe the political dimension of experience because they are especially relevant to the political aspect of our lives, roughly in the way harmony, integrity, and consummation are relevant to the aesthetic in life and experience. The less general features of our political lives flow from the interaction of the individual, community, and the pursuit of interests in experience: conflict, domination, liberation, conquest, compulsion, liberty, exploitation, rights, rebellion, revolution, genocide, and the many other concepts and categories that arise in political theory and practice. Our political theories depend to some extent on how we understand these three concepts and how we wish to describe their relation with one another and their relative importance. And specific forms of political life and organization also flow from the ways these three general traits of our experience are exercised: constitutional monarchy, absolute monarchy, democracy, dictatorship, anarchy, authoritarian rule, etc.

For example, in the pursuit of our interests we may generate, or at least find ourselves in, situations of conflict or harmony. Some political theorists make much of conflict, for example Chantal Mouffe today and Carl Schmitt in the previous century. Schmitt regarded irreconcilable differences as inherent in political life, which made political liberalism untenable in his view. Mouffe agrees that conflict is inevitable, but it moves her to articulate a conception of democratic political forms that do not attempt to smooth over conflict with consensus, but manage in other ways to incorporate it.[10] But as important as is the recognition that conflict and antagonism happen, and regularly, in our political lives, it is a mistake to take it to be a necessary trait of political experience because conflict and contestation simply do not function at that level of generality. The general category, and feature of the political dimension of experience, is interests and our pursuit of them. The process of pursuing our interests may lead to antagonism, but it need not.

One form of evidence we may offer to support the plausibility of identifying individual, community, and interests as traits of political experience, and of the idea that more specific forms of political experience derive from them, is the intellectual value Dewey demonstrated them to have by identifying common interests among members of communities as a definitive trait of democratic experience. As is well known, though still underutilized in analysis, Dewey developed his conception of democracy by noticing two features of our experience, as we have mentioned: that in all social groups their members have interests in common and that social groups necessarily engage in interaction with those beyond their own boundaries, specifically, we may add, most valuably in the form of the pursuit of common interests.[11] If that observation is accurate, then conflict is no more a necessary feature of political experience than is commonality. Dewey built his understanding of democracy on these two features of community. In other words, he drew his conception of democracy from the very features of experience that we are here using to characterize the political dimension of experience.

Just as democracy may be defined in terms of a certain form of the interaction among individual, community, and interests, so too may other political categories and forms of political experience. We may pursue interests in common, as in a democratic model, or we may pursue them at each other's expense, as other forms of political organization may enable or encourage; we may recognize the importance of a rough equality of opportunity among individual members of communities in the pursuit of interests, or we may let the differences in power and access of various individuals fall where they may; we may rely on rights or on social utility in the ways that we structure our organizations and the pursuit of our interests; we may fail to pursue common interests across borders and engage instead in imperialist adventures; we may pursue our interests intelligently or carelessly; we may emphasize collaboration and persuasion, or we may rely on power in our political structures.

Each of these alternatives will generate a different political picture, and a different form of political organization. In short, our political experience will differ depending on which of these forms of action and structure we promote. But all of them are forms of political experience, and all of them involve individual, community, and the pursuit of interests, and a specific relation among the three, as their defining traits. The reason for that is that these are the traits of political experience, or the political dimension of experience.

Experience in general, we may then say, has a political character, much as it has an aesthetic character. And as the most fulfilling and satisfying experience is, in the end, that in which the aesthetic dimension plays a prominent and intelligent role, so the most rewarding and enriching experience is also that in which we engage its political dimension intelligently. This, I take it, is more or less what Dewey meant by experience growing in ordered richness, and it seems that he was right. Moreover, it is the rich, interactionist theory of experience and the related theory of judgment that enable us to understand experience as thoroughly as we need in order for its aesthetic and political dimensions to be apparent.

NOTES

I would like to thank James Campbell, Larry Hickman, Krzysztof Skowroński, and Leszek Koczanowicz for helpful comments on the substance of this paper.

1. See Richard Shusterman, *Pragmatist Aesthetics: Living Beauty, Rethinking Art* (Lanham: Rowman and Littlefield, 2000), and "Aesthetic Experience: From Analysis to Eros," *Aesthetic Experience*, eds. Richard Shusterman and Adele Tomlin (New York: Routledge, 2008), pp. 79–97. For Skowroński, see Krzysztof Piotr Skowroński, *Beyond Aesthetics and Politics* (Amsterdam: Rodopi, 2013), and "The Constitutive Role of Social Values and Political Power in G. H. Mead's Reflections on Aesthetic Experience," *George Herbert Mead in the Twenty-First Century*, eds. F. Thomas Burke and Krzysztof Piotr Skowroński (Lanham: Lexington Books, 2013), pp. 189–202. Also see Richard Rorty, *Contingency, Irony, and Solidarity* (Cambridge: Cambridge University Press, 1989); and *The Rorty Reader*, eds. Christopher J. Voparil and Richard J. Bernstein (Oxford: Wiley-Blackwell, 2010). Though not contemporary, also see George Herbert Mead, "The Nature of Aesthetic Experience," *International Journal of Ethics*, 36 (1926), pp. 382–92, and at http://www.brocku.ca/MeadProject/Mead/pubs2/papers/Mead_1926a.html.
2. Justus Buchler, *Nature and Judgment* (New York: Columbia University Press, 1955); *The Main of Light: On the Concept of Poetry* (New York: Oxford University Press, 1974).
3. John J. McDermott, *The Drama of Possibility: Experience as Philosophy of Culture*, ed. Douglas R. Anderson (New York: Fordham University Press, 2007).
4. The source of all of it is, of course, John Dewey, *Art as Experience*, in *The Later Works of John Dewey*, vol. 10, ed. Jo Ann Boyston (Carbondale: Southern Illinois University Press, 1987).
5. See Michael Eldridge, *Transforming Experience: John Dewey's Cultural Instrumentalism* (Nashville: Vanderbilt University Press, 1998), pp. 37–8, 117–23.
6. Larry A. Hickman, *Philosophical Tools for Technological Culture: Putting Pragmatism to Work* (Bloomington: Indiana University Press, 2001), especially chap. 1.
7. James Campbell, *The Community Reconstructs: The Meaning of Pragmatic Social Thought* (Champaign: University of Illinois Press, 1992), and *Understanding John Dewey* (Chicago: Open Court, 1995), pp. 68–75, 144–57.
8. Justus Buchler, *Toward a General Theory of Human Judgment* (New York: Columbia University Press, 1951), for the relevant concepts of proception, proceptive domain, and proceptive direction.
9. Chantal Mouffe, *The Democratic Paradox* (London: Verso, 2009); Carl Schmitt, *The Concept of the Political*, trans. and ed. George Schwab (Chicago: The University of Chicago Press, 2007).
10. John Dewey, *Democracy and Education*, in *The Middle Works of John Dewey*, vol. 9, ed. Jo Ann Boyston (Carbondale: Southern Illinois University Press, 1980). See especially chap. 7.

Six

AESTHETICS AS DUTY OR AESTHETICS AS FAITH: NOTES ON RICHARD SHUSTERMAN'S *PRAGMATIST AESTHETICS* WITH REFERENCE TO ADORNO AND CASTORIADIS

David Schauffler

Two of the most prominent efforts of Richard Shusterman's *Pragmatist Aesthetics* – and, it might be thought, of the philosophical thrust of pragmatist aesthetics generally – are, first, to endorse and elaborate on John Dewey's concept of "art as experience," and second, to advocate the serious study, or serious appreciation (it is not always clear which), of certain cultural products heretofore considered beneath such study and not worthy of such appreciation. In general, Shusterman thinks we should focus on the life-enhancing pleasures of aesthetic experience and, in doing so, erase what he considers an artificial and invidious distinction between "gloomy and ascetic" high art, and the "potent pleasures" that "are typically declassed as mere entertainment."[1]

The fundamental question that is raised by these two proposals, namely, that of the relation between "art" and "ought," at root derives from pragmatism's signature stance of anti-foundationalism, which Richard Rorty celebrated and which Shusterman endorses. It is not within the scope or purpose of this paper to argue the merits or the nature of the foundationalist and anti-foundationalist positions (neither of which is as clear as their simple contrast might seem to suggest); rather I would like to break the general question into two parts, and then refer to two different conceptions of how to frame the notion of aesthetic experience, to see if the pragmatist theme might be clarified and perhaps strengthened by comparing it with these other approaches.

In the first place, let us ask why, on pragmatist grounds, we "should" conceive of art as experience – or, indeed, as anything at all – and why we "should," in concert with that, discard the distinction between high and low art, and embrace all the products of human ingenuity with equal enthusiasm and pedantry. While the pragmatist epistemic menu of local, temporalized, contingent, rhetorical, and infinitely revisable truth claims has many merits, I suggest that such claims supply especially feeble tools for the making of normative statements about art and aesthetics. For one thing, the absence of immediate function that is generally recognized in works of art and other "cultural" artifacts makes their meliorative role hard to specify, absent any existing hypothesis about what this role might be (see remarks below on the essentially conservative thrust of pragmatism). And, if we should broaden our criteria of both art and amelioration enough to be certain we have left nothing out, we may come close to vacuousness, as Shusterman himself recognizes ("if aesthetic experience is essentially indefinable, to explain art in terms of it will not take us very far").[2] Beyond this problem lies the surrounding one, namely, that normative views of any kind are hard to sustain, in both criticism and metacriticism, if one is committed to the idea that there are no secure, universal or universalizable grounds for such views. Why, from a dogmatically pragmatist standpoint, should we take the trouble to define art? Why should we occupy ourselves with such questions? In what sense is it "better" to view art on an experiential rather than an object-based plane, and how are we to measure the "betterness" of life that is stimulated by an experience of art or for that matter by a theory or anything of the kind?

Secondly, the question of the possible evaluation of art precisely on aesthetic grounds becomes problematic under a pragmatist epistemology. It is, without doubt, rather easy to assemble a schedule of qualities in an art object (or any other object) according to whether a person using (or experiencing) an object with or without such qualities is better able to function in a given environment, so long as we have agreed on what "better functioning" means, which is also not difficult to do. John Dewey in his 1926 article "Affective Thought in Logic and Painting" makes an argument of this kind based on Albert C. Barnes's study *The Art in Painting*, and comes up with a definition of quality in art (more precisely, in painting) which anyone today would recognize as the argument from successful adaptation:

> It is the kind and degree of integration of plastic means in achieving each of the elements of design taken by itself, and also the integration of each with all the others, which constitutes the objective standard for value in painting. From the psychological standpoint, this integration in pictures means that a correlative integration is effected in the total set of organic responses (...). In other words, integration in the object permits and secures a corresponding integration in organic activities. Hence, the peculiar well-being and rest in excitation, vitality in peace, which is characteristic of aesthetic enjoyment.[3]

A definition of this kind, despite Dewey's characteristically apposite description of "aesthetic enjoyment" at the end of the passage, displays all the shortcomings of a pragmatic search for criteria of artistic quality. In the first place, there is no "objective" way to assess the "integration of plastic means" in a work of art, unless it might be by measuring the "corresponding integration in organic activities," though any association between these two, whatever they may independently mean, is simply an occult claim of early 20th-century pseudo-science – as is, likewise, the attribution of the feeling of "rest in excitation" to the foregoing organic integration. We are left to fall back on the art recipient's subjective reports of feelings of excitation, vitality, etc. upon experiencing the artwork, which are all only rather elaborate ways of saying that he likes it.

There is nothing wrong with a naïve-response view of artistic merit, but such a view excludes the possibility that there are formal conditions of quality for various genres of art or for artworks as a whole, by which they can be judged better or worse in relation to one another. A pragmatist may indeed wish to dispense with formal criteria for artistic quality, though this is likely to lead him into inconsistency,[4] and will furthermore seem to abrogate the need for theory entirely, perhaps turning it, as in the passage just quoted, into something like self-parody. But the naïve-response view will also trouble the pragmatist, again, on the original aspect of the normative judgment: namely, why "should" we want to derive pleasure from works of art, and, if doing so may improve our lives or make us better people or citizens, by what criteria is such improvement or betterment to be measured and why, again, should it matter?

The answers to these issues that appear in *Pragmatist Aesthetics* are essentially of two kinds and are in keeping with the general tenor of pragmatist argumentation. The first is pleonastic in tone: "Dewey," writes Shusterman, reconceives philosophy "as aimed not primarily at the resolution of abstract philosophical puzzles but at bringing us closer to achieving more and better concrete goods in experience (…). So a good definition of art should effectively direct us towards more and better aesthetic experience."[5] The reiteration of the comparatives makes this work of aesthetic theory read a little like the motto of the Olympic Games ("higher, faster, stronger") or, perhaps, the selling-point of a modern sex manual, but Shusterman is unembarrassed by such associations and directly repeats the same terms still more emphatically. To define art as experience "helps us to recognize and valorize those expressive forms which provide us aesthetic experience but which could provide us far more and far better, if they could be appreciated and cultivated as legitimate art."[6] The obvious questions begged by these assertions are, first: why cannot the resolution of abstract puzzles (i.e. traditional philosophy, or, for that matter, formalist aesthetics) also bring us closer to more or better concrete goods, or whatever it might be that we are aiming for? And second: what can "more and better concrete goods in experience" possibly mean, if not the endless accumulation of superfluities that marks our economic behavior and that art, one might be tempted to think, can be a relief from, rather than another instance of? We do not, at any rate, generally desire "more and better" wives or husbands, children, philosophy lectures, walks in the park, and other things we greatly value, and if we do, we take it as a sign that something in our life has gone badly wrong. Nowhere does Shusterman address[7] the possibility that aesthetic experience is subject to the law of diminishing returns (either in quantity or in quality), or that, on separate grounds, some aesthetic experiences (like some experiences of all kinds) may have meaning or value for us because of their mildness of intensity or rareness of incident. Third, by what means shall the quality, and improvement in quality, in aesthetic experience, granting that such things are measureable, be measured? And fourth, what role can the critic, or anyone, have in helping us to enhance our aesthetic experiences so that, as Shusterman urges, they should be both better and more frequent? If we concede, as the burden of *Pragmatist Aesthetics* is to get us to do, that certain despised popular forms of entertainment should qualify as "art" and be appreciated as such, what is the manner of that appreciation, how does it differ from our appreciation of mere entertainment, and how, without appeal to objective (formal, historical, intentional) qualities in the work, can the critic hope to improve our experiential performance, what Dewey calls the "correlative integration in the total set of organic responses"?

The second kind of answer that is proffered in *Pragmatist Aesthetics* as a reason for viewing art as aesthetic experience of a certain quantifiable kind is that, in one fashion or another, viewing art this way will enhance or enrich human life, or make individuals happier, or lead to a better society. There is no way to refute such ambitions and, since they are perfectly amiable, no reason to try to do so. But they remind us that pragmatism is not only meliorist and utilitarian (and thus possessed, in spite of itself, of a very broad and largely unexamined foundation), but is also an inherently conservative, indeed traditionalist, school of thought, and this most clearly in the moment when it expresses the liberalism of its great practitioners. For it can only coherently gauge the quality, and thus the worth, of objects or actions (or ideas) by the subjective assessments of those affected by them, and these assessments are inevitably embedded in the traditions that have gone to make up the outlooks of the subjects. When Shusterman writes of the failure of Dada and Surrealism to break the grip of the "cultural establishment" on the definition of art, because that establishment simply appropriated the revolutionary forms as high art,[8] leaving the uncultured masses to continue toiling along with Charlie Chaplin and Sunday Pops and other mere entertainment, he is describing the same process by which bourgeois "high" culture continually appropriates new art forms, finding in them excitement and individuality and self-expression and other good liberal virtues, just such qualities as he himself finds in rap music. Surrealism could improve and enrich people's lives, and make society happier, by becoming an interesting aesthetic experience, but not if it convinced some people that society was absurd and art meaningless, and drove them to despair or suicide. Likewise, rap music can enrich people's lives and make society happier, if it gives a voice to talented youths, and broadens our cultural horizon with a refreshing dose of linguistic creativity, but not if it convinces some people that society is absurd and their lives are meaningless, and drives them to murder or suicide.

If we ask in what other terms the definition or quality of art might be discussed, we soon enter a thicket of metaphysical speculation, such as Shusterman walks through during his exegesis of T.S. Eliot's "Portrait of a

Lady." Here Schiller's *Letters on the Aesthetic Education of Man* are held up as an example (indeed, as the "paradigm text") of the romantic doctrine of art, which Shusterman (speaking of Eliot's poem) suggests is likely to lead either to effete aestheticism, or to moral callousness, or to both.[9] But even if this were found to be the case, Schiller in the *Aesthetic Education* offers a succinct and supple account both of what art (or great art) is, and of what it does, i.e., why it is art (or great art), which Shusterman is not able to do. In Schiller's letters, beauty appears to both the *Stofftrieb* and the *Formtrieb* as that which is, respectively, attractive to them; that is, beauty is the feature of a thing that in one way or another draws us to it, makes us wish to master it, to possess it. But aesthetic beauty, that which appeals to both of our original drives, can therefore attract neither of them; our nature in recognition of this impasse is thereby freed from the control of these drives, and it is precisely this liberation that comprises the general response we feel to the work of art.

Schiller famously goes on to argue that the spiritual freedom evoked by (genuine) aesthetic experience (which he describes in terms similar to those used by Dewey, quoted earlier[10]) is the key to our true humanity, and the precondition for life as a citizen and as a wholly competent and happy being. But Shusterman has little interest in this line of argument. He first accuses Schiller of a kind of aestheticism, according to which "our great human potential for feeling and deep emotion will be directed not at fellow humans but at works of art,"[11] and, worse, suggests, that Schiller was a rank elitist: "What Schiller (and also Hume and Kant) meant by universality was not the natural taste of all people in all classes, including the common taste of the vulgar, but was basically the shared taste of culturally privileged society."[12] Nothing that Schiller says about aesthetic experience, or its role in human psychology, in the *Aesthetic Education* remotely supports either of these claims; the first is a direct contradiction, and therefore displays a sad misunderstanding, of Schiller's principal argument; the second finds no corroboration whatsoever in the letter of Schiller's text and is contradicted, too, by the spirit of it. But Shusterman's two points, which are apparently the result of bringing to his reading of Schiller his own prejudice, betray his deep commitment to the two convictions that I mentioned at the outset: first, that art, or the aesthetic experience, is "supposed" to beneficially affect human behavior and bring about, in whatever way we might choose to conceive them, "good outcomes," and second, that there is in fact a distinction between "high" and "low" art (a distinction which, as remarked above, never appears in Schiller) but that, in some way, this distinction should be dismantled or abolished.

The argument that our experience of the beautiful does, or ought to, lead us into better ways is one which is explicitly rejected by Schiller,[13] for which he has been often criticized, and Shusterman and other pragmatist aestheticians are (as in other things) quite traditionalist in restating the charge. But here we may turn to Theodor Adorno, who in *Aesthetic Theory* offers an

argument, different from Schiller's but more detailed, for the moral inertia of
aesthetic experience.

Adorno means definitively to sever the evaluative link between art and
behaviour – or, as we might say, the meliorative outcome of aesthetic
experience – by theoretically asserting the artwork's complete autonomy. This
effort is undoubtedly related to his preoccupation with the role of economic
forces, technology, and ideology in the creation of cultural products, and the
perpetual Hegelian-Marxist anxiety that all cultural expression, and indeed
almost everything else in human affairs, is to be interpreted merely as an
effusion or expression of economic and political structures and their
sustaining ideologies; such a worry may well incline the critic to posit a way
in which art (or some art), while indeed arising out of its parent society, can
stand in opposition to that society, or be independent of it, and thus stand
independent of the various beliefs and expectations of the members of that
society, and precisely in this way offer them a relief from, or a perspective
upon, their own habitual beliefs and social circumstances. Adorno writes:

> The transition from natural beauty to art beauty is dialectical as a
> transition in the form of domination. Art beauty is what is objectively
> mastered in an image and which by virtue of its objectivity transcends
> domination. Artworks wrest themselves from domination by
> transforming the aesthetic attitude, shaped by the experience of natural
> beauty, into a type of productive labor modeled on material labor (…).
> Artworks have this much in common with idealist philosophy: They
> locate reconciliation in identity with the subject; in this respect idealist
> philosophy – as is explicit in Schelling – actually has art as its model,
> rather than the reverse. Artworks extend the realm of human domination
> to the extreme, not literally, though, but rather by the strength of the
> establishment of a sphere existing for itself, which just through its
> posited immanence divides itself from real domination and thus negates
> the heteronomy of domination.[14]

The thrust of Adorno's aesthetics is transcendence, but this consists in
identity with the absolute self-sufficiency of the artwork as such. It is in this
regard that I speak of Adornian aesthetics as an aesthetics of duty: not civic
duty or Kantian duty or eudaemonic duty, but a duty inherent in the being-
present of the art. Under this view, it is almost meaningless to speak of
amelioration, of the good, bad, or mixed "effects" of the art upon the recipient
or, through him or her, upon society.

> What is true in positivism is the platitude that without the experience of art
> nothing can be known about it and there can be no discussion of it. But
> precisely this experience contains the distinction that positivism ignores:
> To put it drastically, this is whether one uses a hit song, in which there is

nothing to understand, as a backdrop for all kinds of psychological projections, or whether one understands a work by submitting to the work's own discipline. What philosophical aesthetics held to be liberating in art – in philosophical argot, what transcended time and space – was the self-negation of the contemplator who is virtually extinguished in the work. This extinguishing is exacted by the artworks and is the *index veri et falsi*; only he who submits to its objective criterion understands it; he who is unconcerned about it is a consumer.[15]

The conception of aesthetic appreciation as self-obligating duty, the idea that the artwork – by virtue of its being an artwork – demands of the recipient *qua* appreciator that he abandon all reference to his personal condition or well-being, clearly has the look of a universal posit, and would seem to leave out of consideration the historical circumstantiality both of the artwork itself and of any given recipient of the work, from its own time and place or another one. Adorno is aware of this and remarks upon it as follows:

> While the effort of aesthetics today presupposes the critique of its universal principles and norms as binding, this effort is itself necessarily restricted to the medium of universal thought. It is not within the purview of aesthetics to abolish this contradiction (...). In the obligatorily universal determinations, historical processes have sedimented what – to vary an Aristotelian formula – art was. The universal determinations of art are what art developed into. The historical situation of art, which has lost any sense of art's very raison d'être, turns to the past in the hope of finding the concept of art, which retrospectively acquires a sort of unity. This unity is not abstract but is, rather, the unfolding of art according to its own concept.[16]

This posited unfolding, this – very Hegelian – notion of art in the present retaining its autonomy because it is the culmination of its own, as it were, independent identity, leads to the second of the two viewpoints I wish in this paper to contrast with the pragmatist approach, and to the second question raised by the two elements of *Pragmatist Aesthetics* with which I began, namely: why should we wish to abolish the high art/low art distinction, or why should we try to reconceive these terms?

In the first place, this distinction is, or rather was, an eminently pragmatic one, and seems to be as old as the practical and taxonomic reasons for maintaining it. Aristotle, for example, distinguishes Epic and Tragedy from Comedy on the grounds that the former treat of noble actions and personages, while the latter is "a dramatic picture of the Ridiculous" and is "an imitation of men worse than the average."[17] That the works of these kinds served different functions, evoked different responses, and to some extent appealed to different audiences, would not have seemed to Aristotle matters any different from their existence as such. Secondly, it may be said that mass culture and its products do not today seem to be in any great need of aid or sponsorship from philosophy; it seems to be much more the case that philosophy and cultural criticism, now functioning as elements of an enormous academic industry, have decided to appropriate products of mass culture as objects for analysis in order to feed their insatiable appetite for fresh material. As a result, despite what Shusterman maintains in *Pragmatist Aesthetics* (and very much more so since the book was first published in 1992), the longstanding distinction between high art and low art has, in the academic if not in the popular mind, already become largely erased. Thirdly, and partly as a result of the foregoing, the quite separate distinction between art that is worthy of serious critical and aesthetic attention and art that is not, or to put it baldly, between great art and bad art, has also become blurred; indeed, the evaluation of art in accordance with notions of its inherent quality has fallen into bad odor in academic circles, to such an extent that even to speak of art that is "good" and "bad" is coming to suggest an unsavory combination of philistinism and political incorrectness.

An interesting avenue towards maintaining both the category and a coherent theory of great art, and also towards recognizing and evaluating the category of art that is not great, is sketched in elements of the work of Cornelius Castoriadis. He was not an aesthetician, and his direct remarks on art appreciation are few, and indirect references to it widely scattered across a diverse body of work; but one can easily extrapolate from these observations the outlines of an aesthetic theory that makes an interesting contrast both with Adorno's and with Shusterman's position in *Pragmatist Aesthetics*.

Castoriadis's theory of the imaginary institution of society is a supple tool for conceptualizing how it is that art functions socio-historically, and how it seems sometimes to transcend, and in most cases fails to transcend, the local conditions in which it arises. Castoriadis posits the "institution" of a given society as a collective, unplanned, unintentional consciousness, an amalgamation of traditions, collective and individual memories, embedded habits of thought, biological drives, language, and economic and other social relations, all existing simultaneously, though non-identically, in all the individuals who go to make up the society and in the society as a whole. The creative element, both of Castoriadis's theory and of the "institution" itself as he projects it, lies in the argument that this institution is simultaneously full of convictions and full of internal contradictions, both in itself and between it and the individual "imaginations" who form it and whom it forms. Art, on this view, is at least in some measure a kind of testament on the part of the artist; an attempt to force a reconciliation between the conflicting elements of the social imaginary that he or she has absorbed, including those parts of it that are "individual" parts of his or her character or circumstances. Art, so considered, is received as an expression of faith in the absurdity of social identity – being who we are because of where and when and to whom we were born, and at the same time perpetually rising out of that identity, becoming but never fully being alienated from it in the direction of differentiation and the universal.

On such a model it is clear, first, that aesthetic experience, as in Adorno, is a matter of identity or reconciliation, rather than of sensual satisfaction. But the implication of Castoriadis's scheme is that the reconciliation that the recipient may feel in the presence of the artwork is essentially a disturbance; reconciliation takes the form not of satisfying, self-enhancing identity but of recognition of a state of conflict, of insufficiency and existential unhappiness. (It may be added here that the close tie between aesthetic and religious experience is affirmed not only on anthropological but also on phenomenological grounds.) Second, Castoriadis's framework provides a clear way to distinguish degrees of artistic quality: leaving questions of technical skill aside, certain individuals, groups, societies, genres of art, art-producing technologies, etc., are simply better able to create portrayals of imaginary convictions and contradictions than others. Moreover, it may be said (and this is a point that Castoriadis himself repeatedly makes) that some of these imaginary convictions and contradictions are more powerful, more disturbing, and more universal than others.

But Castoriadis adds a further level to the discussion. In a late essay, "The Crisis of Culture and the State," he elaborates on the possibility that most contemporary art – both "serious" and "popular," "high" and "low" – is simply not very good.[18] He asserts this as a fact and one which, moreover, is acknowledged by virtually everybody – that is, as a fact which functions in the society as a social imaginary, to use his own formulation. The task of contemporary aesthetics, he believes, is not to obscure or deny this fact but to explain it.

Castoriadis holds that

> The two poles, the two nuclei of imaginary significations which have coexisted in Western societies for centuries are in a state of crisis. One of these nuclei is the capitalistic nucleus properly speaking, the imaginary signification of unlimited expansion of pseudorational mastery over nature and over humans. To this is opposed the other nucleus, the project of social and individual autonomy (or the emancipatory project, or the democratic movement, or the revolutionary movement).[19]

These two movements, he believes, are the intellectual, emotional and political driving forces of Western modernity; in them, and in the tensions and conflicts between them, we would expect to find the convictions and contradictions, the sources of great emotional triumph and tragedy that it would be the role of great works of art to bring forth, and that were brought forth by the great works of the modern period. But, continues Castoriadis,

The imaginary signification of unlimited expansion of "rational" mastery is in deep crisis today. One has only to look at the hollowness of the revived "liberal" rhetoric of the free market, free enterprise, etc.; there is nothing new in it, not even new arguments – it is a plastic, cheap thing, miles below the level of discussion of the great liberals of the early 19th century. On the other hand, a crisis equally deep has corroded the democratic, or emancipatory, or revolutionary project (…). Revolution is radical change in the institutions of society. After (…) the decline of the ideology of "progress," be it liberal or Marxist, there is now a stalemate. Even people who would like to work to change things look around, and cannot see any direction in which they could work.[20]

Castoriadis adduces further examples contrasting periods or societies that produced great art with those that did not, and concludes by saying,

I would tentatively suggest that the creation of great works, œuvres, in a society presupposes that there are meanings in that society which are very positively and strongly cathected, invested by the people living in the society in question. I think that all the great works we do have, including the modern ones (…) have been created in a sort of positive relation to positive values (…). What I mean is not an edifying function of the work, not a moralizing function, not what the Germans would call *Erbaulichkeit* (…). What I mean is not even Aristotelian catharsis. Rather, I refer to the strange relation existing between the work and values or imaginary significations of a society, relations consisting in the fact that the great work of art simultaneously reaffirms those values and calls them into question.[21]

We have here, then, a sketch of artistic accomplishment – and hence, of potential aesthetic appreciation – which can be in some fashion measured along a scale, one which does not, at least essentially, depend upon the relative merits of individual technique. It also has not to do directly with the much-labored distinction between low and high art, and at least, in this respect, it disputes the charge implicit in the arguments of Shusterman and others, that "low" and "high" art are code terms intended by intellectual elitists to signify that "high" art is "good" and "low" art is "bad." Castoriadis, as mentioned above, gives reasons for thinking that almost all contemporary art, low and high, is "bad" in the sense he goes on to develop, but he would also no doubt say that on the same grounds, much of history's "low" art was and is very much better than that which has been considered "high." On the other hand, Castoriadis's formula (as I have interpreted it here) for measuring the worth of artistic achievement preserves the sense in finding and understanding variation in the quality of that achievement, on grounds that, as Adorno pointed out in a passage quoted above, are necessarily universal in import though historical in application. Most importantly, in light of the questions with which this discussion opened, the aesthetic scheme of Castoriadis does not locate the quality of the art object in the response of the observer, but in the potential for evoking a response that inheres in the work. To have a high potential of this kind, the work must be created under conditions in which its creator, or creators, are conscious of problems, challenges, and emotional dilemmas of great importance; they not only must possess a high degree of talent and technical skill, but also they (and therefore, to some substantial degree, their society) must have vital convictions about past, future, and present, a deep sense of human dignity and lively awareness of moral conflict, and some intuition of charity.

So much, Castoriadis concludes, for the chance of great art being created in any quantity in today's world. But the most telling aspect of his notion is that understanding and appreciation of greatness in art requires, as it were, imaginative recognition of those convictions, challenges, aspirations, and conflicts on the part of the recipient; the viewer, listener, or reader who lives in a culture in which nothing is held too seriously, in which irony is the default setting of almost all discourse, will neither recognize nor appreciate what is great in great art – and may be inclined, therefore, to call "great" whatever sells well or is marketed with the label of genius – but can still approach art, any art, with a kind of faith in the sense best described by Kierkegaard, precisely not for what it will bring him, but because the idea of art itself demands it.

NOTES

1. Richard Shusterman, *Pragmatist Aesthetics: Living Beauty, Rethinking Art* (Lanham: Rowman and Littlefield, 2000), p. 53.
2. *Ibid.*, p. 56.
3. John Dewey, "Affective Thought in Logic and Painting," *John Dewey on Education: Selected Writings*, ed. Reginald D. Archambault (Chicago: University of Chicago Press, 1974), p. 146.
4. Shusterman himself, while generally rejecting formal criteria in *Pragmatist Aesthetics*, actually employs them frequently, above all in discussing the genre of rap music, which he maintains is (contrary to the view of hostile critics), "full of songs firmly structured either on clear narrative development or on coherent logical argument." Shusterman, *Pragmatist Aesthetics*, p. 233.
5. *Ibid.*, p. 57.
6. *Ibid.*, p. 57.
7. At least, not in *Pragmatist Aesthetics*; he makes what can be construed as an argument, or several arguments, of this kind in the later book *Thinking through the Body: Essays in Somaesthetics* (Cambridge: Cambridge University Press, 2012).
8. Shusterman, *Pragmatist Aesthetics*, pp. 144–45.
9. See *ibid.*, pp. 153–68.
10. „When we have abandoned ourselves to the enjoyment of genuine Beauty, we are at such moments masters in equal degree of our passive and our active powers,

and shall turn with equal facility to seriousness or to play, to rest or to movement, to compliance or to resistance, to abstract thinking or to beholding." Friedrich Schiller, *On the Aesthetic Education of Man in a Series of Letters*, trans. Reginald Snell (New York: Frederick Ungar, 1984), p. 104.

11. Shusterman, *Pragmatist Aesthetics*, p. 155.

12. *Ibid.*, p. 156.

13. „We must therefore acknowledge those people to be entirely right who declare the Beautiful, and the mood into which it transports our spirit, to be wholly indifferent and sterile in relation to *knowledge* and *mental outlook*. They are entirely right; for Beauty gives no individual result whatsoever, either for the intellect or for the will; it realizes no individual purpose, either intellectual or moral; it discovers no individual truth, helps us to perform no individual duty, and is, in a word, equally incapable of establishing the character and clearing the mind." Friedrich Schiller, "Twenty-first Letter," *On the Aesthetic Education of Man in Series of Letters*, p. 101.

14. Theodor W. Adorno, *Aesthetic Theory*, trans. and ed. Robert Hullot-Kentor (Minneapolis: University of Minnesota Press, 1997), p. 77.

15. *Ibid.*, pp. 265–6.

16. *Ibid.*, p. 263.

17. Aristotle, *Poetics*, trans. Ingram Bywater, in *Introduction to Aristotle*, ed. Richard McKeon (New York: Modern Library, 1947), pp. 628–30.

18. Cornelius Castoriadis, *Philosophy, Politics, Autonomy: Essays in Political Philosophy*, ed. David Ames Curtis (New York: Oxford University Press, 1991), pp. 222–4.

19. *Ibid.*, p. 221.

20. *Ibid.*, p. 222.

21. *Ibid.*, pp. 227–8.

Part Three

ETHICS, HUMANISM, AND SOCIAL HOPE

Seven

THE LINGUISTIC WORLD: RORTY'S AESTHETIC MELIORISM

Rosa M. Calcaterra

1.

An overall look at the wide international reception of Rorty's neo-pragmatism certainly shows that it has received more criticism than consent, both on the part of those who continue the philosophical line inaugurated by Charles S. Peirce and William James, and on the part of the representatives of philosophical currents from outside the pragmatist tradition. While the consent comes from the post-postmodernist or post-philosophical side of contemporary culture, which appreciates especially Rorty's call to reassess the role of philosophy in relation to other human expressions of intelligence, it is easy to see that the criticisms derive instead from a sort of "cross-party group" of our theoretical scenario, which underscores the difficulty of taking up the skeptical challenge that Rorty launched against a series of canonical tenets of Western thought. In particular, it is a challenge that seems, to many, to be incongruous precisely because it makes an appeal to the pragmatism of James and Dewey, proposing a reading that results in a remarkable contrast with the fallibilist, but at the same time anti-skeptical and constructivist spirit that permeates their work.

More or less like every other philosophical work, Rorty's work certainly contains a number of ambiguities, but what in this case seems more problematic is his often rash, or even fanciful, manner of addressing certain themes and authors. One can easily practice historiographic or philological scrupulousness on various exegetical pronouncements made by Rorty. But this is probably not the most appropriate way to evaluate the theoretical and ethical-political influences that come from the research of a thinker generally placed alongside the most prominent figures of American philosophy of the second half of the twentieth century: Willard Quine, Hilary Putnam, and Donald Davidson.[1] On the other hand, it is worthwhile to consider that a provocative style is an integral part of Rorty's commitment to fostering a cultural climate in which one can do without a series of theoretical-methodological criteria that are profoundly rooted in the Western philosophical tradition. This should be a climate in which, above all, one is able to give up the defining mentality that pervades the origins and the most influential developments of our history of ideas. It is equally important to take note that, at various points, Rorty himself realized that his contributions regarding thinkers he considered essential to his neo-pragmatism were mainly attempts to freely develop their most relevant suggestions for the purposes of his philosophical project. Thus, for example, in his Preface to *Philosophy and Social Hope*, Rorty asserts that his references to James and Dewey have no pretence of being faithful to their thought but seek rather to offer his own, "sometimes idiosyncratic, restatements of Jamesian and Deweyan themes."[2]

2.

I look forward to an era in which the question "Are there absolutes?" has no resonance. To ask that question betrays an inability to live with one's own finitude, and I should like to think that someday human beings will no longer try to escape the historicity and contingency of their existence.[3]

This is what Richard Rorty declared in the conclusion of the autobiography he submitted in 2007, a few months before his death, for the volume of the "Library of Living Philosophers" dedicated to him. It is an expression which definitively confirms the leitmotiv underlying his philosophical journey throughout. In fact, in his work a battle against the search for "absolutes" and a firm conviction that it is necessary to accept the contingency and historicity of human life are fused in a cultural project marked by a trust in the accomplishments as well as in the further ethical potentialities of liberal democracies. More precisely, Rorty was committed to supporting the hope for consolidation, dissemination, and growth of the meliorist spirit, which Ralph Waldo Emerson, Walt Whitman, and John Dewey saw as distinctive of American democracy. In fact, they identified its essential characteristic as the "the ability to believe that the future will be unspecifiably different from, and unspecifiably freer than, the past."[4]

One can view Rorty's philosophy as a renewed expression of the meliorism which characterizes the cultural tradition of the United States. Within this tradition, he certainly favors the "aesthetic" strand, that is, those components that emphasize the value of emotions, or even declare their effectual priority over other human faculties. In Rortian discourse, the meliorist-aesthetic orientation becomes specific in the call to revive the hope for a continuous increase in feelings of human solidarity and in their irreplaceable capacity for resistance to oppression and cruelty, relying not on the need for rationalism, but rather on the power of imagination and literary narratives. Imagination and literature are seen as tools into which both individual and political energy should be invested, for the safeguard of the value of free interpersonal and intercultural communication, a value that democratic societies identify as one of their most salient criteria.

The strong emphasis on the future and the importance of communicative interactions – of the "human conversation," to use Rorty's words – constitute not only the two basic aspects of his image of American democracy but also the pivotal points of the particular version of pragmatist philosophy that he proposed on the basis of a close criticism of the concept of philosophical work as an activity intended to provide the universal and necessary foundations of a certain knowledge of reality, that is, knowledge capable of accurately reflecting its phenomena and essential traits. Alternatively, Rorty's neo-pragmatism proposes an image of philosophy as an edifying commitment founded on the principle of *social hope* and, in parallel, on a trust in the potential of individual human self-creation, building on the consonances between the work of James and Dewey and the anti-foundationalist orientation that marks much of contemporary European thought as well as post-neopositivist philosophy in the United States.

It should be pointed out immediately that the themes chosen by Rorty from Dewey and James relate primarily to the criticism of the distinction between appearance and reality, which, in his view, extends from Plato to modern and contemporary foundationalism. In other words, he credits James and Dewey with the merit of having shown the difficulties inherent in the way of thinking centered on metaphysics of a Platonic sort, and of having at least opened the way toward a philosophical style capable of going beyond the conviction that the most important human ability is an ability to discover the reality behind appearances. Having shifted attention from this problematic goal to the question of the practical function of philosophical knowledge, and, in particular, of our cognitive endeavors, James and Dewey are, for Rorty, a source of great support for a cultural perspective that intends to foreground the value of human happiness, as he himself declared he wanted to do. It is precisely in such sense that Rorty took the two classical representatives of pragmatism as support in his journey as a public intellectual: a journey guided by the idea that "the most distinctive and praiseworthy human capacity is our ability to trust and to cooperate with other people, and in particular to work together so as to improve the future."[5]

As mentioned above, the focus on the future and on communicative interaction is the key factor both in Rorty's image of American democracy and in his neo-pragmatism. The crucial section of *Philosophy and Social Hope*, with the eloquent title "Hope in Place of Knowledge: A Version of Pragmatism," offers interesting indications in this direction. Leaving James aside, no doubt because he does not refer to social issues, these pages reflect the specific anti-foundationalist angle from which Rorty identifies a close relationship between Dewey's pragmatism and the orientation of U.S. democracy:

What he [Dewey] had in mind is that both pragmatism and America are expressions of a hopeful, melioristic, experimental frame of mind. I think the most one can do by way of linking up pragmatism with America is to say that (…) we can, in politics, substitute *hope* for the sort of knowledge which philosophers have usually tried to attain. (…) If there is anything distinctive about pragmatism it is that it substitutes the notion of a better human future for the notions of 'reality,' 'reason,' and 'nature.' One may say of pragmatism what Novalis said of Romanticism, that it is "the apotheosis of the future."[6]

Rorty clarifies that Dewey's thought, shifting philosophical attention "from the eternal to the future," is committed to ensuring that philosophy is established as a tool for changing preconstituted beliefs and behaviors: a commitment that, in his view, Dewey brought forward "by denying – as Heidegger was to deny later on – that philosophy is a form of knowledge," that is, denying that "there is or could be an extra-cultural foundation for custom." And, citing Dewey himself, Rorty asserts that all of this means recognizing that "in philosophy, 'reality' is a term of value and choice."[7] The connection between the pragmatists' philosophical attitude and the democratic image of the United States is an integral part of the ethnocentrism which Rorty wished to voice with his neo-pragmatism, and it is precisely on this level that we encounter the theme of communicative interactions, which accompanies Rorty's emphasis on the future.

3.

As can already be evinced from Rorty's words quoted above, he interpreted, from an ethnocentric perspective, also Heidegger – one of the philosophers that he counts among the contributors to the "post-philosophical" atmosphere in Europe. "[I am trying to] adapt pragmatism to a changed intellectual environment,"[8] declared Rorty in order to explain the project that had started with *Philosophy and the Mirror of Nature* and *Consequences of Pragmatism*,[9] in which he concentrated precisely on the instances of consonance between the thought of James and Dewey and the reflection of a large and also heterogeneous group of philosophers (Nietzsche, Heidegger, "later" Wittgenstein, Gadamer, Derrida, Foucault, and others) who shared, in his opinion, a post-philosophical attitude, that is, an attitude centered on the commitment to set aside the age-old philosophical attempts to discover the absolute foundations of knowledge, truth, and the good. In his view, this aspect of European thought could invigorate the pragmatist tradition, precisely because in both cases the anti-foundationalism was supported by means of a strong appreciation of the role of language and of communicative interactions in the entire range of philosophical issues. In particular, already in the first phase of his philosophical research, Rorty indicated the value of communication as a mainstay of the link between, on the one hand, European and American post-philosophies, which were alternatives to the analytic current inspired by neo-positivism, and, on the other hand, the pragmatist epistemology offered by Dewey.

The first step in this direction was Rorty's *The Linguistic Turn: Essays in Philosophical Method* (1967), in which he criticized the attempt of analytic philosophy to follow, in an updated way, the foundationalist criteria of classical metaphysics, translating philosophical problems into a theoretical framework which was set up "scientifically," that is, based on the presumed neutrality of scientific knowledge.[10] Above all, in this context, there was a foreshadowing of an irreversible crisis of this approach, a crisis that Rorty later clearly attributed to the identification of philosophy with epistemology. In the epistemological attitude, he in fact found a strong continuity between analytic philosophy of a neo-positivist type and the idea shared by Descartes, Locke and Kant, according to which the task of philosophical research is to devise a general theory of our relationship with the external world and of the manner in which our mind represents it.

The "professionalization" of philosophy, its confinement within academia, and its estrangement from the rest of culture and of civic history are inevitable outcomes of this theoretical project of modernity and, more specifically, of the idea of the mind as "a great mirror, containing various representations – some accurate, some not – and capable of being studied by pure, nonempirical methods."[11] It is necessary, instead, to revisit the "therapeutic" or "edifying" practice of authors, such as Nietzsche, "later" Wittgenstein, Heidegger, James, and Dewey, who had the merit of promoting a philosophical attitude no longer aiming at the construction of systems, but rather at taking problems in philosophy textbooks back to the personal, social and historical dimension.

From his earliest writings on, Rorty asserted the propositional nature of our relationships with the physical and human world,[12] and on this basis he continued trying to dissolve the ontological-metaphysical implications that underlie representationalism: what matters are our statements regarding the facts and the objects of our both "internal" (psychological-affective) and "external" (empirical-rational) experiences, and this means that all the knowledge that we can obtain comes to us through the linguistic and symbolic forms that one by one come into play.

In *Philosophy and the Mirror of Nature*, the elaboration of these themes concludes with contrasting Gadamer's hermeneutics with epistemology, and "the conversation" among subjects of different cultures with the commensuration of the specialized languages of the sciences. The philosophers concerned with edifying themselves and others, among whom Rorty indicates Sartre, Kierkegaard, and Santayana, advocate a commitment to discovering new ways of speaking, more interesting and more fruitful vocabularies, rather than to searching for certainty or the "essences" of reality. And it is in this light that he channels into the "post-philosophical" atmosphere the two strands of American thought in which he would also later continue to recognize the contemporary sources of his neo-pragmatism: on the one hand, Quine, Sellars, and Davidson, who – together with "later" Wittgenstein – represent, for Rorty, the culmination of analytic philosophy, i.e., the phase in which it "transcends and abolishes itself," and, on the other hand, James's and Dewey's pragmatism, which, in his view, suggested to us that we should "liberate our new civilization by giving up the notion of 'grounding' our culture, our moral lives, our politics, our religious beliefs, upon 'philosophical bases.'"[13] Similarly to the above mentioned "post-philosophers," according to Rorty, anti-foundationalism and the edifying philosophy of James and Dewey are also centered around the enhancement of communicative practices:

> pragmatism (…) is the doctrine that there are no constraints on inquiry save conversational ones – no wholesale constraints derived from the nature of the objects, or of the mind, or of language, but only those retail constraints provided by the remarks of our fellow-inquirers.[14]

The acceptance of this position is equivalent to an invitation to emancipation from logocentrism, which is defined by Rorty, in the wake of Derrida, as a need to find non-historical and universal truths. And emancipation from it entails developing the idea of the human subject as an "interpreter" of reality who is historically determined yet able to intervene in history through the freedom of self-creation and re-description of his/her relationship with others. Thus, what comes to the fore is the task of ethics and morality to safeguard freedom, and this means promoting and defending the values of democracy. Rorty's assertion "If we take care of freedom, truth can take care of itself,"[15] which sparked outrage by many philosophers, perfectly encapsulates this perspective. In fact, these words refer to the recognition of "truth" as everything upon which a social reality free and open to the possibilities of profitable innovations can achieve an operational convergence. This is not a mere consensus about assertions concerning the world or the reality of the facts, but a suggestion that it is worthless to search for an ultimate normative criterion that would be, by definition, independent of the practice in which we are immersed and of the limits it imposes.

Responding to those who deny that maintaining a distinction between the consensus notion of truth and the notion of objective truth does not necessarily mean an exit from our language, Rorty reiterates his Wittgensteinian and pragmatic distrust in the possibility of identifying anything external to linguistic practice, which is itself operative with respect to the objective world. Of course, the notion of objective truth is certainly more in line with common sense, but one should also admit that it entails a metaphysical option that is difficult to accept. The fact that the value of science is its usefulness in predicting and controlling natural reality does not depend on whether it is able or unable to grasp "the true nature of the world" or "true reality." These expressions are actually tautologies because, according to Rorty, the scope of the relationship between science and reality consists of Science's capability to achieve certain objects. Moreover, it is not clear what advantage there might be in an effort to fit our statements about the world into an alleged "true essence," since in any case it is not possible to escape from the terms of our languages.[16] In the ethical sense, renouncing the notion of objective truth simply means promoting, as we have said before, freedom and democracy as prerequisites for the achievement of shared truths made possible by the "human conversation."

Summing up, Rorty's objective is to deny the possibility of acquiring an *extra-linguistic* point of view, by indicating that our statements are not intended to express the presumed inherent truth of something, its "true being," because actually we always speak in view of the conformity of what we say with the set of intentions, purposes, and possibilities that are ours individually or socially. For this reason, the battle against "representationalism" is accompanied by the dismissal of the essentialist approach to classic philosophical problems, ranging from truth and knowledge to language and morality.

Accepting the contingent nature of all our points of departure requires recognizing ourselves as participants in human history, which is actually a linguistic history. It is thus made up of a variety of "vocabularies" corresponding to the particular forms of life that gradually come into being, and of "influential metaphors" rendering the descriptions of human experience and their changes in the course of socio-cultural contingencies. Before we return to this subject, some brief observations can be made about Rorty's debt to the twentieth-century hermeneutics and to Davidson's thought on communication. Interestingly, in both cases steps were taken to show that any form of communication implies the activity of understanding, which itself is meant as a process coextensive with any relationship of the human subject with alterity, whether that of another human or that of an object. In particular, it is emphasized that understanding is a process of interpretation, the nature of which is in principle indeterminate, that is, never guaranteed by absolute prior certainties or by certainties consequent to concrete interpretative practices. In Davidsonian thought, this view implies the idea that it is linguistic communication that is precisely the terrain of emergence and, at the same time, of semantic evolution of the notion of truth, but it also contains the affirmation of the causal and not representational relationship between the beliefs that we call "true" and certain aspects of the natural physical environment to which they refer.

Rorty agrees with Davidson's suggestion that there are such causal links between external reality and our beliefs about it, but emphasizes the linguistic factor of Davidsonian positions on truth, recognizing in it a "disquotationalist" option, which, in his opinion, makes his view very close to Dewey's. Thus, despite Davidson's denials, Rorty enrolled him in the list of neo-pragmatists for whom, according to Rorty, the key pursuit is to promote the possibilities to realize "human hopes for happiness," and not to find certain and timeless criteria to justify the correctness of beliefs regarding the physical and social environment. To be more precise, he asserted: "The attainment of such happiness is not something distinct from the attainment of justified belief; rather, the latter is a special case of the former."[17] In this light, the attempt of Emerson to promote "self-creation on a communal scale" should be taken up again, and this really corresponds to what Rorty meant when he affirmed that one must replace knowledge with hope. As already mentioned, "Hope in Place of Knowledge" is the expression Rorty coined to present his personal version of pragmatism, and he described its continuity with the Emersonian project in this way:

> To say that one should replace knowledge with hope is to say much the same thing: that one should stop worrying about whether what one believes is well grounded and start worrying about whether one has been imaginative enough to think up interesting alternatives to one's present beliefs. (...) In the context of post-Kantian academic philosophy, replacing knowledge with hope means something quite specific. It means giving up the Kantian idea that there is something called 'the nature of human knowledge' or 'the scope and limits of human knowledge' or 'the human epistemic situation' for philosophers to study and describe.[18]

4.

The "communitarian" concept of self-creation offered by Emerson and Rorty's interpretation of Davidson's work merge into the sentiment of *solidarity* invoked by Rorty to support the hope for a better future of humanity. This concept is also presented as a site for the development of the "narrative" model of personal identity proposed in *Contingency, Irony and Solidarity*. Generally speaking, the model confirms the widespread tendency of twentieth-century thought to downplay the traditional hypothesis that there is a human essence of which philosophy should formulate a precise definition, upon which the "truth" of the assertions regarding knowledge and values can then be founded. Rortian thought offered a scathing critique of this hypothesis, emphatically expressive of contemporary mistrust of the universalist repertoire of modern thought. As its many variations, this skepticism foregrounds the linguistic nature of every exercise of the abilities of human subjects, that is, the always symbolically mediated nature of their various experiences and, therefore, of their logical-cognitive parameters and their ethical parameters. For Rorty, language is specifically conceived of as a basic function of individual and social behavior, in which the historical and cultural constraints that underlie thinking and philosophical activity itself emerge, or rather, are clearly demonstrated. Recapitulating, it is a question of attributing to the practices of language the assumption of certain cognitive and ethical criteria, together with the arguments and motivations that support them all along or denounce their insufficiency.

This approach to the question of language is entirely in line with Rorty's intention to pursue and reinforce the ancient "edifying" task of philosophy, retrieving it – as already stated – beyond the currents of twentieth-century thought. In the wake of Descartes and Kant, these currents restricted the field of philosophical research to epistemological questions, and, one could say, reduced it to a kind of *ancilla scientiarum*. Against the intention of likening the analysis of cognitive activity to a search for its atemporal "foundations," its formal structures and its a priori principles, Rorty insisted on giving to philosophical reflection an ethical value as a criticism of culture, which will thus be able to carry forward "the conversation of mankind." In this way, Rorty seeks to show that philosophy itself emerges as an art rather than as a scientific discipline. Philosophy "is not a natural genre" but rather a cultural expression closer to human auto-creative activities than to the activities of the physical-natural sciences, and it is precisely in this difference from scientific knowledge that a possibility lies for it to contribute to social and ethical progress.[19] In this respect, Heidegger's criticism of the idea of the subject as a source of necessary truths and his insistence on the importance of historical awareness are placed alongside Wittgenstein's commitment to a philosophical practice intended to deconstruct "the enchantments of language" and alongside some crucial aspects of Dewey's thought: his conception of science as a social phenomenon and of truth as "justified assertability," and, finally, the idea of philosophy as an aesthetic improvement of human life and not as a search for certainty.

The image of philosophy as criticism of culture obviously involves the Rortian emphasis on linguistic dynamics and, in particular, entails the idea that philosophical historiography must consist in the narration of the genesis, development, and final dissolution of the metaphors that determine the various philosophical theories. It is precisely the creation and the dissolution of metaphorical expressions that reflect the mode in which individual philosophers tackle the specific needs of the moment as well as the cultural tradition to which they belong. It is within this framework that the two crucial factors of the "ethnocentric" vision endorsed by Rorty emerge from the 1980s on: namely, the concept of *final vocabulary* and the concept of *irony*.[20]

Rortian ethnocentrism sparked widespread aversion, but it should be acknowledged that it offers, in fact, a courageous invitation to explore the question of individual and social identity without too many philosophical illusions. This is particularly significant in a historical situation like ours, notoriously characterized by the economic and cultural processes of globalization and, no less, by the clear antagonisms among the various subjects, each of them "naturally" intent on defending his or her particular identity. And in fact, what Rorty's ethnocentrism intends to suggest is the need to abandon the pretension of setting aside the languages in which the various cultural traditions are expressed,[21] and thus the need to respect the differences that mark the human world. Moreover, Rorty is not willing to regard his ethnocentric view as an extreme form of relativism, reiterating insistently that it is not a question of supporting the equality in principle of all the axiological and epistemic criteria, but rather of giving importance to the encounter of different subjects for the discussion and justification of their respective points of view. More precisely, ethnocentrism is, in his opinion, a necessary condition to promote a practice of interpersonal and intercultural solidarity that makes room for conversation among different subjects. According to Rorty, the more distant such practice is from the metaphysical claims to identify the universal foundations of human nature, the more authentic it will be.[22]

In *Contingency, Irony and Solidarity*, the project of an "edifying" and "therapeutic" philosophy is specified in the intention to replace the traditional notions of truth, rationality, and moral duty with those of metaphor and self-creation,[23] which are effectively applied also to the theme of personal identity. Nietzsche and Freud are referred to as the cornerstones of a contingentist notion of subjectivity which, on the one hand, implies the creative power of language, and, on the other hand, pits the value of personal history against generalizations. More precisely, Nietzsche is credited with having theorized the subject, accepting his or her radical contingency and, at the same time, with having sanctioned the right-duty of self-creation through the paradigmatic definition of the artistic genius as an individual who knows how to tell a story that has not been told yet and to transform the "thus it was" into "thus I willed it."[24] In Freud, Rorty finds, in turn, the premises for a description of the individual conscience as if it were woven from contingencies, centered on the value of details and of the particular circumstances that cause the formation and development of personal identity.[25] Thus, based on the idea that language "is a tool for doing something" rather than a means for formulating lucid representations of external reality or of one's inner world,[26] the concepts of metaphor and self-creation merge into a "narrative" model of self-knowledge, in which self-knowledge is equivalent to a process of *self-description* that brings into play a plea for recognition from others.

Briefly, in this way the relationship among language, social interaction, and self-awareness is favored,[27] showing that the choice of a certain vocabulary, of a certain way of speaking, is contingent, that is, tied to an intellectual history that proceeds through a gradual acquisition of new metaphors corresponding to new cognitive and normative attitudes. Therefore, on the basis of the concept of "causal history of language" introduced by Davidson, Rorty argues that the creation of new vocabularies is equivalent to an empirical process that includes pragmatic interpersonal demands for management of the surrounding world: a process that does not have predetermined rules and criteria, but takes place in view of the possibility of an intersubjective convergence to address new problems and experiences. Linguistic evolution is thus, in principle, infinite, which can be seen in the dynamics between "dead" metaphors, that is, those that are no longer able to exert any concrete effect, and new metaphors, which instead are claimed to have truth value, that is, they remain susceptible to acceptance or rejection.[28]

5.

Against the background of this description of the contingency of languages, we can see a clear outline of the concept of final vocabulary, which – as mentioned before – plays a key role in Rorty's ethnocentrism and in the narrative model of personal identity that derives from it.[29] To give up the idea that the human subject has a universal and pre-ordained "intrinsic nature" means to maintain that each person is made up of a network of beliefs, behavioral attitudes, and desires, which are an outcome of the interaction among a series of contingent factors, such as family and education, the overall cultural tradition to which a person belongs, and the forms of language which he or she happens to speak. All these factors are condensed in the "final vocabulary" of individuals, that is, a tightly cohesive group of expressions that feed individuals' strategies for justifying their logical and practical criteria. These strategies cannot in turn be justified unless their specific semantic validity is encroached upon.[30] Rorty notes that the justification of one's "final vocabulary" inevitably implies the use of the words and concepts that it makes available, and he thus intends to highlight the fact that our logical-rational processes inexorably draw on an already functioning system of moral values, descriptions of physical reality, projects, and desires, and thus that all our practices of justification are in some way self-referential, that is, they cannot be founded on any other bases but those bound up with the linguistic mechanisms of individual and social self-creation.

The final vocabularies of individual people contain elements that relate to both the private and the public spheres; consequently, the differences among them are both intra-cultural, that is, due to each individual's history, and inter-cultural, that is, relative to the socio-historical context to which each person belongs. Since final vocabularies do not represent the presumed objectivity of the facts, but are rather a set of logical-semantic elements that serve as the foundation in the self-descriptions of those who embody them, there is no criterion to determine a priori which is most "real." However, this does not entail denying the importance of a critical examination of one's own final vocabulary and of its possible adjustment. On the contrary, once again the contingent nature of our logical-semantic criteria is highlighted, and this also implies the contingency of the "final vocabularies" which form the vital horizon of these criteria. Thus, Rorty clarifies the role of the ironic stance in the processes of self-realization in individual existence, setting it as the basic condition for the possible changes of a final vocabulary. In other words, Rorty links the ironic stance to a comparison with others, which should be based on the recognition of and respect for those who use a "final vocabulary" different from one's own. The following passages help to clarify this point:

> The ironist spends her time worrying about the possibility that she has been initiated into the wrong tribe, taught to play the wrong language game. She worries that the process of socialization which turned her into a human being by giving her a language may have given her the wrong language, and so turned her into the wrong kind of human being.[31]

> For us ironists, nothing can serve as a criticism of a final vocabulary: save another such vocabulary (…). Nothing can serve as a criticism of a person save another person, or of a culture save an alternative culture – for persons and cultures are, for us, incarnated vocabularies. So our doubts about our own characters or our own culture can be resolved or assuaged only by enlarging our acquaintance.[32]

Rorty tends to reserve irony for the private sphere, setting it in contrast with the sense of community, of rootedness in one's own history and culture, which should instead prevail in the public sphere. However, his lessons about the effects of the ironic stance on social ethics must not be underestimated. Beyond his controversial criticism of the common philosophical tendency to unify the public dimension with the private dimension, a precise link can be seen between irony and that peculiar concept of human *solidarity*, which is one of the crucial features of his meliorism. In particular, the theme of suffering and humiliation emerges, which is the basis for the Rortian proposal to regard the moral principle of solidarity as a typical expression of liberal democratic societies, and not as a fruit of the metaphysical definitions of the human being. Rorty wrote:

> The liberal ironist just wants our *chances of being kind,* of avoiding the humiliation of others, to be expanded by re-description. She thinks that recognition of a common susceptibility to humiliation is the *only* social bond that is needed. Whereas the metaphysician takes the morally relevant feature of the other human beings to be their relation to a larger shared power – rationality, God, truth, or history, for example – the ironist takes the morally relevant definition of a person, a moral subject, to be 'something that can be humiliated.' Her sense of human solidarity is based on a sense of a common danger, not on a common possession or a shared power.[33]

The moral principle of solidarity and the hope for its continuous expansion seem thus to belong to a non-cognitivist metaethics, or rather, to an integration of the classical model of this theoretical orientation with a historicism that in fact distances itself from emotionalism. Moreover, emotionalism is certainly out of the question, according to Rorty, if one is willing to go beyond the sharp distinction posed by neo-positivism between sentiments and reasons.[34] Furthermore, tackling Kantian ethics and all forms of universalism, Rorty always accentuated the historical framework of values, which he considered to be central to moral progress: the ability to enter into communicative contact with others, tolerance towards cultural subjects who are different from us and, above all, the feeling of solidarity, which he indicated as the main driving force behind this progress, that is, as an irreducible value to which all other ethical criteria should be adapted. These moral values originate from the development of democratic societies and not from the Kantian "tribunal of reason." Consequently, the validity of these values cannot be guaranteed by arguments that seek their origins in the presumed universality and necessity of rational principles. On the contrary, their validity must be justified by showing that concrete advantages flowing from the practice of such values surpass the advantages generated in the practice of other values. In other words, the typical invitation by Rorty to substitute argumentative justification for the anxiety to find the universal foundation of our cognitive criteria is reflected with regard to ethics.[35] In any case, the link between ironic attitude and solidarity suggests an approach to the self that gives precedence to interpersonal and intercultural communicative relationships, assembling their complex dynamics together in a philosophical view that discards the opposition between emotion and reason.

The idea of solidarity cannot signify a mere sentiment of closeness to others. Rather, such an idea evokes the vital interference between the affective sphere and the logical-argumentative sphere. This interference – as a matter of fact – is what allows solidarity to be placed in the same social path as values, purposes, and common practices. In fact, it must be admitted that those with whom we enter into relationship, even if only accidentally, call no less for our intelligence than for our feelings, that is, they induce us to try to understand the beliefs underlying what they affirm or the behavior with which they present themselves to us, in addition to involving us in some aesthetic attitude. In other words, one should bear in mind that every interpersonal and intercultural relationship sets in motion a process of interpreting the *reasons of others*: a process which may be more or less conscious and precise, but which we are "normally" inclined to undertake, setting aside the classical philosophical urge to clearly demarcate sentiments from reasons.

We can agree with Rorty that literary works conveying "detailed descriptions of particular varieties of pain and humiliation" have contributed more to promoting human solidarity than philosophical treatises have. It must be understood, however, that ultimately it is up to each person to make room in his or her own experience for the conviction that moral progress exists and "this progress is indeed in the direction of greater human solidarity." And then perhaps we will also feel committed to reflecting critically and constructively on Rorty's affirmation that solidarity "is not thought of as recognition of a core self, the human essence, in all human beings. Rather, it is thought of as the ability to see more and more traditional differences (of tribe, religion, race, customs, and the like) as unimportant when compared with similarities with respect to pain and humiliation – the ability to think of people wildly different from ourselves as included in the range of 'us.'"[36]

Rorty's neo-pragmatism deliberately disregards Peirce. After an initial favorable comment that Peirce foresaw that logical positivism would be left behind,[37] Rorty dismissed the founder of the pragmatist movement, considering him still too conditioned by foundationalism. And yet, it is precisely from Peirce that very strong suggestions come regarding the theme of hope, so dear to Rortian post-philosophy. I am referring to the so-called logical socialism, which runs through Peirce's semiotics, and more precisely to the assertion that the necessity for logical principles upon which our cognitive inferences are founded is based on an "infinite hope" – on the reasonable hope/possibility – that if we apply these logical principles, conclusions can be reached that are intersubjectively and in the long run shareable.[38]

The feeling of "infinite hope" thus appears as the core of an idea of rationality modeled on the awareness of the deep intertwining between the aesthetic-affective plane and the rational-logical plane, an intertwining that underlies the "infinity" of the path of the meanings that emerge along the semiotic dynamics of human society. This is a journey of which, according to Peirce, it is impossible to identify the absolute foundation, just as it is impossible to identify its definitive conclusion, because human intelligence always deals with signs – with their prior configuration of things as well as with the complexity of the interpretative developments that they set in motion.

The semiotic structure of Peirce's logic allows thus space for the awareness that we do not possess a certain criterion of rationality: "There is no royal road to logic," Peirce asserted – we can only place our trust in the probability that experience and future reasonings of the human community may validate our reasonings, but even before that we must place our trust in the "infinite hope" that the search for truth will never cease. This, very briefly, is the meaning of what Peirce defines as the "social foundation of logic": a foundation which, however, cannot find full justification, except through recourse to sentiment, that is, to that "infinite hope" which in itself transcends the means that more properly belong to logic, and yet constitutes one of the essential requirements of logic: to use his words, "This sentiment is rigidly demanded by logic."[39] But is there not in all of this perhaps an allusion to the normative value of certain sentiments, and, therefore, also an invitation to set aside the classic dichotomy between the dimension of sentiment and the dimension of knowing, the dichotomy that Rorty himself sought to resolve in his neo-pragmatism? On the other hand, is it not possible that Rorty's aesthetic challenge to rationalism and to foundationalist claims might be profitably strengthened by the intimate connection among logic, ethics and aesthetics, theorized in one of Peirce's last writings, in which, indeed, aesthetics appears as the true and most concrete support for logic and ethics?[40] A comparison between Rorty's ideas and these components of Peirce's thought would probably clarify how far we are willing to follow a philosophical perspective that does not admit absolute criteria of knowledge and ethics, but which, at the same time, does not give up looking for points of reference that are sufficiently solid, precisely because they are constructed and justified by means of communicative cooperation among human individuals.

NOTES

1. Rorty declared that he did not at all consider himself among the most eminent philosophers of American philosophy after World War II, and maintained that his contribution and that of Putnam to post-neopositivist philosophy were less important than the contributions of Quine, Sellars, Davidson, and Brandom, whom he in fact enumerated as the four most important American philosophers. Cf. Richard Rorty, *Truth and Progress: Philosophical Papers,* vol. 3 (Cambridge: Cambridge University Press, 1998), p. 147 ff.
2. Richard Rorty, *Philosophy and Social Hope* (London: Penguin Books, 1999), p. xiii.
3. Richard Rorty, "Intellectual Autobiography," *Library of Living Philosophers: The Philosophy of Richard Rorty*, vol. 22, eds. Randall E. Auxier and Lewis Edwin Hahn (Chicago: Open Court, 2009), p. 23.
4. Rorty, "Education as Socialization and as Individualization," *Philosophy and Social Hope*, p. 120.
5. *Ibid.*
6. *Ibid.*, pp. 24–7.
7. *Ibid.*, p. 29.
8. Rorty, "Comments on Sleeper and Edel," *Transactions of the Charles S. Peirce Society*, 21:1 (1985), p. 47.
9. Richard Rorty, *Philosophy and the Mirror of Nature* (Princeton: Princeton University Press, 1979); *Consequences of Pragmatism* (Minneapolis: University of Minnesota Press, 1982).
10. Richard Rorty, *The Linguistic Turn. Essays in Philosophical Method* (Chicago: The University of Chicago Press, 1967), in particular pp. 1–38.
11. Rorty, *Philosophy and the Mirror of Nature*, p. 12.
12. Interesting criticisms of Rorty's notion of the linguistic nature of all knowledge as well as of Rorty's tendency to view language as the exclusive interest of philosophy can be found in James T. Kloppenberg, "Pragmatism: An Old Name for Some New Ways of Thinking," *A Pragmatist's Progress? Richard Rorty and American Intellectual History,* ed. John Pettegrew (Oxford: Rowman and Littlefield, 2000); and in Barry Allen, "What Knowledge? What Hope? What New Pragmatism?" *The Pragmatic Turn in Philosophy: Contemporary Engagements Between Analytic and Continental Thought*, eds. William Egginton and Mike Sandbothe (New York: State University of New York Press, 2004).
13. Rorty, *Consequences of Pragmatism*, p. 161.
14. *Ibid.*, p. 165.

15. Richard Rorty, *Contingency, Irony and Solidarity* (Cambridge: Cambridge University Press, 1989), p. 176.

16. Cf. Richard Rorty, "Response to McDowell," *Rorty and His Critics,* ed. Robert B. Brandom (Oxford: Blackwell, 2000), pp. 123–28; *Ibid.,* "Response to Conant," pp. 342–50.

17. Rorty, *Philosophy and Social Hope*, p. 33. For a succinct overview of Rorty's interpretation of Davidson's positions on the question of truth in the 'disquotational' sense and the respective polemics of Davidson himself and of Jeff E. Malpas, cf. *Ibid.,* pp. 41–3, notes 22–4.

18. Rorty, *Philosophy and Social Hope*, p. 34.

19. See, in this regard, the essays in section III of Rorty, *Truth and Progress,* pp. 245–350.

20. Rortian ethnocentrism uses themes taken both from the pragmatist tradition in the United States and from the analytic and hermeneutic currents of European thought; the most significant texts in this sense are Rorty, *Contingency, Irony and Solidarity*; *Objectivity, Relativism, and Truth: Philosophical Papers,* vol. 1 (Cambridge: Cambridge University Press, 1991), third part; *Philosophy and Social Hope*; *Achieving Our Country: Leftist Thought in Twentieth Century America* (Cambridge, MA: Harvard University Press,1998); Balslev Anindita Niyogi, Richard Rorty, *Cultural Otherness: Correspondence with Richard Rorty* (New Delhi: Indian Institute of Advanced Study, 1991).

21. Davidson and Heidegger are in this regard essential sources; see, for example, Rorty, *Contingency, Irony and Solidarity*, p. 50, in which Rorty cites the following assertion by Davidson: "speaking a language (...) is not a trait a man can lose while retaining the power of thought. So there is no chance that someone can take up a vantage point for comparing conceptual schemes by temporarily shedding his own," and adds: "Or, to put the point in Heidegger's way, 'language speaks man,' languages change in the course of history, and so human beings cannot escape their historicity. The most they can do is to manipulate the tensions within their own epoch in order to produce the beginnings of the next epoch."

22. See Rorty, *Consequences of Pragmatism*, chap.1; see also *Contingency, Irony and Solidarity*, p. 51 ff.

23. Rorty, *Contingency, Irony and Solidarity*, pp. 44–5.

 24. *Ibid.*, p. 29.

25. *Ibid.*, pp. 29–38.

26. *Ibid.*, pp. 11–2.

27. *Ibid.*, pp. 19–20.

28. Cf. *Ibid.*, pp. 15–9.

29. I restate here some observations included in my article "Individuale, sociale, solidale. Armonie e dissonanze," S*emiotica e fenomenologia del sé*, ed. Rosa M. Calcaterra (Turin: Aragno, 2005), pp. 25– 44.

30. Rorty, *Contingency, Irony and Solidarity*, p. 75 ff.

31. *Ibid.*, p. 75.

32. *Ibid.*, p. 80.

33. *Ibid.*, p. 91.

34. Cf. Richard Rorty, *Essays on Heidegger and Others: Philosophical Papers,* vol. 2 (Cambridge: Cambridge University Press, 1991).

35. Cf. Rorty, *Philosophy and Social Hope*, pp. xxxi, 36–8.

36. Rorty, *Contingency, Irony and Solidarity*, p. 192.

37. Cf. Richard Rorty, "Pragmatism, Categories, and Language," *Philosophical Review*, 80 (1961), pp. 197–233.

38. Cf. Charles S. Peirce, *Collected Papers of Charles Sanders Peirce*, vol. 5., eds. Charles Hartshorne and Paul Weiss (Cambridge, MA: Harvard University Press, 1934), para. 318–57.

39. *Ibid.*, para. 357.

40. Cf. *Ibid.*, para. 120–50. For an analysis of these aspects of Peirce's philosophy, I draw on my *Pragmatismo: i valori dell'esperienza. Letture di Peirce, James e Mead* (Rome: Carocci, 2003), pp. 17–65; "Psicologia e normatività epistemica. Figure dell'esternalismo," *Le ragioni del conoscere e dell'agire. Scritti in onore di Rosaria Egidi*, ed. Rosa M. Calcaterra, (Milan: Franco Angeli, 2006), pp. 30–43.

Eight

THE CONCEPT OF MAN IN THE SHADOW OF THE SHOAH: GERAS, RORTY AND SHUSTERMAN IN DIALOGUE

Katarzyna Liszka

The issue of human nature has come to occupy the central place in several discussions concerning the ethical consequences of the mass annihilation of six million Jewish people, called the Shoah. How does the terrible knowledge of 20th-century crimes and unimaginable suffering caused by them impress upon and affect our understanding of who we are, of humanity, and of human nature? These queries have been tackled across different philosophical traditions and disciplines of the humanities and social sciences.

The attempt to situate this problem in the field of contemporary pragmatist philosophy seems a challenge worth undertaking. The task of rethinking the consequences of the Shoah for the ideas, institutions, and practices of the Western culture seems very much in alignment with the general pragmatist concept of dynamic relations among the human being, culture and discourse expounded, among others, by Richard Shusterman: "Pragmatist philosophy celebrates the idea of culture. Recognizing that culture is both an essential value and the ineliminable matrix of human life, pragmatism further insists that philosophy itself is the product of culture, changing with cultural change."[1] I will proceed by answering consecutively two broad questions: "Is the issue of human nature after the Shoah addressed in the current reflection of pragmatist thinkers?" and "In what way can pragmatism inspire the study of human nature after the Shoah?"

I begin from the position external to pragmatism, by referring to *Solidarity in the Conversation of Humankind: The Ungroundable Liberalism of Richard Rorty*,[2] a book written by the leftist political thinker Norman Geras, who focuses exactly on rethinking the idea of human nature in the face of the Shoah, in a polemical dialogue with Richard Rorty's philosophical views. The reconstruction of arguments on both sides is to explain why it is so important for Geras to defend the idea of human nature as well as why it is so important for Rorty to reject it. The controversy between them is not only about human nature, though: it concerns other issues crucial to pragmatism, too, such as democracy, solidarity, human potentialities and modes of self-creation, suffering and cruelty, the body, ethical universalism versus ethical particularism, and language versus nonlinguistic experience. Although Richard

Shusterman, in general, does not thematize the Shoah – nor does he reflect on its ethical or political consequences[3] – several aspects of his work may illuminate the discussion between Rorty and Geras. I mean here especially Shusterman's profound attention to bodily experience and his critical reading of Rorty. Therefore, passing from the first question (about the actual pragmatist engagement with human nature in the face of the Shoah) to the second one (about the possible pragmatist inspirations in dealing with the problem), I will draw on Shusterman's thought. Putting the body at the center of his philosophy, referred to as somaesthetics, Shusterman develops a particular way of thinking about the issue that is both essential to Rorty's and Geras's argumentation concerning the human vulnerability to pain and suffering and, at the same time, the very one that they curiously seem to ignore.

In his polemical book *Solidarity in the Conversation of Humankind*, Geras takes issue with Rorty's assumption that human solidarity does not need to be associated with the idea of human nature. Geras analyzes how this assumption is inscribed in the wider theoretical framework of Rorty's criticism of foundationalism, essentialism, and universalism, his affirmation of ethnocentrism, and his vision of a liberal ironic utopia.

I will start by focusing on the details of Rorty's argumentation against the idea of human nature presented in his lecture titled "Human Rights, Rationality and Sentimentality" (1993). Referring to the war in former Yugoslavia, he offers the following account of the status of the idea of human nature in Western democracies:

> We in the safe, rich democracies feel about the Serbian torturers and rapist as they feel about their Muslim victims: They are more like animals than like us. (...) We think of the Serbs and the Nazis as animals, because ravenous beast of prey are animals. We think of the Muslims or the Jews being herded into concentration camps as animals, because cattle are animals. Neither sort of animal is very much like us, and there seems no point in human beings getting involved in quarrels between animals.[4]

Rorty describes what he views as symptomatic of generations after Auschwitz and Srebrenica: a rupture in the solidarity of human species, a refusal to feel solidarity with the victims as well as with the perpetrators. He states that this refusal paradoxically corresponds with the foundationalist philosophical grounds of reflection on human nature, derived from the Western tradition of rationalism shaped by the Platonic and Kantian canon. Identification of reason as the attribute that distinguishes human beings from animals and the proposition of the affinity of human beings as rooted in the "rational" determinant of their humanity do not suffice, for Rorty, to construct grounds for human solidarity. The idea of universal humanity fails the very moment that an individual, answering the question "who is my neighbor?"

points to a "rational" person similar to herself, and at the same time denies rationality, and thus humanity, to someone else, to the other.

In other words, the rejection of the idea of universal human nature is motivated here by the observation that this idea, as formulated in the Western tradition, does not strengthen human solidarity, and the education informed by it failed to help us avoid cruelty towards and lack of compassion for the victims of the 20th-century genocide. This seems to be one reason why Rorty posits the dismissal of the idea of universal human nature as the only way to affirm the culture of human rights. Rorty postulates a rearrangement of priorities: sentimentality instead of reason and sentimental stories instead of the universal humanity discourse offer, in his view, more effective grounds for the human rights-oriented education. The question that is central to the ethics of human rights is not an ontological one – "what is man?" – but an ethical one – "who is my neighbor?" or "who can I be responsible for?" If we are to hold out some hope for the discourse of human rights, as Rorty concludes, their functioning must be supported and sustained by the education of sentiments which would foster individual responsibility for those who are ultimately alien, for "people whose appearance or habits or beliefs," as he says, "seemed at first an insult to our own moral identity, our sense of the limits of permissible human variation."[5]

The important question is: Why does Rorty's state that men and women develop a sense of responsibility for the Other only after making another human being – through the work of imagination and sentiments – "one of them"? They need to discover a way to identify with strangers through detecting similarities under the surface of (apparently) insurmountable differences. The idea of solidarity as larger loyalty that is to be enacted only through an active identification with other people, for example on the basis of nationhood, religious beliefs, gender, age, and the like,[6] differs substantially from Geras's approach, but also from Emmanuel Lévinas's influential reflection on responsibility for the Other as infinite alterity.[7]

Is the affirmation of human rights without universal humanity a sound response to the crisis of the idea of human nature after the Holocaust? Perhaps. But let me focus on another attempt to cope with this crisis.

Norman Geras also recognizes the crisis of the idea of human nature, but he consistently defends this idea in his works *Marx and Human Nature: Refutation of the Legend*, "Socialist Hope in the Shadow of Catastrophe," and *Solidarity in the Conversation of Humankind*.[8] His general thesis is that without a concept of human nature, the projects of progressive social change – Marxist, socialist, liberal, or any other ones – are impossible. Geras begins his rejoinder to Rorty by referring to the last chapter of *Contingency, Irony and Solidarity*, and, in particular, to the way Rorty construes attitudes of people who saved Jews during World War Two. Rorty argues that "if you were a Jew in the period when the trains were running to Auschwitz, your chances to be hidden by your gentile neighbors were greater if you lived in Denmark or Italy than if you lived in Belgium."[9] According to Rorty, the reason why Danes and Italians were more inclined to take risk and save their Jewish neighbors was the possibility of imaginative identification with them, which enabled one to say "this particular Jew was a fellow Milanese, or a fellow Jutlander, or a fellow member of the same union or profession, or a fellow bocce player, or a fellow parent of small children."[10] We can thus see that Rorty finds in this rescuing disposition an illustration of his thesis on human solidarity understood as rooted in some sense of identification. Rorty states: "our sense of solidarity is strongest when those with whom solidarity is expressed are thought of as 'one of us,' where 'us' means something smaller and more local than the human race. That is why 'because she is a human being' is a weak, unconvincing explanation of a generous action."[11]

In the chapter titled "Richard Rorty and the Righteous Among the Nations," Geras draws on several works on rescuing activity and numerous sources documenting narratives of people saving Jews in order to present an opposing anthropological reflection. Geras indicates that rescuing strangers was not a marginal occurrence: according to the Holocaust scholars those cases were even more common. Moreover, despite the divergent conclusions about who more tended to support the Jews – women or men, workers and peasants or the middle-class people and intellectuals, believers or not believers – there is a considerable consensus among the scholars concerning the universalist motivation of those who were later called the Righteous among the Nations.[12] Most rescuers explained their generous action in terms of ethical universalism: "Only because they were human beings."[13] Geras concludes: „It could be that these rescuers are, all of them, mistaken; that they are really wrong about their reasons. Or it could be, on the other hand, that Richard Rorty is wrong about the Righteous."[14]

According to Geras, Rorty overestimates individuals' inclination to aid people on the basis of identifying with them as members of one nation or ethnic group, etc., without recognizing all those cases in which the only impetus for giving shelter and support to the people in danger came simply from their being in need. The Universalist motivation for saving the other is not less plausible than the ethnocentric motivation. For Geras, the fragility of Rorty's vision of solidarity through identification becomes clear when children are involved:

> Consider, as coming from an adult, the appeal, 'We should do something; they are (only) children.' Again, I just take it this carries some persuasive force. Perhaps part of the reason it does is that, having all been and still knowing children, we can identify with them, although children ourselves no longer. But another part, I contend, has to do with a particular fact we know and feel about children; it has to do with their vulnerability. On account of this, however, children may be taken as simply highlighting what is a possibility for anyone, for any human

being: the possibility in virtue of his natural needs and limitations, in virtue of her acquired values, loves or hopes, of being hurt. In that respect all human beings are potentially children. They can be made very easily to suffer – innocently, for nothing.[15]

In his commentary to Rorty's Amnesty International lecture cited above, Geras insists that if effectiveness of human rights is to rely on an individual's ability to feel responsible not only for the near and dear, but also for strangers when in their suffering they crave help, protection, and asylum – so for the people who are only people in need, and not friends or members of the same party, nation, or culture – it is only the idea of universal humanity that can ground such solidarity. "I put it in the form of a simple question. Is there not something rather implausible about insisting on the communal sources of strong solidarity, and insisting at the same time on the irrelevance of the idea of a common humanity to the goal of more expansive solidaristic relations?"[16]

In other words, following Geras we can ask: If Rorty sees the need to expand our responsibility, why does he reject the notion of the widest horizon of solidarity, that is human race? Why does he repeatedly insist on ethnocentrism as a strong ethical rule of one's commitment and responsibility, as if there was no other rule and possibility to act? Geras asks further not without irony: "What on earth motivates supporters of Amnesty International today? Do we say that people should not be locked away for their beliefs, should not be tortured, because (that is *if*) they are fellow city-dwellers? Or fellow academics, baseball-lovers, nationals even?"[17]

Rorty builds his vision of the human being in opposition to the idea of an ahistorical human nature conceived as a solid essence unaffected by cultural, social and historical change. And yet, according to Rorty, the human being is vulnerable to pain, suffering, and humiliation, has a capacity to use language, is subjected to contingency, but also has an ability to transcend it, and is capable of self-creation. I will phrase this, surprising perhaps, discrepancy in the form of a question that seems as pertinent as it is difficult answer. If people share these attributes and potentials across cultures and ages (despite differences in the modes and conditions of expressing them produced in particular historical, social, cultural, economical, political conjunctures), why does Rorty at the same time decidedly reject the lexicon which could enable us to understand this kinship in terms of human nature?

Returning to Geras, we should emphasize that his defense of the idea of human nature as a ground for human solidarity formulated in his polemics with Rorty's philosophical position is accompanied by simultaneous critical analyses of basic socialist assumptions about human nature. In the essay "Socialist Hope in the Shadow of Catastrophe," Geras points out the urgency of rethinking the concept of man in the socialist tradition in the face of the Shoah.

Geras discusses four ethical theses on human nature: human nature is intrinsically evil, good, mixed or blank (it does not exist). According to Geras, we cannot discount or suspend the conception of brutality, destructivity, and sadism as related to the nature of the human being. But neither should we assume that the cruelty of the Nazi genocide defines definitively who we are and who we can become in terms of the naturalistic explanation that man is intrinsically evil and that only through socialization and enculturation can his or her pathological tendencies be restrained. Such a premise, according to Geras, ruins the hope for building a better world. But neither should we espouse the socialist vision of human nature, which brims with a fundamental optimism inherited from the Enlightenment, because it would entail accounting for the Nazi behavior by tracing and attributing cruelty, sadism, and thoughtlessness only to the contingent shape of institutions, ideas, and cultural practices. Therein the naturalistic explanation of the Nazi genocide is replaced by a culturalist approach that assumes that the problem raised by the Holocaust does not pertain to the nature of man, and is instead related to the economic, social, political, and cultural conditions shaping human lives.

Geras rejects also the third thesis that the Holocaust showed that human nature is infinitely flexible and fluid, in other words, that it does not exists. Stanley Milgram's and Philip Zimbardo's experiments are worth mentioning at this point, as they have widely been taken to corroborate the thesis that social situation can easily transform normal people into subordinated, passive individuals or ruthless sadists. Yet, in *The Anatomy of Human Destructiveness*, Erich Fromm claims that, despite the dominant interpretation of those experiments, what they really illuminate is the power of reaction to one's own cruelty and fright against one's own sadistic behavior, both revealing the immediate consequences of crossing the limits inscribed in humanity.[18] Fromm adds that if human nature was infinitely plastic, judgment on and critique of a particular behavior or social order would lose its rationale and remain essentially unfounded. At this point, Fromm's argumentation is convergent with Geras's assumptions. What is at stake in the rejection by Geras (and Fromm) of the idea that human nature does not exist is the viability of critique and the hope to change the world:

> The goal of a much better and a more just society is to be fought for not because human beings are by nature overwhelmingly or essentially good, nor because they do not have an intrinsic nature; but because and in spite of the combination in their nature of bad impulses with good ones. Because of the bad impulses, this struggle is necessary. In spite of them, it is to be hoped, a socialist society may yet be possible.[19]

It is only on the basis of the assumption that human nature is intrinsically mixed – prone to good and to evil, as Geras suggests – that we can defend essential and indispensable component of the socialist projects, that is hope, but also criticize ambient practices and work towards a more equitable society:

At the limit the Holocaust then becomes, more than a tragic, ghastly event with its own historicity and conditions, the symbol of inexorable human fate, in a reversal of the very idea of progress. Humanity's accumulating crimes live on, not, and as they ought to, as a memory of the evil man and women do, of what has to be guarded against, fought. They live on, in the minds of all those who succumb to learning this as 'the truth,' in the shape of the thought that such is what we are and have to be. This is an option, it has to be said, that is not only not appealing. It is repellent. We cannot give up on utopian hope of socialism. We cannot give up on progress. They are not *less* apt in light of what we know about the bad side of human nature. They are more necessary.[20]

In my reading of Geras and Rorty, I have situated their thought in the context well described by Alain Finkiekraut, who referring to the crimes of the two totalitarian regimes of the 20th century asks: "How was it possible for the concept of universal humanity to fall into such massive and radical oblivion in the center of the very civilization where it reached its most spectacular development?"[21] For Finkielkraut, the urgent challenge posed by those events was: "to preserve the idea of humanity and to make sure the idea does not kill."[22] I believe that both thinkers, each in his different mode, attempt to face up to this challenge, suggesting answers so as to salvage hope for better, more just, solidarity-based human relations.

At the heart of Geras's and Rorty's philosophical projects lies profound anthropological reflection on human vulnerability to pain, suffering, oppression, and humiliation. And the hope to minimize pain, suffering and humiliation, to avoid institutional cruelty is central to their utopias. But their utopian projects seem to be polar opposites when it comes to the understanding of the nature of man.

Vulnerability to pain, as well as seeking the way to minimize it, is also a perennial theme in Richard Shusterman's philosophical reflection. But he pursues it against a wider background of studies devoted to the body and bodily consciousness. I think that Shusterman's work on the experience of pain and cultural practices and ideas associated with it can help us answer our opening question about pragmatism's possible contribution to the discussion about human nature after Auschwitz.

In his critical reading of Rorty, Shusterman comments on the presence of the body issues in Rorty's philosophy. Shusterman puts it explicitly in "Postmodern Ethics and the Art of Living," a chapter from *Pragmatist Aesthetics*: non-linguistic bodily experience underestimated by Rorty returns in his description of shared human vulnerability to pain and humiliation, where pain is understood as the loss of language and "the reality of the world which cannot be vanquished by our transformative narratives."[23] The claim that the only untransformable reality is "just pain and power," as Shusterman assumes, "betrays a deep and particularly troubling absence in the Rortian vision of aesthetic living. For it is a very sad and unsatisfying aestheticism that affirms the pervasive presence of non-linguistic pain but ignores the sensual bodily pleasures."[24] This passage is essential if we read it in the light of Shusterman's philosophy of the body as he developed it later. In his later writings, as well as in the excerpt cited above, Shusterman consistently rejects two assumption: that the reality of pain and power is untransformable and that pain is the central experience of an embodied self.

The author of *Body Consciousness* notes: "Recent philosophy has strangely devoted so much inquiry to the ontology and epistemology of pain, while so little to its psychosomatic mastery or transformation into pleasure."[25] Shusterman's account is one of radical repositioning: a physical or psychological wound indicates that there is something (someone) that can be wounded. Only the body can be physically wounded; only a subject can be subjected; and only a human being can be dehumanized. His philosophy is underpinned by the tenet of the positivity of the "soma" as "a living, feeling, sentient body."[26] The body can be hurt, tortured, dominated, oppressed, it can also be cured, cultivated, transformed, and it can become a powerful source of resistance, emancipation, and the art of being.

Embodiment is a universal and essential fact of human existence. But the body is pliable (not infinitely, though: the malleability of the body has its limits), shaped by various disciplines, regimes, habits and practices, and individuals can deepen their body consciousness. The art of living begins in the body. Shusterman cites the classic Daoist thinkers Laozi and Zhuangzi: "You have only to take care and guard your own body … [and] other things will of themselves grow sturdy."[27] The body as a renewable source of subjectivity necessarily preexists any attempt at consciously caring about the body. Even after a severe illness, excruciating pain, or atrocious torture, something remains, something that can feel the wound. Ability, decision, or attempt to favor the body and care about it is only a subsequent step – the first one is always the very fact of the living body.

Shusterman shows various possibilities of attention to the body and its influence on an emotional, cognitive, and ethical transformation of the self and its relations with other people. He insists that care about the body is not contained within the private sphere only: "Not only is the body shaped by the social, it contributes to the social. We share our bodies and bodily pleasures as much as we share our minds, and they can be as public as our thoughts."[28]

I will discuss briefly three examples, analyzed by Schusterman, of ethical contribution of active bodily consciousness to fostering a new quality of relations among people. The first example is Michel Foucault, for whom the body remains a site of struggle where the self experiences various disciplinary regimes and power relations which produce it. Therefore, the body, as described by Foucault, may become a source of resistance (cultural, social and political) and a source of self-transformation. Shusterman appreciates making the bodily experience (especially when it comes to sexuality and gender) central to the project of self-creation, but he also expresses his doubt about the mode of transformation of the self suggested by Foucault, that is liminal and intense homosexual sadomasochistic sexual practices and hard drug use. Once again, his balanced critique of Foucault's somaesthetics targets the tendency inherent in the Western culture to prioritize the vision of the body in pain over any other – softer, slower, peaceful – bodily experience. According to Shusterman, these practices, rather than being "a perverse transgression of our culture's values," convey "an explicit, intensified expression of deeply problematic tendencies that historically subtend those values and the practices they generate, even in our spiritual and religious experience."[29]

The second example is Simone de Beauvoir, commenting on whom Shusterman emphasizes that: "Beauvoir's future-looking, activist, meliorist approach to our open, malleable human nature (itself shaped by a malleable world that is partly the product of human interventions) is an existentialist orientation convergent with the pragmatist tradition that motivates somaesthetics."[30] Recognizing the significance of Beauvoir's existentialism to pragmatism and somaesthetics, Shusterman tries to explain the ambivalent approach to the body in Beauvoir's writings, as if the body featured as an obstacle on the way of women's emancipation understood as becoming an active person and creating the self by transcending the existing conditions. Shusterman points out:

> Beauvoir seems to be arguing that by improving their awareness of bodily experience, women would be reinforcing their passivity and withdrawal from the world into immanence as well as underlining the very dimension of their being (namely, bodily experience) that most expresses their oppression. Being identified with the body and the passive interiority of its feelings, women find it more difficult to assert themselves in the public world of action and intellectual projects.[31]

Shustermann asks: "Why should scrutiny of one's somatic experience necessarily confine oneself to immanence and passivity?"[32]

The utmost relevance of deepening one's own bodily consciousness, understanding the cultural specificity of body gestures and transforming habits of the body to the performance of gender roles, as well as to the goals of feminism, can be readily inferred from, for instance, Martha Nussbaum or bell hooks. In *Not for Profit*, Nussbaum shows how Rabindranath Tagore, a teacher and founder of schools and Visva-Bharati University in India, used dance, music, and drama to strengthen the body consciousness of girls and boys in order to help them become more aware of the way they performed gender roles. "Women were his particular concern," writes Nussbaum, "since he saw that women were typically brought up to be ashamed of their bodies and unable to move freely, particularly in the presence of men. A lifelong advocate of women's freedom and equality, he saw that simply telling girls to move more freely would be unlikely to overcome years of repression, but giving them precisely choreographed moves to perform, leaping from here to there, would be a more successful incentive to freedom."[33]

In the chapter of *Feminist Theory* devoted to the problem of solidarity among women, bell hooks recounts her experiences of teaching a course titled "Third World Women in the United States" in multi-ethnic groups.[34] hooks describes the difficulties in communication among students, rooted in mutual misunderstanding of cultural codes of bodily and verbal behavior. For example, the loud, expansive, and ironic communication style of black students was perceived as aggressive and hostile by white students, whereas fast and immediate exchanges of views in discussion by white American girls were difficult to accept for a Japanese student, who had been taught to speak only after having considered her voice's meaning to and impact on a dispute. The awareness of cultural codes shaping their ways of speaking – e.g., speed, audibility, pauses, and silence – helped them establish a better atmosphere for dialogue.

The third example is Shusterman's reading of Wittgenstein, in which he foregrounds the analogy and relation between the feeling of one's own body – its integrity or vulnerability, familiarity or strangeness, cleanness or dirt – and the attitude toward others. He begins by revisiting Wittgenstein's remarks on the body and the concept of man: "our sense of the body, he argues, provides the ground and often the symbol for our concept of what it means to be human."[35] And he continues: "Our ethical concepts of human rights, the sanctity of life, our high ideals of moral worth and of philosophical, and aesthetic achievement all depend, Wittgenstein argues, on a form of life that takes as a premise the ways we experience our bodies and the ways that others treat them."[36]

In this framework, the author of *Body Consciousness* offers an illuminating interpretation of Wittgenstein's views on the roots of anti-Semitism in Europe as expressed in his 1931 diary: "This seemingly irrational hatred of the Jews may in fact have a deep compelling logic of its own that seems to operate on a visceral model or analogy. The Jews, in this unhappily familiar analogy, are a diseased tumor (*Beule*) in Europe, though Wittgenstein is prudent enough not to call this tumor a fatal cancer."[37] Let me quote, after Shusterman, the following passage from Wittgenstein: "'Look on this tumor as a perfectly normal part of your body!' Can one do that, to order? Do I have the power to decide at will to have, or not to have, an ideal conception of my body? (…) We may say: people can only regard this tumor as a natural part of the body if their whole feeling for the body changes (if the whole national feeling for the body changes). Otherwise the best they can do is *put up with* it."[38] Shusterman concludes that it is precisely because anti-Semitism and other forms of ethnic hatred are deeply rooted not only in ideas but also in visceral images and bodily habits of experiencing otherness that they usually remain unaffected by rational arguments of multicultural tolerance. According to Shusterman, somaesthetic awareness can help control, distance oneself form, and even transform or overcome the visceral feelings of enmity and disgust. "Somatic feelings," writes Shusterman, "can be transformed through training because they are already the product of training."[39]

At this point, we could ask how Shusterman's reflection on human nature understood in terms of an embodied self open to cultivation and transformation can contribute to the discussion about human nature after the Shoah. I would tentatively suggest that there might be a possibility to read Shusterman's philosophy of the body as a kind of "response" to the difficult questions emerging in the aftermath of the Holocaust. One of the problems widely discussed in the context of the Western and Jewish philosophical traditions is the relation between memory of the catastrophe and hope as an orientation toward the future. The tension this relation is fraught with is aptly conveyed by the Jewish philosopher Emil Fackenheim: "We are forbidden to turn present and future life into death, as the price of remembering death at Auschwitz. And we are equally forbidden to affirm present and future life, at the price of forgetting Auschwitz."[40] There is a risk that such a catastrophe will crush not only the past but also the future and the hope. As Geras notices, it has already become for many people "the symbol of inexorable human fate," and the only truth about "what we are and have to be."[41]

If we turn to responses to the Holocaust stemming from the Jewish tradition and philosophy, we could identify points at which some of those responses, Geras's defense of hope and the concept of human nature in socialism, and Shusterman's somaesthetics converge. Jewish culture boasts a rich and long tradition of responses to the catastrophes afflicting Jewish communities throughout ages, which serves as a reservoir of strategies and instruments for balancing the tensions among memory of the catastrophe, grief, and messianic hope.[42] Over centuries rabbis, intellectuals and artists have repeatedly sought to reestablish the equilibrium among dark times, the tradition, and the messianic future and to curb the grief, in order to prevent a singular event from destroying the past and the future.

Richard Shusterman's body-focused approach, consistently underscoring the need for establishing the sound proportion between experience of pain and other experiences of the living body, offers one more source of inspiration in seeking to balance memory of the catastrophe and the future after the Shoah. The essential postulation of his philosophy of the living and sentient body is that our wound is not all-encompassing, that there is always something more, something that feels the wound. How important is it in the face of experiments on the limits of human vulnerability to pain, hunger, and suffering experienced in the death camps? I think that it can hardly be overestimated, especially when we also consider countless testimonies of torture victims from across the globe, and the compelling impression they convey. As Elaine Scarry writes in her book *The Body in Pain*: "It is the intense pain that destroys a person's self and world, a destruction experienced spatially as either the contraction of the universe down to the immediate vicinity of the body or as the body swelling to fill the entire universe."[43]

NOTES

1. Richard Shusterman, *Surface and Depth: Dialectics of Criticism and Culture* (Ithaca: Cornell University Press, 2002), p. 191.
2. Norman Geras, *Solidarity in the Conversation of Humankind: The Ungroundable Liberalism of Richard Rorty* (New York: Verso, 1995).
3. The omission seems to be a personal choice, as Shusterman does not mention the events of the Shoah even in his essay about the contemporary problems of Jewish identity in America and Israel. Cf. Richard Shusterman, "Next Year in Jerusalem? Jewish Identity and the Myth of Return," *Practicing Philosophy: Pragmatism and the Philosophical Life* (New York: Routledge, 1997).
4. Richard Rorty, "Human Rights, Rationality and Sentimentality," *The Politics of Human Rights*, eds. Belgrad Circle, intr. Obrad Savić (New York: Verso 2002), p. 68.
5. *Ibid.*, p. 80.
6. Richard Rorty, "Justice as Larger Loyalty," *Justice and Democracy: Cross-cultural Perspectives*, eds. Ron Bontekoe and Marietta Stepaniants (Hawaii: University of Hawaii Press, 1997), pp. 9–22.
7. Emmanuel Lévinas, "The Rights of Man and the Rights of the Other," *Outside the Subject*, trans. Michael. B. Smith (Stanford: Stanford University Press, 1994).
8. Cf. Norman Geras, *Marx and Human Nature: Refutation of the Legend* (New York: Verso, 1983) and "Socialist Hope in the Shadow of Catastrophe," *The Contract of Mutual Indifference: Political Philosophy after the Holocaust* (New York: Verso, 1998).
9. Richard Rorty, *Contingency, Irony, and Solidarity* (Cambridge: Cambridge University Press, 1989), p. 189.
10. *Ibid.*, p. 189.
11. *Ibid.*, pp. 190–91.
12. Geras, *Solidarity in the Conversation of Humankind*, p. 18.
13. *Ibid.*, p. 8.
14. *Ibid.*, pp. 40–1.
15. *Ibid.*, p. 80.
16. *Ibid.*, p. 90.
17. *Ibid.*, pp. 80–1.
18. Erich Fromm, *The Anatomy of Human Destructiveness* (New York: Holt, Rinehart and Winston, 1973), pp. 45–65.
19. Geras, "Socialist Hope in the Shadow of Catastrophe," p. 68.
20. *Ibid.*, p. 120.
21. Alain Finkielkraut, *In the Name of the Humanity: Reflections in the Twentieth Century*, trans. Judith Friedlander (New York: University of Columbia Press, 2000), p. 24.
22. *Ibid.*, p. 83.
23. Richard Shusterman, *Pragmatist Aesthetics: Living Beauty, Rethinking Art* (Lanham: Rowman and Littlefield, 2000), p. 259.
24. *Ibid.*, p.259.
25. Richard Shusterman, *Body Consciousness: A Philosophy of Mindfulness and Somaesthetics* (Cambridge: Cambridge University Press, 2008), p. 21.
26. *Ibid.*, p. 1.
27. *Ibid.*, p. 18.

28. Shusterman, *Pragmatist Aesthetics*, p. 260.
29. Shusterman, *Body Consciousness*, p. 45.
30. *Ibid.*, p. 84.
31. *Ibid.*, p. 97.
32. *Ibid.*, p. 98.
33. Martha C. Nussbaum, *Not for Profit: Why Democracy Needs the Humanities?* (Princeton: Princeton University Press, 2010), pp. 104–5.
34. bell hooks, *Feminist Theory: From Margin to Center* (London: Pluto Press, 2000), pp. 57–8.
35. Shusterman, *Body Consciousness*, p. 127.
36. *Ibid.*, p. 127.
37. *Ibid.*, p. 128.
38. *Ibid.*, p. 128.
39. *Ibid.*, p. 130.
40. Emil L. Fackenheim, *To Mend the World: Foundation of Future Jewish Thought* (New York: Schocken, 1982), p. 22.
41. Geras, "Socialist Hope in the Shadow of Catastrophe," p. 120.
42. See Yosef Hayim Yerushalmi, *Zakhor: Jewish History and Jewish Memory* (Washington: University of Washington Press, 1982); David G. Roskies, *Against the Apocalypse: Responses to Catastrophe in Modern Jewish Culture* (Cambridge: Harvard University Press, 1984).
43. Elaine Scarry, *The Body in Pain: The Making and Unmaking of the World* (New York: Oxford University Press, 1985), p. 35.

Nine

SOMAESTHETIC ENCOUNTER WITH ONESELF AND THE OTHER

Robert Dobrowolski

The encounter with the Other tends to be tainted with the fear of the unknown but also with the fear of that which is known only too well, when the alter-ego materializing in front of us reveals the principle of our own violence. The impersonal voice of universal Reason promises to lead us out of the state of secret or open war. We know that "the sleep of reason produces monsters"; however, it often happens that only after it awakens do they take full possession of us, not annihilated by its light. They continue their stealthy workings, lurking in the dark corners of our senses, feeding on our bodies.

The voice of reason is not enough. We have to exorcise not only our minds but also our bodies, harnessing their dormant demons of fear and prejudice. We should adjust our bodies so that they can recognize the Others as neighbors; not just as narcissistically distorted mirror reflections of ourselves, but rather as the living proof that we are not doomed to confinement within our own selves.

Therein, we need to attend to factors that interfere with the mechanicity of notions. Despite digital claims, symbolic communication is never performed in the immaterial ether, but it is always rooted in the particular, analog, real media. Therefore, attempts to regulate interpersonal relations cannot be confined to the abstract limits of autonomous reason. Only transcendent phantoms, rather than beings of flesh and blood, meet in the Habermasian world based on the "ideal speech situation" (*ideale Sprechsituation*). "( ) If there is no Thing to underpin our everyday, symbolically regulated exchange with others, we find ourselves in a 'flat,' aseptic, Habermasian universe in which subjects are deprived of their hubris of excessive passion, reduced to lifeless pawns in the regulated game of communication."[1]

The theory and practice of social life need to be complemented by aesthetics, because they all too often fail to acknowledge the personally undifferentiated social background space we inhabit in virtue of our shared bodily being in the world. On that shared background, we exist with others, alongside them, not over against them.

Friedrich Schiller was aware of it when he implanted Kant's rationalism onto the sensuous ground of the Greek *kalos kagathos*. The question remains, however, how to continue his classicizing ideas of aesthetic education when disintegration and uncertainty, *Sturm und Drang*, have become the norm.

Contemporary projects of an aesthetization of social discourse have long been insensitive to the innocent harmony of beauty, seeking their self-justification in the rhetoric of the sublime rather, where they are confronted with the reality of the defragmented world and the split subject. While declaring anti-foundationalism, these projects focus on such categories as "body," "flesh," "unconscious," or "Other". Although not all of them resist the temptation of final justification, they can serve as sources of mutual inspiration. The somaesthetics of encounter with the Other has been studied by such thinkers as Maurice Merleau-Ponty, Julia Kristeva, or Richard Shusterman, within such diverse theoretical frameworks as phenomenology, psychoanalysis, and neopragmatism.

1. The Bodily Experience of Sympathetic Harmony

Maurice Mearleau-Ponty has transferred the study of social relations from the plane of the rational and conscious to that of bodily interconnectedness. Therein he found the primal source of genuine interpersonal bonds. In his view, each discourse aiming at the rational conciliation and communion among alienated individuals must find its validity in the immediacy of precognitive and non-epistemic experience of the sympathetic harmony, which constitutes the profoundest foundation of the social perception of the Others.

A rational and linguistic communion of any kind can thus be experienced only through the primal communion of bodies, as Merleau-Ponty claims: "Consciousnesses present themselves with the absurdity of a multiple solipsism, such is the situation which has to be understood."[2] Merleau-Ponty's phenomenology seeks to pierce through the layers of the objectifying order of ideas and arrive at the bodily being-in-the-world, pointing out that the intentionality of consciousness is always preceded by the pre-reflective intentionality. In this acategorial world, revealing the ontological kinship of bodies, "man is a mirror for man"[3] primarily through the bodily medium. "Other minds are given to us only as incarnate, as belonging to faces and gestures."[4]

If being the particular body is the essence of consciousness, the validity of any act of understanding with others has to be tangibly confirmed by a sentient body. For we transcend towards that which is other just because our perception fulfills itself not as a constitutive thought about an object, but rather as a sensory opening-up to the potential being of things. Obviously, according to Merleau-Ponty, we do not reach the Kantian "things in themselves" in the process, but arrive rather at a certain, independent set of potentialities that require particular actualization. The light of perception is guided through the glow of primal, silent being, which urges us to pronounce its countless names. Evidently, even though the creative expression of a bodily subject co-creates the Other, specifying its *Gestalt*, it does so only when passively opened to its otherness, in the bodily coexistence with that which resists conceptual arbitrariness.

It is only being-in-the-world mediated by the body, Merleau-Ponty argues, that ultimately allows experiencing transcendence, suspending the dialectics of consciousness, which has endlessly deferred the Husserlian "return to the things themselves."

> Our relationship to the social is, like our relationship to the world, deeper than any express perception or any judgment. It is as false to place ourselves in society as an object among other objects, as it is to place society within ourselves as an object of thought, and in both cases the mistake lies in treating the social as an object.[5]

The transition from the "philosophy of consciousness" to a corporeal existence does not only make the pre-reflective existence of Objects available to a perceptual individual, but it also reveals alterity of the Other. In consciousness defined as thinking, the Other is always given as always already constituted by it, never as an effectively independent "You," a constituting subject, "I which is an other." It is the body that releases us from the solipsistic cage of ideas and opens up the sensual space of being, where encountering the Other is made possible.

According to Merleau-Ponty, the Other becomes available as a bodily familiar other. Before reflectively recognized as "not-I," a negation of ourselves, he or she is first encountered in the shared, intercorporeal area of being. This common place which we inhabit together, or which inhabits us, is a non-personal being of flesh, a co-experienced fabric of corporeality. An encounter with the Other, Merleu-Ponty claims, in this bodily, pre-personal subject is more primal and penetrates into deeper levels of existence than the subsequent experience of each other as separate, individual subjects. It enables us to recognize immediately familiar patterns of behavior in the Other's body:

> A baby of fifteen months opens its mouth if I playfully take one of its fingers between my teeth and pretend to bite it. And yet it has scarcely looked at its face in a glass, and its teeth are not in any case like mine. The fact is that its own mouth and teeth, as it feels them from the inside, are immediately, for it, an apparatus to bite with, and my jaw, as the baby sees it from the outside, is immediately, for it, capable of the same intentions. 'Biting' has immediately, for it, an intersubjective significance. It perceives its intentions in its body, and my body with its own, and thereby my intentions in its own body.[6]

When we touch our touching hand, in the hiatus of dual sensation, in the doubled transmodality of our own being, we experience ourselves as both the constituting and the constituted – I experience being seized by some other I. In this opening of oneself by oneself, an outline of the spherical structure of experience can be discerned, where the intertwining perspectives of my own and the Other's existence reveal the community of expression and sensing. The act of making ourselves available to each other is only possible because we become embodied for each other in the same texture of being.

2. The Other as a Bleeding Wound

From Merleau-Ponty's perspective, it is exclusively the body that can counter the horror of consciousness, where "Hell is other people" (*L'Enfer, c'est les autres*), by allowing us to experience tangibly a communion with the Others. Although the French philosopher is perfectly aware that in the process of social identity formation the perception of personal separateness is deepening, the body remains, for him, the primal principle of opening onto the Other.

In Merleau-Ponty's domesticated, perfectly familiar world, the Other's alterity, however, seems to be left out of account. "Our own body is in the world as the heart is in the organism,"[7] but the heart suffers numerous, often unrecognized arrests when the intrusion of the unfamiliar makes it miss a beat. The notion of redeeming properties of the body cannot obliterate the experiences in which the body becomes an inadvertent source and a reservoir of enmity towards other people. The body in question may mean both a "naked," unconscious body, which is a precondition for the cultural and psychological biography, and a corporeality already subject to symbolic determination. From this perspective, the Other may appear as a painful, unsettling stain in our sensory perception field, as someone blurring the clarity of the symbolic order embedded in our innards, or a sensorily felt threat to the unconscious processes of acquiring bodily self-identity.

A rapid breach of consensus with the Other may occur at the level of bodily expression. If a Bulgarian person wished to disagree with this statement, he would nod his head instead of shaking it, as we customarily do, and an apparently kind smile of a Japanese person might express his angry indignation. Traveling in space and time, we can often experience how very divergent intentions are transmitted in similar gestures. Despite Merleau-Ponty's universalist views on this matter, ("every gesture is comparable to every other. They all arise from a single syntax")[8], a particular bodily expression does not always convey the same meaning. A good illustration would be Hitler's gestures and facial expression and their rendition by Chaplin's dictator Hynkel, in which the sublime and the ridiculous are coextensive.

For the French phenomenologist, the encounter with the Other takes place at the most fundamental level of perception; in the phenomenal field where, beyond the dialectics of opposing consciousnesses, our bodily intensions correlate with each other. At times, the mode of the intercorporeal exchange process changes suddenly not only because of different cultural codes, but also due to the phenomena which occur within the domain of the body itself. It is here that, alongside the principle of universal communion, another – contrary – principle of separation is realized. For individuation already starts within a non-personal body, under its lining and in the fissures of flesh, prior to the subsequent involvement of consciousness.

A sensory transmission belt can always be corrected by heuristic explication whenever it slides and veers off upon symbolic differences. What was lost in translation can be recovered in its contextual repetition or in an explicitly elucidated gesture. Matters become complicated when we chance upon obstacles, gaps, and knots in the very matter of flesh itself, and our harmonious interaction with the Others and the world is thwarted. A bodily communion can be transformed then into the horror of abjection by a powerful, penetrating sensual discord.

Although the sensory nature of the abject is always qualified by its particular cultural context, it cannot be recognized as an effect of discourse alone. As Kristeva argues,[9] the abject, even though retroactively qualified by culture, is a precondition of discourse as such. Owing to the abject delimitation of the body, the subject and the object emerge. Therefore, paradoxically, if it was not for the abject, there would be nobody to fraternize with.

To make it possible for the Other to appear as a particular *Gestalt*, both his/her and our bodily shapes have to be defined by the unconscious action of our sensory abjectness. Just as Eros always takes shape in the shadow of Thanatos, similarly the sense of beauty is animated by sublime reason. Therefore, a genuine relation with the Other cannot be based on the phantasms of sensory wholeness, as Merleau-Ponty argues. In the bodily communion, while sensing our non-substantial absence, we should be able to recognize rationally an inalienable alterity in ourselves and in the Others.

Merleau-Ponty, as Jacques Lacan comments, "(...) hangs on to the notion of totality, of unitary functioning, he always presupposes a given unity accessible to what in the end will be an instantaneous, theoretical, contemplative apprehension, to which the experience of the good form, so very ambiguous in Gestaltism, gives a semblance of support."[10]

This non-perceptive dissonance can drive an aesthete into the state of morbid disappointment with himself and the Others. On the other hand, it can form an underlying sensory-cognitive motive for objective liberty to discover, in one's "I" and the Other's "You," a difficult affinity, an identified potential for coexistence which will be immunized against the whims of narcissistic phantasms.

When we see the face of our fellow man turned upside down or at an unusual angle, a commonly shared body scheme suffices to sustain his identity. But in these short moments of perception disturbances, it appears to be the face of a monstrous Thing. Therefore, the chiasmatic flesh postulated by Merleau-Ponty reveals cracks and fissures through which an amorphous plasma leaks out, causing nausea and a-bjects in our bodies.

Our ability to incorporate the world and the Others prior to applying concepts to them is indispensably conditioned by a transcendental, corporeal ability to cut and loosen up the threads which link us with the flesh of the

World. The sublime perspective of the unfamiliar, in which the Other evades our grasp, cuts across the perspective of sensory unification, in which the Other is given as part of the experienced World, "a set of manipulanda."[11] Merleau-Ponty rightly observes that in the flesh of the world "there is a germination of what *will have been* understood."[12] But it is also true that what is entirely unfamiliar germinates in the fissures of this very flesh. The structuring of the unconscious affects the visibility of the visible and the sensibility of the sensible, not always bringing about "beautiful" results, but sometimes disturbing the sensory equilibrium. Apparently, the "umbilical cord" metaphor used by Merleau- Ponty to describe intercorporeal connectedness falls short here. The flesh is rather a diversified plentitude of threads connecting us with the Others and the world, with some of them thinner, more jagged, and weaker than other ones and some of them completely missing. These gaps and this absence cause a sensory shock and the feeling of alienation.

In the same sensory seat of the unconscious where, Merleau-Ponty claims, we commune with the Other, a sudden clash with an unfamiliar gaze of the Other may take place. The otherness of the Other, while his gaze splits our vision, is perceived as a tantalizing, and alluring at the same time, hazard of dissolution of our personhood. Our eye, unable to appropriate the point of view of the Other, circles helplessly as an object of the scopic drive, as a lost object of the m/other's or the Other's gaze, unsealing our bodily limits.

"The gaze is thus, like the phallus itself, the drive under which the subject's identity and certainty fail."[13] The infirmity which we so experience exposes the fragility of our bodies; the phantasms of their phallic cohesion seep through open cracks and fissures. This uncanny gaze alienates the familiarity of our body. We experience ourselves as strangers. To our dismay, the delusion of the immediate, bodily contact with the substantial self is dispelled.

To be able to "love one's neighbor as oneself," we have to acknowledge that the Others are the hell which can be found in ourselves, too. We can experience it when we sense in our bodies some amorphous remnants eluding our conceptualizations. In the dimension of conceptual identification, even love for the Others is tinged with psychotic aggression. Therefore, all the orgiastic phantasms of fraternization within the real m/other lead to the elimination of the truly Others. Only by ignoring what is fundamentally unfamiliar in the Other could Merleau-Ponty experience disappointment in his passing love affair with the communist party. Moreover, this ideological romance stood clearly in contrast with his own admonitions.

"If the patient hears voices in his head, this is because he does not absolutely distinguish himself from others and because, for example, when he speaks, he can just as well believe that someone else is speaking. The patient, says Wallon, has the impression of being 'without boundaries' in relation to the other, and this is what makes his acts, his speech, and his thoughts appear to him to belong to others or to be imposed by others."[14] Working through such a bodily self-consciousness, an exposure to the alterity in me and in the

Other may not only serve to relieve the fear of alienation but also provide an embodied reason for making self-consciousness more flexible and, consequently, for increasing tolerance for the dissimilarity of the Others. The narcissistic desire to regain mine-ness results in aggression towards the Other. The gesture of love does not entrap the Other in its murderous grip exclusively on condition that my identity is not only realized but also experienced bodily as an open project. The tag "Perception itself is never finished"[15] refers to our bodies and the body of the Other.

3. Somaesthetics of Otherness

It is not enough to understand the Other; we must envelop the Other's alterity in aesthetic sympathy and, going far beyond any verbal declarations, touch him/her, sometimes literally. An indispensable condition for such a sensual self-transcendence is the ability to recognize appearances of substantial identity within the somaesthetics of one's own body. Our bodiliness is much too often shaped as a cultural armor which, while preserving the illusion of an invariable I, protects us from the truth of variable reality.

Also an apparently naturally marked emotional borderline, which closes off whatever is disgusting and frustrating, is actually drawn as a result of social indoctrination. In an open society, it is worthwhile, therefore, to reflect upon, or perhaps modify, the widespread forms of bodily regimes. The melioristic effort would thus aim at constituting and then promoting those forms of both one's own and the social body which are most conducive to conscious sensation.

To illustrate in what way the lack of somaesthetic awareness may expose us to an unconscious influence of the bodily entrenched prejudices, let me use an example. I have once heard quite a shocking confession from a person brought up in communist Poland, in conditions precluding any external influences, in an ethnically homogenous society. Namely, this educated and purportedly non-racist man admitted that when he had shaken hands with a black foreigner for the first time, he had wiped his hand against his trousers, a gesture as involuntary as it was secret. Unfortunately, we far more often fail to notice that our body language belies our verbal attitude.

The meaning of declarations, even those made in good faith, may take very long to really sink in and nestle in our innards, or may even fail to do so at all. Empty words always miss physical fulfillment.

If another human being reveals him/herself to us as utterly inimitable, his/her presence inevitably disturbs the conciliatory grammar of logos: in an unspeakable embodiment, a ghost of flesh and bones appears in front of us. The encounter with the Other always entails a traumatic immersion in a vast abyss of irreducible Otherness. What disturbs us are not the very words that the Other addresses to us, but the unique, sensual, material way in which they are uttered.

As Richard Shusterman rightly notices,

If the familiar forms and normal feelings of our body ground our form of life, which in turn grounds our ethical concepts and attitudes toward others, then we can perhaps better understand some of our irrational political enmities. The fanatical kind of hatred or fear that some people have for certain foreign races, cultures, classes, and nations does display a deep visceral quality, which suggests that such enmity may reflect profound concerns about the integrity and purity of the familiar body in a given culture. Such anxieties can be unconsciously translated into hostility toward foreigners, who challenge that familiar body and threaten its corruption through ethnic and cultural mixing that can alter the body, in both external appearance and behavior.[16]

Apparently, the socioanthropologically ascertained interdependence between the closure of one's bodily boundaries and the consolidation of the unity and power of a social group in which they materialize overthrows any somaesthetic attempt at increasing tolerance towards the Others. Wittgenstein thought along these lines when he referred to the metaphor of Jews as the tumor of Europe. In the sinister light of such symbolism, anti-Semitism seemed a wholly justified phenomenon to him – one could not possibly expect strongly shaped nations to treat the imminent disease, i.e. the Jews, in the way they treated their own healthy social organism. Shusterman questions the aesthetic and ethical inevitability of such rhetoric.

He says: "If the seductive image of body purity and uniformity fuels the deep prejudice that incites fear and hatred toward alien groups (whether of racial, ethnic, or sexual difference), then one strategy for overcoming the problem would be to make vividly clear and visible the impure and mixed nature of all human bodies, including our own. Somaesthetic disciplines can give us such a heightened experiential awareness of the impure mixture of our bodily constitution and remind us that our body boundaries are never absolute but rather porous."[17]

History, especially that of the past century, confirms that the ideal of the purity of the social body, even if it served indispensable integrative functions at critical moments for a given society, in the long run leads to a weakening or even to the annihilation of the social body. The aesthetics of immaculate unity functions equally badly at the level of a real body, when an individual defines his/her identity through the experience of his/her own bodiliness as modeled upon the image of a tightly closed, stiff, strained body. According to Shusterman, an appropriate modification of aesthetic experience, of both one's own as well as somebody else's body, might help us become more tolerant towards other people, especially when they represent and embody a totally dissimilar sensuality and culture. Systematically scanning our bodily sensations, we could identify the impressions that are marked by hostility towards the Other, which in turn would give us an opportunity to neutralize or even to overcome them. The consciousness of such bodily quasi-prejudgments, which enables a critical detachment from them, would significantly enhance the comfort of meeting the Other. If for a true hermeneut interpretation is a never-ending process, then for a true somaesthetician, the discovery of sensual prejudices proceeds in a spherical structure of ever-renewed scanning of one's bodiliness. The somaesthetic self-knowledge, gained in this interminable process, exposes the pretence of the phantasmatic substantial body.

How erroneous the belief in an impeccable autonomy and unity of our bodies is can be evidenced, among others, by psychoanalysis, with its accounts of how the inevitably de-centered, split subject takes on an embodied form. In the mirror phase, described by Lacan, a child's bodily self-consciousness is constituted by means of outer images and representations, as the French theoretician posited. At this stage of development, the imaginary represses the Real, and a fragmentary sense of bodiliness is replaced by an illusory perception of a substantial, filled, and united body. The specular identification with the image of the Other partially compensates for the frustrating sense of lack caused by the lingering absence of the already separate mother.

This narcissistically cast specular body of the Other becomes an integration model, which allows a more successful control of one's organism and the outer world. Fascinated by his/her own image, an ideal which reflects the promise of regaining the symbiotic bond with the fullness of m(other), a child tries to go through the looking glass. Nevertheless, he/she always slides down its ideally smooth surface, rubbing roughly against the rugged bottom of the Real. That generates aggression towards all imaginary others, who cannot be fully comprehended, who are unpalatable.

The cannibalistic body of the imaginary Narcissus can only be tamed by a symbolic presence of the big Other – language and law, cultural mediation between the subject in the making and the real others. Shuttering the specular bonds between the newly-born ego and its imaginary alter-ego from inside, the big Other largely takes control over the somaesthetic attitude of the subject, which has so far been developing within its symbolic field. And, desiring its loving gaze, the subject inscribes the abstract rules of the law in its own body.

Apart from bringing ethical advantages, becoming open to the experience of our body's flexibility, its processualness, and certain unpredictability would effectively enhance our creativity. As Nietzsche's Zarathustra spoke: "One must still have chaos in oneself to be able to give birth to a dancing star."[18] However, not everybody can become a superman, and only few are ready to sacrifice everyday little pleasures for the ecstatic and deadly *jouissance*.

Therefore, it is urgent to create a project of common somaesthetic education, which would not only facilitate an increase in our bodily awareness, but also help develop our abilities of aesthetic and ethical self-education, for the sake of ourselves and for the Other. Popular art is of paramount importance here. It is therefore worth examining whether the aesthetic forms which are being promoted foster participation in democratic life.

Richard Shusterman finds the right aesthetic form in the culture of hip-hop, and not without reason. One cannot fail to observe that the body which is stretched in break-dance vortexes can foster an open, mercurially flexible mind far more easily than all mechanical, industrial, and digital forms of popular art, in which body-mind is either torn into pieces or compressed into stiff stupor. If I were asked to point out the popular art form best fitted for these educational purposes, it would be music whose rhythmical heart beats in a free, improvised atmosphere of the so-called blue notes. Typical of blues and jazz, these notes, swaying beyond the piece's major scale, when aptly selected, interrupt the musically disciplined structure with moments of indefiniteness and indeterminacy, which provide room for specific, temporary and fleeting individual intuitions, adroitly reconciling the need for self-expression with the needs of a group.

The aesthetic preparation for encountering the sensory dissimilarity should involve its more pronounced presence in the public space. The positive manifestation of such openness can be increasingly often – though still not often enough – seen in the mass media: cultural, racial, and sexual dissimilarities, as well as disease and disability, are no longer taboos of the aesthetic unpresentability. For instance, in one of the most popular Polish TV stations a well-known news program was run by a presenter suffering from cancer. The viewers learnt about his disease after he had died. I can still remember my hesitant reaction, when instead of seeing a smooth face of a typical plastic man on the screen, I was captured by the view of a strangely gaunt, ugly face.

Such a traumatic confrontation with both oneself and the other can take place when a symbolic web, dominant in a given culture, is torn by the repressed Real. An excessive manifestation, disrupting conventional systems of presentation, means – in Julia Kristeva's terminology – that whatever is semiotic, whatever precedes the symbolically arranged language, returns as a splitting of apparently substantial identities. At this level, our somaesthetic self-consciousness regains the pre-oedipal flexibility to some extent, revealing its materiality as a kind of Aristotelian potency – the matter which is capable of much more differentiated actualization than that which is apportioned to us by the dominant symbolic order. "It is for this reason that Kristeva seems fascinated with the avant-garde text, the 'texts' of Mallarmé, Lautréamont, Artaud, Joyce, Schoenberg, Cage, Stockhausen, and even Giotto and Bellini."[19]

Such sublime fascinations cannot be neglected, but one must remember also about those that constitute the majority of the social body of democracies. Hence the need to promote somaesthetics appropriate for an everyman, who is not necessarily prepared for the psychotic experiments with the modern abject art. Perhaps we should begin as early as at school, providing children, who acquire social identities, with ample opportunities for positive, cathartic confrontation with sensual prejudices. And by that I do not mean any perverted happenings, like those of Viennese actionists. What I mean is rather a meeting with, for example, a disabled person, so that one could literally touch him/her and, thus, stop being scared of him/her.

NOTES

1. Slavoj Žižek, *Interrogating the Real* (New York: Continuum, 2005), p. 321.
2. Maurice Merleau-Ponty, *Phenomenology of Perception*, trans. Colin Smith (London: Routledge, 2005), p. 418.
3. Maurice Merleau-Ponty, "Eye and Mind," trans. Carleton Dallery, *The Primacy of Perception: And Other Essays on Phenomenological Psychology, the Philosophy of Art, History and Politics*, ed. James Edie, (Evanston: Northwestern University Press, 1964), p. 168.
4. Maurice Merleau-Ponty, *Sense and Non-Sense*, trans. Hubert L. Dreyfus and Patricia A. Dreyfus (Evanston: Northwestern University Press, 1964), p. 16.
5. Merleau-Ponty, *Phenomenology of Perception*, p. 421.
6. *Ibid.*, p. 410.
7. *Ibid.*, p. 235.
8. Maurice Merleau-Ponty, *Signs*, trans. Richard McCleary (Evaston: Northwestern University Press, 1964), p. 68.
9. See Julia Kristeva, *Powers of Horror*, trans. Leon S. Roudiez (New York: Columbia University Press, 1982).
10. Jacques Lacan, *The Seminar of Jacques Lacan. Book II: The Ego in Freud's Theory and in the Technique of Psychoanalysis, 1954–1955*, trans. Sylvana Tomaselli (London, New York: W. W. Norton & Company Ltd, 1988), p. 78.
11. Merleau-Ponty, *Phenomenology of Perception*, p. 120.
12. Maurice Merleau-Ponty, *The Visible and the Invisible*, trans. Alphonso Lingis (Evanston: Northwestern University Press, 1968), p. 189.
13. Elizabeth Grosz, *Jacques Lacan: A Feminist Introduction* (London: Routledge, 1990), p. 79.
14. Maurice Merleau-Ponty, "The Child's Relations with Others," trans. William Cobb, *The Primacy of Perception*, p. 134.
15. Maurice Merleau-Ponty, *The Prose of the World*, trans. John O'Neill (Evanston: Northwestern University Press, 1973), p. 56.
16. Richard Shusterman, *Body Consciousness: A Philosophy of Mindfulness and Somaesthetics* (Cambridge: Cambridge University Press, 2008), pp. 127–28.
17. *Ibid.*, pp. 131–32.
18. Friedrich Nietzsche, *Thus Spoke Zarathustra: A Book for All and None*, trans. Walter Kaufmann (New York: Modern Library, 1995), p. 17.
19. Grosz, *Jacques Lacan*, p. 152.

Part Four

ART OF LIVING AND LIFE POLITICS

Ten

MAKING THE PRAGMATIST ART OF LIVING EXPLICIT

Emil Višňovský

1. Introduction

I want to explore whether pragmatism in any of its classical and/or contemporary versions includes some tenets of what has become known in the history of philosophy as "the art of life." Or, to put it simply: Is there "a pragmatist art of living," and if so, what might it imply? I will try to show that pragmatism is a distinctive philosophy of life, or, for that matter, philosophy of "the art of life," applicable to and adoptable by the individual. But before we move on, some introductory caveats are in order.

Firstly, I prefer to see philosophy as *an open project*, and here I want to side with those who have recently advocated yet another turn or return – to philosophy as a practice whose center or goal is the art of living, i.e., philosophy whose primary subject matter is human life itself and the central question is "how to live?" Although Greek philosophy did not originate as one of many "scientific disciplines" we have today, but rather as a style of thinking-cum-living, this ancient conception of philosophy lost its centrality after Socrates and has not dominated ever since, with the exceptions of the Hellenistic and Roman eras or, perhaps, the Renaissance of Montaigne. Nonetheless, even modern systematic philosophers, such as Descartes, Spinoza or Marx, took the ultimate purpose of philosophy to be helping people live a good life.

Secondly, I also prefer to conceive of philosophy as *a pluralist endeavor*. Thus I would not like to "kill off" metaphysics or epistemology or other more or less traditional philosophical areas. Let a thousand philosophical flowers bloom and not block the road to inquiry for anybody. But let us see this pluralism in a differentiated way: there are many areas and topics in philosophy which are not of the same importance and meaning. So let those who wish to do metaphysics ask: why and with to purpose? What is the meaning and value of doing metaphysics or epistemology? What does knowing about the world (metaphysics) or knowing about knowing (epistemology) provide us, human beings, with in terms of quality of life? I share one of Sami Pihlström's "deepest convictions," that "in considering philosophical issues such as reality, language, knowledge, and science, we are

ultimately dealing with the problem of human life, that is, facing the question
of the value or significance of our existence in the world."[1]

Basically, I see two fundamental motivations for philosophizing: 1.
anthropological, and 2. cosmological; or put another way: 1. ethical-aesthetic
including political (which jointly may be dubbed as "humanistic" or "artistic"),
and 2. metaphysical-epistemological including logical (which jointly may be
dubbed as "scientistic" or "technological"). Since Plato and Aristotle, and
particularly since Descartes and Kant, the latter has prevailed over the former.
Philosophy has kept pursuing knowledge, truth, and method in order to become
a technology-serving science rather than searching for good, beauty, and
community in order to become life-serving wisdom. But returning to its ancient
roots, philosophy can and should be practiced as wisdom rather than
knowledge; i.e., philosophy as a search for practical wisdom of life, of which
knowledge and science are just parts. Philosophy is neither particular nor
general knowledge, but knowledge for philosophy is just a means rather than an
end. Thus conceived, philosophy should be an inquiry into all that is substantial
for human life. I also share John Lachs's conviction that "[m]etaphysics must,
accordingly, always remain in the service of ethics."[2]

Thirdly, I prefer philosophical "mergers" (fusions) rather than "pure"
philosophies, even if one might call the former "eclecticisms." But I see them
as creative combinations, such as "Stoic pragmatism" or "Epicurean
pragmatism" most recently proposed by John Lachs and Charlie Hobbs,
respectively, in their works.[3] And why not try another one under the label
"existential pragmatism"? One of my intentions here is to provide some
prolegomena to such a version of pragmatism.

2. Pragmatism and Philosophy of Life

The philosophy of pragmatism has been accused of many failures, such as
distorting or even missing the conception of human life. On the other hand,
pragmatism is very often regarded as radical "anthropocentrism," tending to
relate all things to human beings and tackling them for the sake of human
beings. But philosophical anthropology and "philosophy of life" have European,
mainly German, roots. These are the areas of philosophy that explore such
issues as the "nature of human being," the "value of human life," the "meaning
of life," the "good life," and the like. The major proponents of these issues in
modern times have been M. Scheler, H. Plessner, A. Gehlen, M. Landmann, E.
Rothacker, but also K. Jaspers, M. Buber, E. Cassirer, as well as the classics,
including S. Kierkegaard, A. Schopenhauer, F. Nietzsche, M. Heidegger, or H.-
G. Gadamer, and also some French philosophers, such as G. Marcel, J.-P.
Sartre, M. Foucault, and J. Derrida. Their insights into human life are reputed
for their depth unparalleled in other philosophical currents and approaches.

However, pragmatism, too, is certainly one of the philosophies that do
not renounce the problems of human life and the human world. The opposite

is in fact true. Ample evidence could be amassed along these lines, starting from such "proto-pragmatists" as Emerson and Thoreau. It was Emerson who, not unlike Nietzsche, in his famous "The American Scholar" called for "philosophy of life" and considered life to be "our dictionary" and "the quarry from whence we get tiles and copestones."[4] And it was likewise Thoreau who, in his *Walden*, when famously contrasting philosophers and philosophy professors, claimed:

> To be a philosopher is not merely to have subtle thoughts, nor even to found a school, but so to love wisdom as to live according to its dictates (…). It is to solve some of the problems of life, not only theoretically, but practically.[5]

Even Peirce, who strongly contested any connection between philosophy and life and, thus, condemned not only James but also the whole Hellenistic conception of philosophy inclusive of ethical and aesthetic practice, respected ethics as a way to a good life. Peirce, a Darwinian, was also an Epicurean in his "metaphysics of life" as expressed in his tychism.

Of course, it was Dewey and James from among the classical pragmatists who were primarily the "humanists" or "anthropologists" and whose philosophy can credibly be termed a "philosophy of life," not only because they declared that the purpose of philosophy was to solve the "problems of men" (and women) rather than the problems of philosophers (according to Dewey), and demanded that it answer the question "why is life worth living?" (according to James), but also because they lived in a way which in many senses embodied their philosophies that sought the betterment of humanity and its lot.

David L. Murray, a now forgotten American philosopher, very succinctly summarized this in the final chapter of his book *Pragmatism* (1912):

> The mission of Pragmatism is to bring Philosophy into relation to real Life and Action. So far from regarding Thought as a self-centered, self-enclosed activity, Pragmatism insists upon replacing it in its context among other functions of life, and in measuring its value by its effect upon them.[6]

Murray refers to Ferdinand C. S. Schiller and he himself advocates the transition from pragmatism to "humanism" based on a different conception of "the place of knowing in human life at large."[7]

Among contemporary pragmatists, we can, of course, name Richard Rorty and Hilary Putnam, whose philosophical projects are quite clearly oriented, albeit in the subtext, toward the pragmatist philosophy of life. Rorty, trying to answer his lifelong question of "what is philosophy good for?" once remarked that "pragmatism is based on the idea that nothing is more important than human happiness, which cannot be transcended by any other idea including the idea of human grandeur."[8] According to Rorty, philosophy's role is to provide "imaginative suggestions for a re-description of the human situation," through which it can serve either as therapy or as poetry, but in both cases it aims at self-creation rather than self-understanding.[9] He was interested in the ever-continuing richness of human life and concerned with becoming more fully human in every possible way as a philosopher and as a human being. He was also a true pragmatist meliorist when surmising that "we all have, given sufficient security, wealth, education and leisure, the capacity to be the artists of our own lives."[10]

Hilary Putnam sees philosophy in general as having "a double task: to integrate our various views of our world and ourselves (…), and to help us find a meaningful orientation in life."[11] In particular, he sees pragmatism, and especially its Jamesian version, as a school for which "the central philosophical question is *how to live*," just as it was for Socrates and his followers, so "the opposition between philosophy which is concerned with how to live and philosophy which is concerned with hard technical questions, is a false opposition."[12] He accepts that the "great insight of pragmatism" is the insistence on the idea "that what has weight in our lives should also have weight in philosophy."[13]

Similar claims, which explicitly confirm a pragmatist orientation to life problems, can be found in a number of recent works. John Lachs, concerned with the menace of the irrelevance of philosophy to life generally, urges that "(…) philosophers have (…) an obligation to address the problems of daily living" and "philosophical reflection can yield results" in "the service of improving life." He himself devotes his writing entirely to becoming "clear about persistent problems of human happiness" and "in the way of understanding human life."[14] The pragmatist philosophy of life balanced with Stoicism, as developed by Lachs, is perhaps the best example today of how this philosophical mission could be fulfilled.[15]

Another example might be the work of Sami Pihlström, who in his numerous publications seeks to develop pragmatist anthropology. He takes pragmatism to be "a vision of the *fullness* of human life in the world."[16] In his first monograph, which in fact focused on ontology, he also tackled anthropology when he wrote: "Pragmatists (…) have constantly argued that philosophy does not merely aim at a deeper understanding of the world, but also at making human life meaningful."[17] The understanding of the world has a practical, i.e. anthropological purpose: we humans do not care about the world for the world's sake; we care about ourselves and our good life in the world, which we cannot achieve without understanding the world first. Ontology should be transformed via anthropology, and not replaced by it or abandoned for the sake of it. Pihlström writes:

The tradition of pragmatism has been guided by the fundamental conviction that philosophy – as well as science and any other practice – is in the service of good life. Ontological discussions and arguments, which aim at a philosophical conception of what exists, of what is real, of what there is in the world, should also serve this ultimate human purpose.[18]

We are responsible for our practices, that is, for our way of life and art of life, which also includes responsibility for the world we create by our practices.[19]

In conclusion of this section, we may summarize and generalize: the contemporary pragmatist turn in philosophy has brought about a change to "promote a style of philosophizing more apt to dealing with the problems of everyday life."[20] This is an important change not only in providing an alternative understanding of what philosophy is but also in its purpose and mission: philosophy should directly help people live a good life, a better life, which includes the construction of a good society as well as good practices as related to the art of life. Pragmatism is a successor to Sophists, Socrates, Stoicism, and Epicureanism in terms of conceptions of philosophy – of what philosophy is good for and what philosophers should do: provide an understanding of the human condition that corresponds with its transformation. I prefer to see pragmatism as a "philosophy of transformation" based on the experience of "life as an ongoing process, capable of transformation,"[21] and as our human response to ever-changing natural and socio-cultural conditions.

3. Pragmatist Understanding of Human Life

Sidney Hook aptly asked: "What, if anything, has philosophy to tell us about human condition, about the fate of man and his works?"[22] What is it then that pragmatist philosophy tells us about this issue?

Firstly, pragmatism understands human life (or existence) within the broadest framework of naturalism. Human beings (organisms) have evolved naturally and live within an "unstable and precarious" natural environment, from which they "must gather all the resources they can muster to survive."[23] Their primordial task is to "adjust or die" (James), but if "human beings are to live and to live well, they must understand the kind of world in which they exist and the kinds of values appropriate to that existence."[24] However, according to pragmatism, "the nature of the world can only be described philosophically by referring to human practice, experience, and culture, after all."[25]

What is most fundamental for life is "the validity of valuations," i.e. our classification of "all objects as 'good' and 'bad,' according as they are ends to be pursued or avoided, or means which further or frustrate the pursuit of ends."[26] As Dewey shows, the process of human adjustment to nature takes two forms: 1. accommodation within conditions we cannot change, and 2. adaptation within conditions we can change.[27] Given that, human life depends crucially on our ability to find out what we can and what we cannot control (which is what Epictetus made the starting point of his conception of the art of living as pertaining to each human being). Life experience has shown that change which is beyond our control is the greatest danger to life and, based on this, humans have come up with an initiative for permanently extending the limits of their control. The more we can control, the better the life we can get. However, experience has also shown that there is, and can be, no absolute human control over nature such that would eliminate any kind of change. "In a world of change and instability there is no basis for an absolute, fixed mode of life, but neither is there a basis for complete resignation."[28] Despite the fact that humanity has embarked on the road from "the precarious to the stable," on a quest for certainty and security, in which people see their survival and life guaranteed, it is flexibility rather than rigidity of life forms, and selectivity rather than fixation of means, that have proved to be the effective ways to these goals.

Secondly, pragmatism understands human life in terms of action (activity) and experience. Human life is practical throughout; the human world is the sum of socio-cultural practices. To solve their life problems, humans must act, be active, and utilize their practical experience. Human life itself is nothing other than action understood as complex interactions and transactions between humans and their natural (not man-made) and socio-cultural (man-made) environment. To adjust to nature, human beings create "second nature," or transform nature into culture. Human action – and *eo ipso* human life – is intelligent, that is purposive, goal-directed, intentional, rational, instrumental, creative, reflective, examined, emotional, symbolic, social, etc. There are many purposes to it and many ways of evaluating them: ethical, aesthetic, intellectual, etc., and the *summum bonum* is "the ideal of the harmonious satisfaction of all purposes."[29] It is through an intelligent action that human beings in principle create the human world, and it is in an intelligent action that they live their lives as human beings.

Thirdly, pragmatism understands human life in terms of "the immediate flux,"[30] which is potentially unstable, precarious, and fraught with conflicting, problematic, and even tragic situations. This is closely connected to the pragmatist concept of contingency as one of the "generic traits of life." There is no natural law, no kind of necessity that would guarantee human beings their good life or happiness. "Life is a chain of problems, so we are born into trouble (…)."[31] Life is a "rat race" that "has more casualties than a war."[32] According to Hook, no one should be bewildered that pragmatism incorporates "the tragic sense of life as a feature of human experience."[33] He does not construe this concept as "merely sensitivity to the presence of evil or suffering in the world."[34] He distinguishes between "the sense of the *pitiful* and the sense of the *tragic*." While the former includes "sickness, old age and even many forms of death,"[35] the latter is a moral fact, by which he means "a very simple thing which is rooted in the very nature of the moral experience and the phenomenon of moral choice."[36] This phenomenon is not simply the existence of evil, but "a situation where good conflicts with good" or good with right, or even right with right. Amidst such circumstances, some good is always sacrificed, and we must all live with it; it is unavoidable, and thus necessarily tragic. The pragmatist method of dealing with this tragic situation (apart from the Hegelian method of historical reason or the Judeo-Christian method of love) is the Deweyan method of creative intelligence: "Its categorical imperative is to inquire, to reason together, to seek in every crisis the creative devices and inventions that will not only make life fuller and richer but tragedy bearable."[37] Hook concludes:

> As I understand the pragmatic perspective on life, it is an attempt to make it possible for men to live in a world of inescapable tragedy – a tragedy which flows from the conflict of moral ideals – without lamentation, defiance, or make-believe.[38]

But he also adds:

> There is more in life than the sense of the tragic. There is laughter and joy and the sustaining discipline of work (...). There is art and science and religion. There are other uses for intelligence besides the resolution of human difficulties. There is intellectual play and adventure (...). Pragmatism, as I interpret it, is the theory and practice of enlarging human freedom in a precarious and tragic world by the arts of intelligent social control.[39]

John McDermott writes in a similar, albeit more explicit existentialist vein, starting from the "first, foremost, and permanent ontological fact of our human situation," that is "that we were born to live but sure to die."[40] He depicts "our living" as "constitutive of our person. Who we are at any moment is precisely our living." Living for him is "a journey" which "involves risk." But despite all the suffering, he chooses "to go on living," and answers "the question 'Is life worth living?' affirmatively" in the fashion of James and Dewey. He comes close to the Stoic and Deweyan art of living, when claiming "that it is not necessary to have certitude in order for a person to live a meaningful life."[41] Commenting on McDermott's conception of life, Jacquelyn Kegley stresses the concept of "creative living" as "an unrepressed life that can sing its own song" and "the only way one can live a distinctively human life."[42]

In conclusion, it may be stated that: 1. the pragmatist conception of human life is naturalist, realist, and activist; 2. it is neither naively optimistic nor hopelessly pessimistic; 3. it stresses change and (self-)creation. Pragmatist humanism refuses "to treat the world, for good or bad, as a given and completed whole."[43] Man "has always an interest in improving his condition," so "is it not futile to forbid him to re-make his world as best as he can?"[44] We cannot know in advance what is and what is not changeable, so "is it not our wisest course, then, to persist trying?"[45] In the end, we may agree with Lachs: "The most notable feature of pragmatists is their commitment to bring life under intelligent and effective human control."[46]

4. Pragmatist Art of Living: An Outline

The ancient theme of the art of life (*technē peri ton bion, ars vitae*) and the ancient ideal of philosophy as the art of living have recently been revived by a number of diverse (non-pragmatist) authors. The French historian Pierre Hadot, relying on his superb research on the history of philosophy, claims that the role of the philosopher has always been, and indeed should continue to be, not only to develop concepts, theories, texts and discourses, but equally to take practical care of him/herself, to answer the question of "how to live?" To philosophize means to know what the good life consists in and to be able to transform one's personality (if needed). This amounts to the art of living as the goal of philosophy, or at least the goal of the life of a philosopher, of a philosophical life. "Philosophy is an art of living that cures us of our illnesses by teaching us a radically new way of life."[47] Hadot himself wrote: "I've always believed that philosophy was a concrete act, which changed our perception of the world, and our life: not a construction of a system. It is a life, not a discourse."[48] Alexander Nehamas considers the art of living from an aesthetic point of view, the core of which is the self-creation of a unique personality with an idiosyncratic, inimitable style of life.[49] John Kekes focuses on a broad ethical perspective from which he defines the art of life as "a form of self-direction that aims at the good life."[50] The Dutch author Joep Dohmen provides a more structured concept of the art of life as a "learning process," comprising four aspects: responsibility, self-knowledge, competence and attitude, the complex result of which, if practiced successfully, is "an authentic lifestyle."[51] Zygmunt Bauman's analysis engages with the concept of happiness, while another Dutch author Teun Tieleman focuses on the concepts of art, virtue, and wisdom.[52] John Sellars reconstructs in detail the Stoic – mainly Epictetean – concept of the art of living as a special kind of art whose "material" is the human life as such, or the way of life, and whose aim is a self-transformation of this life in order to achieve the highest values of goodness, beauty, wisdom, and the like.[53]   Nietzsche, Foucault, and Deleuze were modern (or postmodern) philosophers who were particularly struck by this ideal of a philosopher whose life is a work of art. In addition, all these authors share the "tragic sense" of the crisis in contemporary philosophy, which in forfeiting this high ideal (or failing to practice it) has also lost much of its attractiveness to ordinary people. And while having become mostly a professional academic discourse, it has compromised one of its important functions, that of helping people understand and guide their lives. Lachs has astutely observed:

Philosophy becomes marginalized only when it distances itself from the problems of life (…). There is no greater social need than guidance in the affairs of life (…). Since philosophers have abandoned their responsibility in this sphere, the public has abandoned philosophers (…). philosophy for its own sake is, in the end, of value only because it makes philosophy for life possible.[54]

However, pragmatism could escape such a demise, as its conception of philosophy is much closer to life and its understanding of human life is realistic and imaginative (as I have tried to show above). This means that pragmatism has good prerequisites for developing its own art of living; the task, however, still lies before us.

So far, the pragmatist art of living has revolved around two axes: an ethical one and an aesthetic one.[55] The former focuses on the concept of a "good life," and the latter on the concept of a "beautiful life." Of course, the division between the two is not, and should not be, sharp.

5. The Pragmatist Ethical Conception of the Good Life

For some, achieving a good life may perhaps be a matter of "good luck," but for the majority of those who are aware of such a concept in the first place, it is a matter of hard work and creation. It is a matter of the art of living. It is a life-long search for and selection from among the options available, and even the creation of new options or a discovery of the previously hidden ones. Striving for a good life is an intentional project, and living a good life means a constant re-thinking, re-assessment and re-creation of the achievements depending on the current situation and the future goals. Such is, for instance, the pragmatist conception of a good life, which is flexible, imaginative, pluralistic, anti-dogmatic, and non-hedonistic rather than a ready-made instruction on how to live well. For a pragmatist philosopher, the issue of a good life is an open question, tackling which entails selecting and forming certain life practices. No life form is ever pre-given.

The ethical line of philosophizing approaches the issue via the concept of human life with the intention of transforming it into a "good life." But what is a "good life" according to pragmatism? We will not attempt to answer this question here, but the key tenet in pragmatism is amelioration, the betterment of life and the human condition through intelligent practice including the pragmatic hope that it is possible to make it better, even if it can never be perfect. Pragmatist meliorism is not perfectionism.

John Lachs' philosophy could be considered a prominent example of the ethical conception of the pragmatist art of living, though Lachs himself does not use the term explicitly. I think he has laid some foundations of the pragmatist concept of good and happy living via his conceptions of the relevance of philosophy to life, of the love of life, of the community of individuals, and most of all, via his creative attempt to articulate the conception of "Stoic pragmatism." He writes:

> Stoic pragmatists are committed to making life better until their powers are overwhelmed. When circumstances render aggressive affirmation no longer possible, however, they surrender to the inevitable gracefully and without complaint. As pragmatists, they insist on the centrality of intelligence in the conduct of life, but they extend the reach of good sense to the acknowledgement of failure or futility.[56]

He takes Stoic pragmatism "to guide practices and express attitudes that shape life and that can meet the pragmatic test of making it better."[57] He shows how both philosophies "are comprehensive views of how to live well," but also how they can "enrich and complete each other" by balancing their attitudes to struggle and surrender, and to power and finitude in human life.[58] In his works, Lachs offers ample inspiration on how to enhance our joy of living as well as on how to withstand the sufferance of living in a humanly dignified way. All this is the pragmatist art of living that deserves to be studied and developed further.

6. The Pragmatist Aesthetic Conception of the Beautiful Life

In pragmatism, the expression "art of life" has yet one more meaning: it concerns art as related to life. Art is embedded in life as a whole rather than in a special human activity. This Deweyan meaning[59] of the term is interestingly linked to the ancient notion of the art of living. For Dewey, the "beautiful life" is not just a life filled with the presence and consumption of artworks. His is a rich idea of art which is very closely tied to the idea of meaning and value of life, and thus the meaning of art and the meaning of life in Dewey are inseparable. Art means the fulfillment and richness of life, rather than "flying high above it" or transcending it. To express and develop this idea, Dewey prefers to speak of "aesthetic experience" rather than simply of art or "artistic experience." Aesthetic experience, according to him, is the fullest and richest experience humans can achieve; it is a "pure" experience devoid of any alienation. Dewey, without making art the highest purpose of human life abstracted from all other human activities and purposes, or the sole source of human satisfaction (the idea espoused by Schopenhauer, Kierkegaard, Nietzsche, Heidegger, Gadamer, and many others), considers the aesthetic experience to be the most satisfactory aspect of life, which, however, neither necessarily nor exclusively involves works of so-called high art, since primordially it is the quality of everyday living. This very (democratic) idea of art is to him the most important and highest human achievement, because only through such an aesthetic experience in the broadest sense of the term does human life become meaningful and valuable. It seems that we may all have a chance to become the artists of life in this Deweyan sense in order to live a good and beautiful life.[60]

The philosophy of Richard Shusterman is explicitly inscribed in the aesthetic conception of the pragmatist art of living.[61] His idea is of "philosophy as an art of living aimed at realizing beauty through creative intelligence and critical reflection (involving both aesthetic and ethical sensitivity)."[62] He draws on the Deweyan idea that art is integral to all human experience and conduct, so we Deweyans can easily join Nietzscheans and Foucauldians, who claim that life itself, not only objects, can become the subject matter of art. Of course, this is a special kind of practical art and, in Shusterman's work, it includes at least two substantial features: 1. practicing philosophy in general, and pragmatism in particular, as the art of life rather than as a purely discursive or textual exercise; 2. practicing the art of life as "somaesthetics," i.e., the aesthetics of the body and embodied human life, rather than as a purely mental or intellectual exercise. Thus in his conception, philosophy, art, and embodied human existence form an amalgam, which, even though it has an aesthetic framework, implies engagement with the ethical as well. In addition to an ideal of an "aesthetic life," it concerns a happy life, too. Shusterman explains:

> When I argue for philosophy as an art of living, am I doing aesthetic theory, ethics, or metaphilosophy, or indeed even metaphysics (...)? It is hard for me to define my theories within a single philosophical category because I see the problems I treat as cutting across traditional philosophical areas.[63]

Shusterman has had a few motivations for this kind of philosophy. Except his endorsement of Dewey's aesthetics and Dewey's own endorsement of the Alexander Technique, they include his critique of Rorty's conception of private idiosyncratic self-creation, which he considers insufficient and overly romantic. The art of life must definitely include bodily practices (together with sexual practices) in order to mold a beautiful (and healthy) human being who can experience her life in a pleasant way. Another source of inspiration for Shusterman is "the exemplary lives rather than formulated doctrines" of Socrates, Cicero, Epicurus, Epictetus, Seneca, Montaigne, Thoreau, Emerson, Dewey, Wittgenstein, and Foucault, among others, serving as exemplars of "living philosophy," or of embodied philosophical lives, which can be seen as "artful lives." Shusterman does not doubt that "philosophy's prime aim is to achieve a life of happiness" and "pragmatism's natural direction is the art of living." This kind of philosophy teaches us "that life should be practiced as an art,"[64] or that a human being should approach life like an artist (at least to some extent). If such an attitude is successfully practiced, life becomes much richer and nicer than a life devoid of such an "artistic" attitude. Life, according to Shusterman, "poses an artistic project in calling for creative self-expression and aesthetic self-fashioning – the desire to make ourselves into something fulfilling, interesting, attractive, admirable, yet somehow true to who we are."[65] Surely, Shusterman's conception also deserves to be studied and developed further (for which, alas, I do not have the time and space here, either).

7. Conclusion

Pragmatism has achieved recognition as an indigenous way of philosophical thinking, bringing a sort of reconstruction into philosophy, and as a social philosophy or ethics as well, but it needs to focus more on the human condition and the conception of the life of the human individual. The pragmatist turn towards the problems of human life most often refers to the problems of social life as if all human problems were social problems. However, this is not the case. There are also individual, private, intimate, personal, human problems, and solving them requires a personal rather than a social change.

The foundations of the pragmatist art of living have been laid in the works of authors I have surveyed in the foregoing. Developing it further is a very exciting project which might demand further "mergers," for instance between Epicurus and Dewey, James and Rorty, Lachs and Shusterman, or Wittgenstein and Brandom, and certainly many other ones – in particular, between non-pragmatists and pragmatists. In the background, the pragmatist philosophy of life must also be developed in order to become not only "competitive" against the influence of the Continental (German and French) philosophies of life, but first of all more attractive to students and people in general, who "search blindly for a worthy life."[66] Last but not least, to expound these lines of pragmatism today, to make them explicit, would mean showing that "pragmatism is humanism," where human life is not an instrument, but a goal in itself (i.e., challenging the invective of instrumentalism in the sense of "instrumental rationality," as posed by Adorno for instance). Rather, *vice versa*, the inherent antidualism of pragmatism amounts to the ancient philosophical ideal of the "harmonization" of various aspects of life.

The pragmatist art of life cuts both ways: it imbues the human condition with genuine happiness and inspires the noble endurance of equally real unhappiness.

NOTES

Some portions of this chapter were read as part of a paper presented at a session titled "Classical American Pragmatism: Practicing Philosophy as Experiencing Life," held at the XXIII World Congress in Philosophy, Athens, Greece, August 4-10, 2013. I wish to thank Krzysztof P. Skowroński and the participants of the session for their stimulating comments, and Sami Pihlström for reading the earlier draft. The work on this chapter was also funded by research grants of the VEGA agency, Slovak Republic, No 2/0053/12, and the KEGA agency, Slovak Republic, No 076UK-4/2013.

1. Sami Pihlström, *Pragmatism and Philosophical Anthropology* (New York: Peter Lang, 1998), p. x.
2. John Lachs, *A Community of Individuals* (New York: Routledge, 2003), p. 58.
3. See John Lachs, *Stoic Pragmatism* (Bloomington: Indiana University Press, 2012) and Charlie Hobbs, "Epicurean Pragmatism," http://www.american-philosophy.org/saap2013/openconf/modules/request.php?module=oc_proceedings&action=summary.php&a=Accept&id=79.
4. Brooks Atkinson (ed.), *The Essential Writings of Ralph Waldo Emerson* (New York: The Modern Library, 2000), pp. 55–72.
5. Carl Bode (ed.), *The Portable Thoreau* (New York: Penguin Books, 1982), p. 270.
6. David L. Murray, *Pragmatism* (Bristol: Thoemmes Press, 2001), p. 70.
7. *Ibid.*, pp. 71–2.
8. Richard Rorty, "Pragmatizmus je politický skrz-naskrz [Pragmatism is Political Through and Through]," *Pragmatizmus. Malá antológia* [Pragmatism: A Short Anthology], eds. Emil Višňovský and František Mihina (Bratislava: IRIS, 1998), p. 549.
9. See Barry Allen, "What Knowledge? What Hope? What New Pragmatism?" *The Pragmatic Turn in Philosophy: Contemporary Engagements between Analytic and Continental Thought,* eds. William Eggington and Mike Sandbothe (New York: State University of New York Press, 2004), pp. 145–62.
10. Richard Rorty, "Intellectual Autobiography," *The Philosophy of Richard Rorty*, eds. Randall E. Auxier and Lewis E. Hahn (Chicago: Open Court, 2010), p. 20.
11. "An Interview with Professor Hilary Putnam: The Vision and Arguments of a Famous Harvard Philosopher," *Cogito*, 3 (1989). Reprinted in *Key Philosophers in Conversation: The Cogito Interviews*, ed. Andrew Pyle (London: Routledge, 1999), p. 52.
12. Hilary Putnam, *Pragmatism: An Open Question* (Oxford: Blackwell, 1995), p. 22. See also his *Jewish Philosophy as a Guide to Life: Rosenzweig, Buber, Levinas, Wittgenstein* (Bloomington: Indiana University Press, 2008).
13. Hilary Putnam, *The Threefold Cord: Mind, Body, and World* (New York: Columbia University Press, 1999), p. 70.
14. John Lachs, *The Relevance of Philosophy to Life* (Nashville: Vanderbilt University Press, 1995), pp. xiii-xvii.
15. See John Lachs, *In Love with Life* (Nashville and London: Vanderbilt University Press, 1998), *A Community of Individuals* (London: Routledge, 2003), and *Stoic Pragmatism* (Bloomington: Indiana University Press, 2012).
16. Sami Pihlström, *Structuring the World* (Helsinki: Hakapaino Oy, 1996), p. 37.
17. *Ibid.*, p. 17.
18. *Ibid.*, p. 379.
19. *Ibid.*, p. 409.
20. Eggington and Sandbothe, "Introduction," *The Pragmatic Turn in Philosophy,* p. 1.
21. Michael Eldridge, *Transforming Experience* (Nashville: Vanderbilt University Press, 1998), p. 107.
22. Sidney Hook, "Pragmatism and the Tragic Sense of Life," *Proceedings and Addresses of the American Philosophical Association*, 33 (1959–1960), p. 5.
23. S. Morris Eames, *Pragmatic Naturalism* (Carbondale: Southern Illinois University Press, 1977), p. 8.
24. *Ibid.*
25. Pihlström, *Structuring the World*, pp. 362–3.
26. Murray, *Pragmatism*, p. 72.

27. See John Dewey, *A Common Faith* (New Haven: Yale University Press, 1934), pp. 15–6.
28. Eames, *Pragmatic Naturalism*, p. 11.
29. Murray, *Pragmatism*, p. 72.
30. William James, *Essays in Radical Empiricism* (New York: Longmans, Green and Comp., 1912), pp. 93–4.
31. Lachs, *In Love with Life,* p. 25.
32. *Ibid.*, p. 42.
33. Hook, "Pragmatism and the Tragic Sense of Life," p. 10.
34. *Ibid.*
35. *Ibid.*
36. *Ibid.*, p. 13.
37. *Ibid.*, p. 20.
38. *Ibid.*, p. 22.
39. *Ibid.*, p. 26.
40. John McDermott, "Why Bother: Is Life worth Living? Experience as Pedagogical," *Philosophy and the Reconstruction of Culture*, ed. John J. Stuhr (New York: State University of New York Press, 1993), p. 274.
41. *Ibid.*, pp. 275–83.
42. Jacquelyn A. K. Kegley, "Living Creatively, While Terminal," *Experience as Philosophy: On the Work of John J. McDermott,* eds. James Campbell and Richard E. Hart (New York: Fordham University Press, 2006), p. 61.
43. Murray, *Pragmatism*, p. 72.
44. *Ibid.*
45. *Ibid.*
46. Lachs, *Stoic Pragmatism*, p. 14.
47. Arnold I. Davidson, "Introduction: Pierre Hadot and the Spiritual Phenomenon of Ancient Philosophy," in Pierre Hadot, *Philosophy as a Way of Life: Spiritual Exercises from Socrates to Foucault* (Oxford: Blackwell, 1995), p. 28.
48. Hadot, *Philosophy as a Way of Life*, p. 279.
49. See Alexander Nehamas, *The Art of Living: Socratic Reflections from Plato to Foucault* (Berkeley: University of California Press, 1998).
50. John Kekes, *The Art of Life* (Ithaca: Cornell University Press, 2002), pp. ix, 26.
51. Joep Dohmen, "Philosophers on the 'Art-of-Living'," *Journal of Happiness Studies*, 4 (2003), p. 363.
52. See Zygmunt Bauman, *The Art of Life* (Cambridge: Polity Press, 2008), Teun Tieleman, "The Art of Life: An Ancient Idea and its Survival," *Scholê* 2 (2008).
53. See John Sellars, *The Art of Living: The Stoics on the Nature and Function of Philosophy* (London: Bristol Classical Press, 2009).
54. Lachs, *A Community of Individuals*, pp. 11, 14.
55. For a similar distinction of conceptions of the art of life see Kekes, *The Art of Life*, p. 149.
56. Lachs, *Stoic Pragmatism*, p. 1.
57. *Ibid.*, p. 2.
58. *Ibid.*, pp. 47, 51.
59. See John Dewey, *Art as Experience* (New York: The Perigee Trade, 2005).
60. For elaboration of this idea, see Thomas M. Alexander, *John Dewey's Theory of Art, Experience, and Nature: The Horizons of Feeling* (Albany: State University of New York Press, 1987); see also his "The Human Eros," *Philosophy and the Reconstruction of Culture,* pp. 203–22; and "The Art of Life: Dewey's Aesthetics,"

Reading Dewey: Interpretations for a Postmodern Generation, ed. Larry A. Hickman (Bloomington: Indiana University Press, 1998), pp. 1–22.

61. See Richard Shusterman, *Pragmatist Aesthetics: Living Beauty, Rethinking Art,* (Oxford: Blackwell, 1992); *Practicing Philosophy: Pragmatism and the Philosophical Life* (New York: Routledge, 1997); *Performing Live: Aesthetic Alternatives for the Ends of Art* (Ithaca: Cornell University Press, 2000); *Body Consciousness: A Philosophy of Mindfulness and Somaesthetics* (New York: Cambridge University Press, 2008), and *Thinking through the Body: Essays in Somaesthetics* (Cambridge: Cambridge University Press, 2012).

62. Shusterman, *Thinking through the Body,* p. 2.

63. Richard Shusterman, "Continuing Connections: Comments on the Preceding Essays," *Shusterman's Pragmatism*, eds. Dorota Koczanowicz and Wojciech Malecki (Amsterdam: Rodopi, 2012), p. 212.

64. See Shusterman, *Practicing Philosophy,* pp. 2–24.

65. Shusterman, *Performing Live*, p. 10.

66. Lachs, *Stoic Pragmatism*, p. 22.

Eleven

THE AESTHETIC COSMOPOLITAN FROM A NEO-PRAGMATIST PERSPECTIVE: THEMES AND CHALLENGES IN SHUSTERMAN

Michael Rings

Let us consider what it might mean to be an *aesthetic cosmopolitan*: in the everyday sense of these words, this may denote an urbane, worldly aesthete, a connoisseur, or perhaps even a collector of art objects from all over the world. In the more philosophical sense of the term, the true "cosmopolitan" is committed to the notion that she is a "citizen of the world," a member of the metaphorical community of all human beings, an idea encompassing ethico-political notions such as moral universalism, pluralism, anti-parochialism, and a belief in the benefits of various kinds of cross-cultural dialogue. Bringing this notion into the realm of aesthetics, we can imagine an appreciator who rejects aesthetic chauvinism of all kinds and welcomes opportunities to engage in open-minded appreciation of other-cultural art objects, in a curious and respectful spirit that does not merely find new objects to evaluate with her own acculturated standards of value, but actively tries on new methods and practices of appreciation. She is also open to the idea that such experiences may leave her changed, perhaps deeply, as an art appreciator. For the aesthetic cosmopolitan, encounters with other-cultural art objects are opportunities to engage in a kind of conversation across various cultural lines.

Though the cosmopolitan may pursue such conversations for various moral motivations – for example, the desire to develop a better understanding of other communities by appreciating their art objects and practices – one may also act from more self-oriented desires: to better understand oneself and one's home culture(s), to enrich or expand one's aesthetic tastes or sensibilities, to shape oneself in fulfilling new ways. Consider the example of an eclectic, "wide-eared" music listener, a U.S. born music enthusiast with her teenage roots in American and British punk and alternative rock, who comes to cultivate an authoritative appreciation for a diverse array of music: old-time Americana, Irish folk, European techno, and Balinese gamelan. With each of these encounters (some traversing more local borders into other-cultural cohorts found within her own community, others crossing greater geographical and musical distances), she not only cultivates new ways to listen to and value music, or to participate in novel, embodied appreciative activities such as American contra dancing or Berlin clubbing – she also actively explores new possibilities for self-fashioning, trying out new ways of listening that may also involve new ways of presenting herself, of situating herself within new communities, new styles of living, of seeing the world, and of seeing herself in it.

Richard Shusterman has explored the pursuit of self-enrichment through art and embodied aesthetic experience extensively throughout his work, and in "Multiculturalism and the Art of Living" he focuses in particular on how transcultural encounters like those described above may function as "self-challenging opportunities to test, deepen, and enrich our own sense of self."[1] He considers a number of different ways in which this may come about. One can develop a contrastive form of self-understanding via an exploratory engagement with the other, learning to place one's own cultural identity within a broader field of contrast, perhaps confronting one's own prejudices and limits in the process. Alternately, one may discover a heretofore hidden or neglected "other" in oneself by exploring a cultural element of one's own unexamined heritage. Finally, one can fashion oneself through the "accretion or absorption" of other cultures; as Shusterman puts it, "we can revise and enrich ourselves by assimilating aspects of the other and by integrating the complex consequences of this cultural interchange."[2]

As enriching and illuminating as such cross-cultural encounters may be, Shusterman warns that they may also prove to be "dangerously destabilizing," shaking one's sense of place in the world, and with it one's sense of self.[3] This phenomenon of cultural estrangement or disorientation is the subject of a similar concern that has long haunted the notion of cosmopolitanism – that of *rootlessness*. In identifying as a citizen of the world, to what degree must one compromise or mitigate one's commitments as a member of more local communities (nation, religion, ethnicity, fan community) that may have a significant impact on shaping who one is, determining one's values, tastes, or worldview? Or, to put it in another way, if one becomes capable of being "at home" anywhere in the world (or at least in many different corners of it), will one cease to be able to be *truly* at home in any one place in particular? In the case of the aesthetic cosmopolitan, this threat of rootlessness may become more clear if we consider Paul Valéry's observation that "tastes are made of a thousand distastes"[4]: if one comes to cultivate an appreciation for a broad and "worldly" diversity of art objects, in a broad diversity of ways, might this threaten to dilute or destabilize one's sense of self as a particular appreciator who perceives and values things in one's own particular way? Or in learning to appreciate new things, might one risk alienating oneself from old favored objects or ways of appreciating that may have served to ground one's sense of identity, to provide a kind of aesthetic "place in the world"?

Shusterman, taking such existential worries of homelessness and destabilization seriously, recommends that one balance the self-expanding impulses of cross-cultural exploration with a simultaneous effort to fashion a sense of self that holds together in an aesthetically satisfying unity. Though I agree with Shusterman to some degree on this point, I will argue that the pursuit of aesthetic unity in one's life is not an adequate strategy for mitigating the potentially alienating effects of multicultural self-fashioning, and I recommend that the ideal of *authenticity* be introduced as a further way to ensure that cultural travelers, be they aesthetic cosmopolitans or otherwise, do not lose themselves to rootlessness.

Shusterman discusses various forms of "multicultural malaise" throughout his work, often illustrating this "confusing tangle of ambiguities and ambivalence" with candid autobiographical examples of how it has impacted his own life as a Jewish scholar who has claimed homes in the United States, Israel, Germany, and elsewhere.[5] For example, he notes how leaving his native America at sixteen to settle in Israel (where he remained throughout much of his education and early career as a philosopher, returning to the States for a post at Temple University), though it brought him "a much deeper realization of [his] Jewish identity," also "deeply alienated [him] from the American culture that had formed [him]."[6] Despite these difficult firsthand experiences in cultural travel, Shusterman nevertheless insists that we not reject it as a form of self-cultivation, but rather "recognize its risks and limits, so as to make it more fruitful." He goes on to add that this is simply "a pragmatic way of putting what can also be aesthetically formulated. We should seek cultural variety for enriching and defining the self, but only to the extent that such variety can be held in a satisfying unity."[7] Because the determination of such a unity is an aesthetic issue, he argues, it is not amenable to any fixed rules that could prescribe it. Shusterman thus invokes *taste* as the appropriate tool for finding this ideal balance between cultural richness and unity in oneself.

Though he does not expand any further on these points in the above quoted essay, he offers a more prolonged discussion in his "Next Year in Jerusalem?," the final chapter of *Practicing Philosophy* and a piece of autobiographical self analysis that finds him considering ways in which to realize a Jewish identity that is "painfully divided" between two possible articulations - roughly put, "an Israeli self (with an American background or penumbra)" on the one hand, and an "American self (with an Israeli shadow)" on the other.[8] In the chapter, Shusterman claims that our notions of personal identity and agency depend on a narrative conception of self, and so any unified sense of self is thereby grounded somehow in a narrative unity. One's fashioning of a unified sense of self is thereby dependent on one's ability to devise an interpretation of one's own life narrative in a way that grounds a unified self-concept and also informs future actions (i.e., possible continuations of one's life narrative) that foster the healthy development and flourishing of that particular self.

In the case of our aesthetic cosmopolitan, the relevant narrative may take the form of a "taste history," her biography as a particular appreciator with her own idiosyncratic and developing aesthetic sensibility, set of preferences, and ways of perceiving and valuing the world about her. Such a story may encompass her adolescent roots as a fan of punk and alternative rock, her branching out first into punk-inflected alt-country, then old-time Americana music and dance, before she crossed even more far-flung borders and became a thoroughgoing enthusiast of Irish folk, techno, and gamelan. This story of her changing cosmopolitan tastes, told in the right away, could present a picture of her that makes a kind of holistic sense of these musical travels, and perhaps offers her guidance on the most fulfilling ways to continue them.

However, as promising as the narrative model may seem as a strategy for self constitution, Shusterman points out that it is burdened with the problem of "the underdetermination of self by narrative": "For any open series of narrative events," he notes, "given an indeterminate future in terms of which these events can be interpreted and also given the future revisability of past narrative interpretations, there will always be more than one narrative that can fit the facts of the individual."[9] This underdetermination not only raises the possibility of multiple selves, but also undermines a single, stable sense of self-identity. In regard to his own Jewish identity, for instance, Shusterman is presented with at least two divergent ways to tell his story: does he see his leaving Israel and coming back to America as a return home after a youthful exploration of an essentially foreign (albeit Jewish) culture, or does he interpret his current stay in the States as a mere "excursion for personal development" that will allow him to better serve his home country when he returns to Israel?[10] Each narrative privileges a different side of his Jewish identity – the Israeli and American Jewish sides, respectively – yet neither can make a more obvious claim to truth than the other. This is not to say, Shusterman notes, that any possible interpretation is as good as any other: the best ones not only offer better explanations of one's past actions, but also facilitate the fashioning of better future selves (one imagines these two things may often be closely linked).[11]

What counts as a "better" future self, on Shusterman's account, involves an artful integration of the contingent yet crucial elements that produce it. "The secret of successful living," he writes, "is not to escape our contingencies but to construct them into an appealing form, a story we can embrace as our own."[12] In the end, neither of the narratives sketched above satisfies Shusterman on this score – each being based on a kind of one-sided essentialism regarding Jewish identity that he rejects – and so he comes to favor a more balanced one built around "a life of continued Jewish self-expression and self-realization through cycles of *yeridah* and *aliyah*, departure and return to Israel."[13] This cyclical narrative, he argues, offers an option for Jewish self-realization that is more flexible and open than a narrative that focuses on either life in the Jewish homeland or life in America, and is also "richer" than certain Zionist notions (e.g., those found in the writings of A.B. Yehoshua).

The problem with this account of how a satisfying, self-unifying narrative might be chosen from the available options is that we seem to have gone far beyond matters of "aesthetic unity" or the exercising of something like aesthetic judgment here. Shusterman's choice to favor the cyclical *yeridah-aliyah* narrative over the first two interpretations does not, at least *prima facie*, seem to be justified by a claim to a greater or more aesthetically appealing unity. The Israeli- and American-centric narratives, after all, each offer a story of a self equally integrated and unified, just in a more hierarchical way than the cyclical story – i.e., in a manner that foregrounds one aspect of the self and backgrounds the other. And while one may rightly claim that the unity found in the cyclical option is, in some respects, more satisfying, it does not seem to be so for obviously aesthetic reasons. One may propose that the self emerging from this narrative has a more *balanced* unity in that the Israeli and American aspects have approximately equal status in it, but such a balance does not seem to be more satisfying on aesthetic grounds alone; it is not imperative for aesthetically unified compositions to place all elements in equal balance, after all - some parts are often subordinated to others. Likewise, the argument that the cyclical self would be more pleasing aesthetically due to some kind of greater richness does not, by itself, offer a compelling reason to prefer it; as Shusterman himself notes, aesthetic unity is often more easily achieved by the self-limiting strategy of relinquishing some elements of a composition. Neither, he argues, is it imperative that a project of self-realization attempt to integrate *all* of the self's contingencies into a meaningful whole, merely for the sake of greater richness.[14]

If we are to understand "aesthetic unity" here by traditional formal notions of harmony and integration of parts into a pleasing whole (and no other sense is offered in these essays), then it seems to run into a similar problem of underdetermination: for any given open series of narrative events, there will always be a plurality of possible over-arching narratives conjoining them that offer a comparable degree of aesthetically pleasing unity. To return to the case of our aesthetic cosmopolitan, there are many different ways in which one might unify her taste history into a satisfying whole, tracing any number of different threads through her progression of musical interests. Her journey from punk to American folk to gamelan may be read alternately as an exploration of the communal or participatory possibilities of music, as a preoccupation with rhythmic vitality and dance, as a musical expedition from West to East, or simply as a constellation of the musical loves associated with the places and relationships that have marked her life. Any of these stories might ground a meaningfully constituted, unified sense of self – and do so in an aesthetically pleasing way – yet it is hard to imagine that any of them would "do" equally well as any other for the appreciator in question. It seems more likely that some would resonate with her better than others, either in terms of their explanations of the past or in terms of the possible future paths of listening and living that they illuminate for her.

In the end, whether or not a picture of a possible self presents an aesthetically satisfying unity is not a sufficiently guiding criterion: it still leaves open the question whether this pleasing unity is one that I can endorse and embrace as *mine*, as a unity that is expressive of the self I strive to be.

Shusterman's endorsement of the cyclical narrative seems akin to such a claim of "mineness"; he favors it over the alternatives because it offers the most meaningful and potentially fulfilling option for building an identity, not just because of how it fits together (or even how *beautifully* it fits together), but because of how it fits *him* - how it fits the past and present contingent conditions of his life and the projects to which he devotes himself within them.

In the spirit of supplementing Shusterman's theory, I propose the incorporation of a value that, I believe, best addresses the concerns above, the historically controversial but potentially helpful value of *authenticity*. I use this term in the existential and moral-psychological senses found in the relevant spheres of the philosophical literature. It is a notion that Somogy Varga, in his *Authenticity as an Ethical Ideal*, glosses as the term we use to describe "a person who acts in a way that we think of as faithful to herself and her principles," while Bernard Williams defines it as "the idea that some things are in some sense really you, or express what you are, and others aren't."[15] This is a notoriously slippery notion, and while I do not have the space here to offer a tolerably complete account of it (or adequately address the points of controversy that riddle its discourse), I will nevertheless conclude with a quick sketch of how a pragmatist-friendly notion of authenticity may be brought to bear on the current discussion.

What will clearly *not* do here, in the question of which narrative is most authentic for one, is a reference to some kind of preexisting metaphysical entity – some kind of personal "essence," or "core" – that one could consult introspectively in order to divine the answer. Such a picture of authenticity, originating with Rousseau, is problematic not only due to its ontology, but also because the notion that determining what is most "expressive" of me is a matter of my discovery of something "inner" and pre-existing (the presence, say, of some particularly strong desire or impulse) leaves no room for the sense of agency or self-authorship we intuitively want to retain in the context of authenticity. At the same time, the most prominent alternative to this Rousseauian account – the Nietzschean view that one does not discover one's true self but rather actively *creates* it, like an artist constructs a work of art – is also problematic for a number of reasons, even if it restores agency to self-constitution. Richard Rorty's model of the "ironist" is one contemporary version of this Nietzschean idea.[16] This figure cultivates an ever-shifting series of selves created via diverse adopted narratives (or "vocabularies") in an ever-expanding and decentered project of self-fashioning. Shusterman is critical of Rorty's model at several points throughout his work, noting that, among other problems, it explicitly disavows the notion of a single unified self, which seems to be required if the very notion of "*self*-cultivation" is to make any sense at all.[17] Varga also argues that the ironic distance that Rorty claims the ironist maintains from all of the various self-narratives he samples precludes him from being able to identify fully with any of them, alienating himself from his own life in the process. Rorty's ironist, perhaps the ultimate "rootless cosmopolitan," would only be able to see himself, in Varga's words, as an "arbitrary placeholder for a shifting set of narratives," finding no real home (even temporarily) in any of them.[18]

Varga suggests a third alternative way to conceive of authenticity that potentially avoids the problems of both of these accounts, and may be a better candidate for our purposes here. Authenticity, for Varga, "is about wholeheartedness concerning the commitments one is involved in."[19] He argues, *contra* the Rousseauian model, that one's relation to a "true self" is not epistemic, but normative, a matter of actively evaluating one's desires or impulses and deciding whether to *endorse* them as desires or impulses *worth* having and cultivating as one's own. Such second order endorsement of one's own projects, attitudes, preferences, and tastes, if enduring and wholehearted, comes to constitute one's authentic identification with them, and over time serves an integrative function, a kind of unifying force, in one's life. Unity thus arises from authenticity here (the former a perhaps necessary though not sufficient condition for the latter), from one's wholehearted commitment to certain self-constituting projects and values that are chosen not only on aesthetic grounds, but on ethical, practical, and political ones as well. The authentic life is thereby constituted not merely by integrating my life's contingencies in a meaningfully beautiful way, but by doing so according to a meaning I wholeheartedly embrace as *mine*, a beauty that is *mine*.

A challenge Varga's "wholeheartedness" model of authenticity faces, especially in the case of cosmopolitan and multicultural subjects, is that wholeheartedness of the kind described above seems to be a fragile and tenuous state, an elusive (perhaps impossible) thing for one to attain or maintain. The cosmopolitan, never comfortably "at home" in any system of cultural values, beliefs, or ideas, may never quite have her whole heart in *any* of her projects, always cognizant of how they could be different, perhaps replaced by something more worthwhile – a restless critical perspective all too aware of the contingent and imperfect nature of her commitments. This may be appropriate, however, as many have argued that authenticity itself is a difficult and fragile (perhaps impossible) thing to achieve. But if the aesthetic cosmopolitan project is to be regarded as a possible program for self-fashioning, a particular form of "the art of living," then it is an ideal that should be taken seriously.

In particular, if a pragmatist, meliorist theory of aesthetic cosmopolitanism (one that treats it as a kind of philosophical project one could actually live by, i.e., the kind that Shusterman is preoccupied with in *Practicing Philosophy*) is to be advanced, then the possibilities for living a cosmopolitan *good life* must be considered. If authenticity, conceived according to Varga's model, is required for such a life, let alone a beautifully constructed one, then virtues and strategies necessary to achieve wholeheartedness must be included in the "art of living." As we have seen above, Shusterman offers the important idea that aesthetic judgment or taste – in the specific form of a capacity to read competently one's own life as a kind of "text" – may be necessary for one who practices this kind of multicultural self-fashioning. But what emerges from his considerations of "multicultural malaise" is the fact that *other* kinds of judgment – perhaps practical, or even those traditionally referred to as "ethical" or "moral" – appear to be needed, as well. Shusterman remarks how, at one point during his stay in Berlin, he found it tough to distinguish between the "healthy asceticism of philosophical self-improvement and the twisted psychological self-torture of pushing oneself beyond where one should go."[20] As I believe I have demonstrated above, navigating such a distinction well requires kinds of judgment (and also virtues) that go beyond a mere sense of aesthetic unity. It requires a reflective, self-attuned brand of practical wisdom, as well as a caring and attentive attitude toward one's own well-being. Shusterman himself demonstrates both of these traits in the insightful meditations I have discussed herein, offering (perhaps unwittingly) a richer picture of the art of living than that presented by his own arguments.

NOTES

1. Richard Shusterman, "Multiculturalism and the Art of Living," *Performing Live: Aesthetic Alternatives for the Ends of Art* (Ithaca: Cornell University Press, 2000), pp. 182–200.
2. *Ibid.*, p. 195.
3. *Ibid.*, p. 196.
4. Paul Valéry, "Things Left Unsaid," trans. William Geoffrey, *The Kenyon Review*, 10:3 (Spring, 1948), pp. 228–39.
5. *Ibid.*, p. 183.
6. *Ibid.*, pp. 198–99.
7. *Ibid.*, p. 196.
8. Richard Shusterman, "Next Year in Jerusalem?: Jewish Identity and the Myth of Return," *Practicing Philosophy: Pragmatism and the Philosophical Life* (New York: Routledge, 1997), pp. 179–95.
9. *Ibid.*, p. 184.
10. *Ibid.*, p. 185.
11. *Ibid.*, p. 185.
12. *Ibid.*, p. 194.
13. *Ibid.*, p. 192.
14. *Ibid.*, p. 195.
15. Somogy Varga, *Authenticity as an Ethical Ideal* (New York: Routledge, 2012), p. 2. Bernard Williams quoted in same, p. 2.
16. Richard Rorty, *Contingency, Irony, and Solidarity* (Cambridge: Cambridge University Press, 1989). See in particular chaps. 4, 5, and 6.
17. Richard Shusterman, "Postmodern Ethics and the Art of Living," *Pragmatist Aesthetics: Living Beauty, Rethinking Art* (Lanham: Rowman and Littlefield, 2000), pp. 236–61.
18. Varga, *Authenticity as an Ethical Ideal*, p. 75.
19. *Ibid.*, p. 83.
20. Shusterman, "Multiculturalism and the Art of Living," p. 199.

Twelve

PHILOSOPHICAL ANTHROPOLOGY IN LIFE POLITICS OF TODAY

Hans-Peter Krüger

In the following essay I will be concerned firstly with understanding the current situation in the Western world as a life-political challenge (part 1). This problematic life-political situation need not, following Michel Foucault, be addressed exclusively in terms of biopolitics, as Giorgio Agamben and Roberto Esposito tend to do even in their criticism of Foucault. It can also be with expanded Anthony Giddens's and Ulrich Beck's diagnosis of a second modernity (as opposed to the first industrial-social modernity). With Bruno Latour's quest for a symmetrical, as opposed to an asymmetrical anthropology, the problem of how anthropology and philosophy relate to each other arises anew in explicit form. In the subsequent two parts of the essay, I try to reconstruct Philosophical anthropology, founded by Max Scheler and Helmuth Plessner in 1928, in a form suited to the life-political task. The theoretical and methodological status of their hypotheses is foregrounded in part 2. In part 3, I provide an introduction to their investigation procedures, since in my opinion this grants a better orientation in the life-political challenge. This amounts to an invitation to interdisciplinary cooperation with both the biological-medical as well as the social and culturally oriented life-sciences.

1. What is Life Politics? Current Contexts and References

In colloquial German, the expression *Biopolitik* (biopolitics) can be evocative of something like environmental politics, which is not actually what is meant by the coinage. Or, it might sound like a new special task to be addressed by the biosciences and their political mediation. Or, one may even suppose a trail leading back to the racial biology of Nazi politics from 1933–1945. The connection to the classical Greek *bios* (life) and *bios politicos* – the actor in a politically understood community – may be apparent to the scholars of the humanities, but it is not self-evident in ordinary language. However, within the social sciences and cultural studies, the expression *biopolitics* has come to describe research that takes up Michel Foucault's program with varying degrees of critical emphasis.[1] By contrast, with *life politics* (*Lebenspolitik*) each and every one of us can feel individually addressed. That is why I have chosen this expression which reflects a matter-of-fact description of the tasks posed biographically in the generational succession by the new possibilities presented by medical therapies in the West.[2] Exemplary questions in this context are: Do we, for our progeny, aspire to a diagnosis of the fertilized egg cell before its implantation in the womb in order to preclude certain diseases and possible life-long disabilities? What should one write in one's own living-will for the case of accidents with critical outcomes? How should one take care of kin who are temporarily unconscious or who may never again regain consciousness? What will become of me if I no longer have kin? What should I insure myself against, and how much should I pay for this? What will happen if I am not insured?

This sense of life politics fits in with another debate. Due to the work of Anthony Giddens and Ulrich Beck, there is an interpretation in the sociological discussion of *life politics* (politics in leading one's life) which consolidates the semantic field within ordinary language. Meant here is the individualization, in the sociological sense, of socio-cultural problem-fields which arise in a "second," or "reflexive" modernity.[3] In contrast to the first modernity, i.e. a modernization characterized essentially by *industrial society and the nation state,* the *second modernity* is concerned with dealing with the mostly indirect, and thus unintentional, negative consequences of the first modernity, e.g., environmental damage, large-scale technological accidents, new diseases. The regulatory capacity of the nation state has long proved insufficient to solve these derivative problems. This capacity must be reproduced subnationally, transnationally, internationally, and globally and be redistributed on these levels so that a "world society"[4] really emerges. The derivative problems have led to a "risk society,"[5] in which attempts are constantly being made to transform the uncontrollable *dangers* into controllable *risks* by means of directing modernity's focus onto its own modernization processes. This bending back of modernity onto its own repercussions proceeds through an intensification of scientific and technological development and new public forms of politics.[6] The *individuation of the negative consequences of modernity* into a reflexive modernity is a *double-edged sword.* On the one hand, it increases the scope of freedom for individuals who, in the processes of innovation, abandon their fixed class and ideological origins. On the other hand, it requires public participation in the transformation of the dangers of these innovation processes into risks which can be described in terms of probability theory. But in this process, in the sum total of individuals' conduct of life though the generations, no-one can reliably tell how big the gap between dangers and risks will prove to be. If one wonders in which class this structural transformational task can best be mastered, then materially and in terms of education, the well-situated middle classes are called upon. In terms of personal biographies and cross-generationally, they are confronted with tasks which elude the old political demarcations between left and right.[7]

The exploration of a second, or reflexive, modernity, which addressed solutions to the negative – originally only indirect – consequences of the first modernity, began earlier in philosophy than in sociology, namely in the 1920s and 1930s in the form of classical pragmatism and Philosophical anthropology.[8] The period between the two World Wars offered sufficient object-lessons in the negative consequences of the first modernity and the necessity of a second modernity without totalitarianisms. To comprehend this object-lesson, the whole relationship between nature, society, and culture was explored anew, an exploration which the sociological investigation of a reflexive modernity has as yet failed to undertake. Particularly lacking in the context of this overall relationship is its own concept of nature. Also, from a cultural perspective, sociology remains bound to strong philosophical assumptions and conditions concerning the political approach to the pluralities of cultures and communities in this pluralistic world society, and thereby it practically invites an anthropological comparison. As Giddens pithily puts it: "Unpredictability, manufactured uncertainty, fragmentation: these are only one side of the coin of a globalizing order. On the reverse side are the shared values that come from a situation of global interdependence, organized via the cosmopolitan acceptance of difference."[9] Can members of the human species afford all of this? Evidently, the social project of a second modernity depends upon very strong and common values if it is not to fail anthropologically: "Consciousness of the sanctity of life and consciousness of the importance of global communication – these are the connected poles of life politics today."[10]

Giorgio Agamben, too, in his *Coming Community,* puts his faith in new "classless" middle classes which emerge in the globalization process. The "planetary petty bourgeoisie" have cast off the nationalistic dreams of the earlier "national petty bourgeoisie": "They know only the improper and the inauthentic and even refuse the idea of a discourse that could be proper to them."[11] If this petty bourgeoisie were, further, to learn to get used to "the frustration of [their] individuality," especially to reconcile themselves to death as "life in all its nakedness, the pure incommunicable," then "they would for the first time enter into a community without presuppositions and without subjects, into a communication without the incommunicable."[12] While Giddens requires strong general values in advance, such as the sanctity of life, so that the risky individuations of the present do not go awry, Agamben sees a chance in just the opposite philosophical direction – in the release of the individuation of events and in the process of profanation. "Revelation does not mean revelation of the sacredness of the world, but only revelation of its irreparably profane character."[13] It is only in the process of this revelation that help arrives in the form of the salvation of the profanity of the world.

How should this orientation be understood? Agamben insists – as do Heidegger and many other philosophers of language – on the "linguistic nature" of humans: he reproaches the mediocracy of spectacles with having restricted languages to "an autonomous sphere," which "no longer even reveals anything – or better, it reveals the nothingness of all things."[14] But it is in this very alienation from the linguistic nature of humans that he sees the revelation of the profanity taking place. With this, "the hypocritical dogma of the sacredness of human life and the vacuous declarations of human rights" are exposed: "*Sacer* [sacred] was the one who had been excluded from the human world and who, even though she or he could not be sacrificed, could be killed without committing homicide."[15] Demonstrating the continuity of this excluded *homo sacer*[16] from antiquity up into the modern era and the present is Agamben's life project, in which he draws on Heidegger to criticize Foucault and relies on Foucault to criticize Heidegger. The liberation of language from its exclusive restriction to an autonomous sphere where reification is revealed and the establishment of "whatever" singularities which can be lovable are the two directions that Agamben pursues in the quest for the salvation of the profanity. If the things are freed from having to present themselves, under dictates of identity, as being economically and nationally exploitable and if one were to liberate language from having to predicate the grammatical subject with attributes, the limits of things could be pushed under a halo to the outer extreme. It would not just be the non-linguistic something, which presents itself aesthetically (in sensual perception) and which is indicated in the act of ostension, that could be taken as *another something* in language. Rather within *language itself* the taking-*as* could be understood differently.[17] Hence Agamben explores firstly the connection between non-linguistic things in their presentation, secondly the relationships within language itself, the self of language, and thirdly the compulsion for the things to present themselves under a certain identity which renders them utilizable. Here a combination of phenomenology – that phenomena can *manifest themselves* – and hermeneutics – their being understood *as* in language – opposes the identity dictate of the things. This combination points to Heidegger's excentricity and attempts to limit the Foucauldian power/knowledge connection to the dictate of identity. Agamben's philosophical criticism of Western modernity is not self-supporting. Similarly, in the reverse direction, Giddens and Beck in their reflexive modernity must presuppose processes of personalization and individualization.

Whilst Beck, Giddens, and Agamben *implicitly* presuppose *anthropology*, for instance in the individuation of socio-cultural problem fields or in the linguistic nature of humans, Bruno Latour *explicitly* thematizes it. The mainstream of Western modernity does not actually think merely in terms of differentiating two sides, but rather in terms of their separation, thus in terms of either-or alternatives. In this, one's own self is essentially identified with one side of dualism in opposition to the other side, whereby the other side is excluded from one's own self. The model is Descartes' dualism of material (*res extensa*) and mind (*res cogitans*), in which the self identifies, qua self-consciousness, with the side of mind and thus releases the material side for manipulation. Latour calls the Western-modern separation of the human being from the non-human being an "asymmetrical anthropology." Against this, he posits a "symmetric anthropology." This consists of networks of mixed beings ("hybrids" in view of the initial dualism) which lie *between* nature and culture.[18] In the anthropological comparison, Western modernity is striking as an ethnocentricity which measures the other and the foreign in terms of its own self. In a historico-cultural sense, it is not a matter of course for differences to be fixed as dualistic separations. And it is also not a matter of course, historico-culturally, for such separations to be used asymmetrically. A long time had passed before ethnology, as the study of other and foreign cultures, was capable of freeing itself from this ethnocentric standard. This liberation of anthropology also bore fruit inwardly, i.e. in its deployment in Western modernity's own science and technology, thus in the sociology of science. Finally, Latour also wants to deploy it in the inner Western political ecology, whose "mononaturalism," he posits, must be replaced by a "multinaturalism."[19]

His counter-proposal consists of a new division of power between a "power to take into account" and a "power to put in order" along with a "power to follow up." Each of these three powers brings factual and normative tasks together, instead of following the old fact-value dualism. The power to take into account connects factual research tasks of exploring new mixed entities with the normative task of determining their relevance for behavioral habits, the aim being to answer the question how many of us there are for the setting up of a collective of hybrids. The power to put in order answers the question of whether the newly explored can live together with the known mixed entities. To do this, it must, on the one hand, publicly run through the contradictory scenarios and thereby debate this cohabitation with all its pros and cons. On the other hand, it must be decided in the here and now, in an institutional hierarchy, which of the hybrid candidates for cohabitation can be excluded in the interim in order to stabilize the inner and outer worlds of the collective. Finally, the power to follow up ensures the maintenance of the division of powers and the quality of the investigative procedures. To this aim, many of the previously opposing professions and partial elites of Western societies will be integrated.[20]

Latour's conception is interesting because it returns to the anthropological focus of Western modernity and poses the problem of the dualistic-anthropological criteria anew. Thus we gain access to the contents of socio-cultural practices and this not just by way of the negative consequences for individuation. Also from a structural-political perspective, the question of a new division of power is cardinal. In the dualistically separating anthropology, which from the outset asymmetrically utilizes the dualisms, there is a hidden ethnocentrism, which, as Agamben says, renders hypocritical such talk as the sanctity of life and the human being in terms of internal and external realms. But Gesa Lindemann has justifiably criticized Latour's alternative division of power as an "expertocracy."[21] All three powers function only through the integration of expertise, which in turn requires experts. Even if one were to limit Latour's new division of powers to the necessary expert consultation within a public plural democracy, important philosophical questions would still remain unresolved. Latour conceives an "experimental metaphysics," which works with "a new exteriority" that contains the negativity of the absolute in the ever renewed processing through the power divisions. He himself notes the relation of this integration of modern constructivism to that which eludes modern construction, the classical American philosophies of W. James, J. Dewey and A. N. Whitehead.[22] Latour is also aware that his proposal for a new division of powers has yet to grapple with Habermas's conception. On the one hand, he would like to benefit from Habermas's model of the communicative reproduction of life forms. On the other hand, with his symmetrical model he wants to overcome those very asymmetries which are characteristic of Habermas's theory of communicative action.[23]

As interesting as Latour's alternative proposal is, it is not yet philosophically self-supporting either, and he is fair enough to refer to its sources in 20th-century philosophy. Much the same can be said of the other discussions which I have signaled referring to the respective catchphrases of Agamben, Beck and Giddens and to the already established Foucauldian *biopolitics*. For a new beginning, more detours, conversions, and reconstructions are necessary than the desired quick-fix solution would have one think. Thus to begin with, I will elaborate on the details which should clarify the approach of Philosophical anthropology. Much like Richard Shusterman regrounds classical pragmatism in the light of present day problems,[24] I intend in the following to reconstruct Philosophical anthropology in view of today's life politics. In this, I attempt to overcome the false idea of Philosophical anthropology which spread in Heidegger's wake.[25] Regrettably, even today Roberto Eposito is of the opinion that Philosophical anthropology, as developed in Germany since the 1920s, only compensates for the alienation of humans by artificially immunizing them against society, which in turn, however, leads to their own autoimmunization.[26]

2. General Introduction to Philosophical Anthropology

Notwithstanding all the cooperation between Philosophical anthropology and biology, Philosophical anthropology (as its founders, Max Scheler and Helmuth Plessner, aspired) is still a self-supporting research project which systematically and *problemgeschichtlich* – using the "problem-historical method" – relates in an equally important manner to historical, social, and cultural studies, and above all to philosophy. By way of introduction, I will pose and answer five questions to offer a quick overview of the whole project and pre-empt the most common misunderstandings.

Firstly:
What is Philosophical Anthropology as Opposed to Philosophical Anthropology and Anthropological Philosophy?

Anthropology is understood as the study (Greek *logos*) of humanity (*anthropos*).[27] Over time, especially between the seventeenth and the early twentieth century, it branched off into a multiplicity of epistemological anthropologies (biological, medical, historical, political, social and cultural anthropologies, or respectively ethnologies). In contrast to these anthropologies, *philosophical* anthropology deals with the nature of humans which – integrating all partial aspects of anthropology – *takes place* as a whole in the conduct of one's life. Since the 1920s, it has been disputed whether philosophical anthropology represents only a particular discipline within philosophy, which in a generalizing manner integrates the empirical anthropologies, or whether over and above this it is capable of taking on the grounding and justifying tasks of philosophy itself. The latter aspiration is known as "Philosophical" anthropology, with "Philosophical" capitalized rather than spelled with a small "p."

This terminological differentiation was introduced by Plessner in his 1936 Groningen inaugural lecture. His lead has been taken to this day;[28] however, the relationally crucial third expression – "anthropological philosophy" – has been left out. The transition from the inner-philosophical sub-discipline "philosophical anthropology" to "Philosophical anthropology" could be understood as establishing the general integration of the empirical anthropologies as the foundation of philosophy. This is exactly what Plessner calls anthropological philosophy.[29] It deploys a generally integrating anthropology to critique philosophy and, above all, to critique the dualistic mainstream modern philosophy (since Descartes and Kant) and its consequences (such as new unity myths). If, however, one stops here at the anthropological critique of philosophy, one disposes of philosophy in favor of the anthropological circle. Thus, the second step is even more important: the question must now be asked what it is that anthropology presupposes practically in life and in its research which it is not itself capable of understanding or explaining. These practical presuppositions which anthropology avails of, but which cannot be understood or explained within it, may belong to the specification of what it is to be human. These presuppositions make anthropology as a human achievement possible. Thereby a philosophical demarcation line is once again retrospectively drawn beneath the anthropologies in their cognitive and practical validity claims.

Today one would speak of an analysis and reconstruction of presuppositions on the practice of life and research inherent within anthropological investigations. It is this double movement from anthropological criticism of philosophy to a renewed philosophical criticism of anthropology which is urged and mostly misunderstood in the phrase "Philosophical anthropology." This double critique is a gap in contemporary philosophy.[30] Philosophical anthropology, treats the border question of humans' conduct of life as philosophy, but treats as anthropology the themes and methods of two comparative arrays constitutive of European modernity. I am referring here to the "horizontal" and "vertical" comparative arrays.[31] In the vertical direction, the genus or species of human life forms is compared with other organic (plant and animal) life forms concerning the question whether the specification of the human being can adequately ensue in the context of living nature or whether, over and above this, it must be justified by and founded in an "essential difference" (*Wesensunterschied*).[32] In the horizontal direction, social cultures of *Homo sapiens sapiens* are compared with one another with a view to finding the minimum of permutations that we humanly need for the specification of the human being. The comparison proceeds both historically (diachronically), including extinct, historical sociocultures, and synchronically, including the differentiation of the currently living sociocultures. In the English and French literature, the latter comparative problem is more frequently discussed under the heading of ethnology than under that of anthropology. The link between the vertical and horizontal specifications of the human as an individual and as a genus is itself a product of history and thus requires a "political anthropology" of the "historical world view."[33]

Secondly:
What Constitutes the Defining Theoretical Nature of Philosophical Anthropology?

Both anthropological comparative arrays are founded independently of each other. This means they can call each other into question or mutually correct each other when necessary in order to pre-empt speciesism (vertical) and ethnocentricities or anthropocentricities (horizontal). For the same reason, both are subject to an indirect process of inquiry. Philosophical anthropology is not directly the better empirical anthropology, but rather indirectly investigates what the latter makes use of in practical life and research without being able to explain or understand it. The practical life presuppositions derive from the practical use of common sense, while the presuppositions of practical research are generated by considerations concerning the future, thus from the continuation of research itself.

For the *natural philosophical founding* of the anthropological *vertical comparison*, Philosophical anthropology's *hypothesis* is that in living nature an *excentric positionality* is availed of for these comparisons. Unlike the "forms of organization" which concern the internal differentiation of organisms, the forms of *positionality* are *behavioral modes* of organisms in their *environment*. *Excentric* positionings are tied *not only* to a *centric* form of organization, but also to a *centric* form of positionality. Thus, there is a possibility of establishing a functional correlation between the center of the organism and the center of the interaction of the organism with its environment. But personal living beings can take up relational stances beyond this centric correlation, outside the organic centre and the behavioral centre in the environment. If they were not able to do this, they would not be able to determine any correlation either, but would rather be trapped within it. But persons can also take up a symbolic perspective from a *world* – especially the *shared world* (*Mitwelt*) – to this same world and position themselves accordingly.[34] Consequently, personal beings are confronted with the problem of having to balance the excentering and the recentering of their behavior. Their behavior is subject to inherent ambivalences, which derive structurally from a break between physical, psychic and mental dimensions of behavior, whereby this *break* must be interlocked in the act of behaving.[35]

The three most important behavioral ambivalences in which processes of excentering and recentering must proceed are a "natural artificiality," a "mediated Immediacy" and a "utopian standpoint" (between nothingness and transcendency).[36] These structures, which enable personal life, are assumed as essential and as a totality when the special characteristic of human as opposed to non-human life forms is *defined*, e.g. by bioanthropologists, medical anthropologists, or brain researchers.

For the *historico-philosophical* founding[37] of the anthropological *horizontal* comparison, the hypothesis of Philosophical anthropology is as follows: the essence of the human in the *totality of the conduct of its life* is to be found in its "unfathomableness,"[38] i.e. in *homo absconditus*. This being cannot be defined as a whole. However, insofar as it is finite, it can very well be defined and qualified in various aspects and perspectives, e.g., by *Geisteswissenschaften* or the humanities. For this definability Plessner developed a theory of playing in and with socio-cultural roles, which is then delimited by the non-acted laughing and crying.[39] If this being did not, in a practical sense, live in a relationship of indefiniteness towards its own future, it would no longer have any more defining tasks ahead. It would already be completely determined. It would perhaps be conditioned by history, but would no longer be capable itself of making any more history. Thus it would not have a future which, in contrast to its past, it could live towards, envision, or realize. The mental imputability of historical processes to human beings remains limited by the natural bodies, the socio-cultural role-playing bodies, and the lived-body performativity of the role players.[40]

Thirdly:
How does Philosophical Anthropology Proceed Methodologically?

Philosophical anthropology modifies four philosophical methods, as it does not believe that one alone suffices for a verifiable philosophy. It does not borrow methods from the empirical sciences. Rather, it reformulates the phenomenological methods (deriving from E. Husserl and M. Scheler), the hermeneutical methods (from W. Dilthey in the form of G. Misch's systematic interpretation), the behavioral critique methods (reconstructing dialectic crises in one's personal behavioral structure), and the transcendental methods (reconstructing the conditions for the possibility of performance). Additionally, these four methods are reintegrated in order to verify or refute the above mentioned ground hypotheses and further intermediary hypotheses.

a) It is Max Scheler's methodology which deserves the credit for having rescued Husserl's phenomenology from slipping back into the transcendental philosophy of consciousness. In order to enable an encounter with and a description of *specifically living* phenomena, Scheler *neutralizes* the phenomenological procedure against the *dualistic pre-decision* that the phenomena must be *defined* as either *physical* or *psychic*. Thus, the phenomenon can *present itself as a living entity* exactly and only *in* this dual aspect *between* the physical and the psychical.[41] On the behavioral level of personal living beings, the above-mentioned distinction between the physical or socio-cultural body and the living body comes into play in a phenomenological sense (English lacks the precise equivalents for "Leib" and "Körper". "Leib" can be translated as a "living body." The "Körper" is a "socio-cultural or physical body," but rather than writing this out in full each time, I will mostly use the original German "Körper" henceforth.)

b) The phenomenon encountering us is interpreted, at the latest in its description, according to habitualized and attentive expectations. How it is conditioned, defined, and rendered finite depends upon the context it is understood in and the horizons of unconditioned, undefined infinities it is viewed against. The interpretation of what is present depends upon what is absent. There is not only an unmediated understanding of the surface of the living expression in the behavioral reaction, but also a variable understanding of the expression and symbolic possibilities of understanding which are disconnected from the behavioral reaction in the here and now (in a clarification of Dilthey)[42].

c) If one runs through the spectra of phenomena and the spectrum of their interpretation, one is confronted with the question of when, where and under what circumstances behavioral crises arise. In such crises, the correlation between the encounter with the phenomenon and its appropriate interpretation at the behavioral level is fundamentally questioned. Breaks in personal behavior emerge. A model example for the dialectical-critical method is put forward by Plessner in his book about play-acted and non-acted *Laughing and Crying* (1941). On a structural semiotic level, he also investigated this question in those cases where a personal functional union of the symbolic integration of sense modalities fails to occur, thus for instance in his books *Einheit der Sinne* [Unity of the senses] (1923) and *Anthropologie der Sinne* [Anthropology of the senses] (1970).

d) Once the behavioral spectra in the investigation procedure have been run through phenomenologically, hermeneutically, and with relation to behavioral crises, the question must be answered what structures are essential as a condition for the possibility of the whole. This can be judged according to whether the behavioral crises can be overcome with new accomplishments in personal life. Sovereignty does not lie in absolute self-determination and self-fulfillment, but rather begins in being able to take up a life-affirming attitude to the limits of the same. Of course, the methodological steps can be run through again for the purposes of correction. A component part of the assessment of the investigation is the self-critical analysis of the semiotic organ which has been employed and which may not have allowed an adequate understanding of the behavioral spectra. In any case, the theoretical level of assessment has been reached. What were the deficits of the behavioral entanglement from psychical, physical, and/or mental perspectives? In what aspects and perspectives did the disabling of personal behavior occur? What was overdetermined, what underdetermined? What is the relationship to the two main aforementioned hypotheses and through what mediating factors?

Fourthly:
How does Philosophical Anthropology Explore the Political?

This is approached in two different ways, namely through the societal public realm of civilizational behavior, which, contrary to community-based forms, takes account of plurality and allows individuals to retain a private sphere. However, society's public realm is *de facto* reduced, marginalized, and possibly even disbanded by way of radical restrictions which are characteristic of European modernity.

To begin with, the political is made possible again through the *public realm* of *society* by contrast to the family-like community forms or the community forms whose goal is intellectual accomplishment. *Community forms* are based on their members sharing the same values, be it in the family-like forms of generational succession, or be it through contribution to the shared intellectual values (e.g. in a *scientific community*). Measured in terms of the shared community values, there is a clear determinability of individual behavior – in the family-like forms through personal hierarchies, and in an objective form through the evaluation of certain accomplishments by independent third parties.[43] Community forms are incommensurable with one another. The inherent ambivalences[44] in the personal behavioral development require both forms of communitization. At the same time, these ambivalences (e.g. the oscillation between restraint and shame, on the one hand, and the need for admiration and exposure, on the other) oppose their dissolution in this one and no other community form. Rather, the individuals also require a value-distantiation from certain community values in their interaction with *others* and *strangers*. Societal forms, as opposed to community forms, develop interaction with others and strangers. This requires a public sphere which diplomatically allows the social interaction and dealings of role bearers who, in order to ensure these tactful dealings, remain free on a private level. Thus, in order to make the diversity of individual lives possible, politics must handle the task of counterbalancing communal and societal claims through law.[45] It fails in the task if it leads to the dualism of either communitarianism or liberalism.

The societal public enabling of new political forms corresponds to the life-philosophical orientation based upon the above mentioned *homo absconditus*. It is a constituent of a society of plural values which attempts to deal civilly with its unavoidable conflicts.[46] It can, however, be restricted in two ways which have become common to European modernity. In one of these ways, politics is built upon an anthropological definition of the essence of the human being, as was the case not only in the Nazi and Bolshevist community ideologies (the human as a racial or class being). Since Hobbes, there have been pessimistic anthropologies, and since Rousseau optimistic ones, upon the basis of which corresponding constitutions have been promoted and enacted. However experience-saturated these anthropologies may already have been before, through constitutions they became, socio-culturally, a functional historical a priori of future experiences of social cohabitation in European modernity (today, for instance, also as *homo oeconomicus*). In the other way of these ways, the political as the condition for empirical politics is left to its own autonomy. Then, it is not subjected to an anthropology which is defined in material or formal terms or that is skeptical against such positive absolutisms. Instead, it is oriented towards the intensification of friend-enemy relationships which, interest-driven, exploits the uncanniness in the human condition for the enforcement of clear either-or alternatives.[47] The struggle for primacy in the human question, whether answered definitively by anthropology, ceded to autonomous politics or, philosophically grounded, kept open in the social public sphere, is – even within modernity – the decisive structural politics in which life power is lost and won, and the borders of life politics are set and disbanded.

Fifthly:
How does Philosophical Anthropology Criticize European Modernity?

The self-image of European modernity has a penchant for interpreting itself as a Copernican revolution. From the perspective of the universe, one could correctly ascertain how incorrect the Ptolemaic life-world assumption was, with the sun and the moon revolving around the earth at the centre. The modern was viewed as that which took up a decentered position in the universe, thus positioning itself in a God-like location. It is a question of taking on the role of God, or at least of taking up an Archimedean point, a god's-eye-view perspective. It takes no account of the living body's necessary recenterings in the development of personal behavior on earth. Philosophically, however, the "Copernican Revolution" (Kant) referred to the movement away from the object to the subject as the condition for the possibility of experience.[48] But this transcendental species subject fragmented socioculturally into conflicts among religions, cultures, communities, individuals, classes. The one "rational" revolution gave rise to many, whose disciples had mutually questioned each other's authorities (Kierkegaard, Marx, Nietzsche, Freud, etc.) until there were no longer any binding authorities. One surrendered, fell into or initiated civil war. One *animal ideolgicum* exposed another *animal ideologicum*. Germany, for historical reasons, was understood as the extreme case according to which European modernity could be studied as a series of involuntary anthropological experiments, since in Germany, unlike in Western Europe, an early habitualization of civil dealings with plurality had not taken place.

But Germany did not only suffer from the imbalance between excenterings and recenterings, which could be repeated elsewhere under today's conditions of globalization. The German case also exemplifies where secularization as a movement towards the worldly can lead if it is equated with profanation. An anthropologically dangerous paradox arises. On the one hand, the "de-deification" is followed by the "dehumanization"[49] on earth in the sense that personal life is reduced to bare life. On the other hand, the "self-empowerment" leads to the "self-deification"[50] of the collective rulers of national state sovereignty. Thus not only is the cardinal difference abolished between the public and the private, but also the old differentiation between the sacred and the profane is artificially turned against the enemy. Each one of us belongs to the sacred which can profane everything one wishes to exclude. During the "axial shifts" (*Achsenverlagerungen*)[51] of modernity, that which this modernity has been exposed to and which cannot simply be excluded from it emerges unresolved and must be given form within this modernity. "The grim, violent trend towards the affirmation of bare life, a heroism of pure action, has recently smitten the most enlightened intellectual classes of Europe."[52]

3. Particular Introduction to Philosophical Anthropology

Anyone wishing to cure people of illnesses, or at least to relieve them from chronic suffering brought on by illnesses, presupposes a minimum of the contrasting concept of health against which to judge processes of healing and pain alleviation.[53] Even the higher good of health cannot be understood in isolation, but is rather one of the many goods constituting a meaningful conduct of life whose given value can vary strongly individually, socio-culturally, and historically. Thus in its two anthropological comparative arrays (horizontal, contrasting humans from different sociocultures and vertical, contrasting humans with other living beings), Philosophical anthropology takes care not to raise any ethnocentrism or anthropocentrism to a standard. Instead, it tries to formulate minima which allow a fair comparison in horizontal and vertical directions. Its conceptual disassociations serve to distance it from hermeneutical prejudices and to promote a methodical control procedure.[54] In any study of the human being, sooner or later a phase begins in which the researchers themselves call their own humanness into question.

a) The *Körper-Leib* Distinction of Persons

I will begin with a phenomenological hypothesis on human beings' conduct of their lives. In this hypothesis, the aspect of being able to differentiate should not be gained at the expense of abstracting from the indeterminedness of life conduct as a whole. One cannot conduct anyone else's life for them, but can help them take up the task anew. Anyone who is not *above* life, but rather moves within it, is always positioned in a relation to their body (*Körperleib*). One's body presents itself in a differential spectrum of modes. In one aspect, which could be described as "having a body"(*Körperhaben*),[55] I treat my body as I treat other bodies. I have a body in so far as I relate to it through the detour of reflexion, through mediation (by objects or by other humans), and through participation in socio-cultural procedures, including medical practices. In this, my body is comparable with other bodies and can be represented by or interchanged with them. In the case of illnesses, their prevention and alleviation, one can be pleased that in this particular aspect one can have one's body renewed like other bodies.

The other aspect, however, is that I *am* and always will be a body, which can be called "being a body" (*Leibsein*).[56] I am this in the here and now in a spontaneous, unmediated, and arbitrary way, i.e. *without* reflexive, mediating, and procedural detours. In being a body I am – like it or not – not comparable with other bodies, interchangeable with them, or representable by them. It may even be that technologies are available which could make a world-record holder out of me with years of training and a special diet. But having a body as a whole has its limits in being a body even if in the here and now I err on the precise demarcation line, which later life-experience can clarify. To begin with, the phenomenological introduction only claims that it is *in* the difference between having a body and being a body that human life becomes a task – which as such must taken up. A total elimination of the living body (*Entleiblichung*) or a total elimination of the *Körper* (*Entkörperung*) would extinguish the difference and thus the task-character of this living being. On the other hand, if one moves within this difference, it continually shifts. What was unproblematically the living body can remain so. Whatever is problematically the living body, for instance a bad habit, must where possible be incorporated within the physical or socio-cultural body. What was once physically embodied, i.e., learned through mediation, sediments into the living body in the process of habitualization. The master-pianist's concert today still draws on what she learned thirty years ago as a five-year-old child. Perhaps at that precocious age she physically embodied (*verkörpert*) an aspect which in the meantime through her life experience can be enacted as a lived embodiment (*verleiblichen*). To a pure empirical scientist, a medical therapy may appear as a mere technique for the physical embodiment of problematic aspects of the living body, which as a means to an end it also has to be. But medical therapies as healing techniques only help when they improve the overall relationship between having a body and being a body over the course of the patient's life.

At the end of this introduction to this hypothesis, it is important to note its emphasis on its question character, which allows a multiplicity of answers in both the aforementioned comparative arrays without anticipating the answer in advance. What should we make use of as a third in order to develop, recognize, and judge the difference between being a body and having a body? Those living in this difference require personhood in order to delineate being a body from having a body and having a body from being a body. Let us call "personhood" (*Personalität*)[57] that which allows the reciprocal interlocking of both in the phases of a biographical process. Without recourse to personhood as the third which allows the difference, the having a body/being a body distinction would degenerate into a tautology or a paradox. A tautology would arise if either being a body (as for instance in the phenomenology of the living body) or having a body (as for example in the naturalism of the empirical sciences) were to be given primacy.

The difference would then only appear as a secondary derivation from a primary identity, on the one hand of the living body, on the other of the *Körper*. We would have a paradox if the having a body/being a body distinction were supposed to express the identity of the *Körper* and the living body simultaneously. Tautology and paradox generally put an end to the investigation before it has begun. Thus the question is kept open in Plessner's Philosophical anthropology by opening it up to that third of personhood, which allows the development of difference, thus keeping it alive in a specific sense. With personhood, a world stage stands and falls against whose background something and someone could appear. The living body/*Körper* distinction, which we started with, moves with*in* the foreground against such a scenic backdrop from which further future surprises could emerge. We ought not to abstract too quickly from this background, without which the foreground of positive defining accomplishments and its own future improvement cannot exist. Our point of departure is not the static closing of the inquiry into human beings as if we had already taken our leave of them, but rather its dynamic opening up into the conduct of their lives. A preliminary answer to the question about personhood is given by social and cultural anthropology at that point where bio-anthropology speaks of the plasticity of a specifically human behavioral development. What can this behavior be shaped for, and what is it shaped for? For the individual execution of personal roles which are not genetically inherited, but rather passed down socio-culturally. Before elaborating on this in point c, I will briefly discuss the world-environment distinction with a view to the philosophical connection between bio-anthropology and social and cultural anthropology.

b) The Distinction between the World (Excentric Positionality) and the Environment (Centric Positionality)

In the development of human behavior, the mammal and primate natures certainly necessarily keep in step, but they are not sufficient for a specification of human behavior. In comparison with other mammals and especially with the primates among them (which, like humans, socially pass down the cultures of populations and, on an individual basis, demonstrate an intelligence which goes beyond pure associated learning on the "trial-and-error"-based model), the human progeny stands out for its particularly lengthy phase of dependency. This refers not only to the first year of life, which Plessner, following Adolf Portmann, describes as "an end phase of embryonic development transferred to the outside concerning sensory performance, motor skills, and language."[58] Nowadays, human beings are only considered adult members of their species after approximately two decades, whereas chimpanzees, our closest relatives, require only a third of this developmental time. In comparison with the pre-adaptation of other primates to specific environments (habitats), human beings appear to be particularly unspecific generalists in their developmental behavior.[59] They require a socio-cultural niche as their environment, in which, from the beginning on, intentionality is furthered, and social interaction and mentality are developed in linguistic communication.[60]

Thus Philosophical anthropology works with the difference between *environment* and *world*. In animal life forms, from a structural-functional perspective, there is a correspondence between the centric *organizational form* (interior differentiation of the organism with a central nervous system) and the centric form of positionality (modes of behavior) in the environment. The organism and the environment are – from an evolutional standpoint – attuned to each other through processes of variation and selection. Even in the play of young mammals, a harmonization of behavioral movements is imparted through social learning within respective populations. But it is only in the primate evolution of human beings that there also seems to be a break in and with the centric pre-adjustment between an organism and an environment. The possible evolutionary reasons behind this must be considered separately. In the modern world in order to be able to speak about this hiatus from the perspective of mankind's known history to date, we must presuppose a personal world. It is from the cultural history of the personhood in the world that social environments for the younger generations of humans as living beings are artificially set up. Humans as centric living beings are still in need of a specifically defined environment. But they must acquire this environment in its particular specificity from elsewhere, namely from a world for persons, setting it up through the mediation of culture and institutions. For the specificity of one environment as compared with the other possible environments to be at all apparent, I must position myself in the world, creating thereby a distance to the environment. The animal is *bios*; it lives in its environment but because of this it does not *have* any bio*logy*. In as far as biologists are personal beings with a world vantage point, they have the distance which is necessary for the recognition of certain environments as opposed to other possible environments.

Humans position themselves frontally towards the things in their behaviorally-suited environment. They also absorb themselves in the interactions with their environment. Insofar as they do all of this, they are moving in a centric form of positionality, which matches their centric organizational form. But in this sense, they live centrically in an artificially pre-created environment, that of everyday life. At the same time, they also end up distancing themselves again from this artificially centric positionality to the extent that they do not only react out of habit. They behave personally towards their interactions, as if from an adjacent position, as if they were moving from behind themselves and above themselves towards their own habitual actions. They feel, hear, and see themselves being moved and observed also from *beyond* their centric behavior. As if from the sidelines, they experience handling the objects which face them or being fully absorbed in an action. Through this sideline experience, they can modify this handling or being absorbed, allow it to happen, or control and change it. They are not just situated in it, like a centre point, but rather also move beyond it: into an *ex-centric positionality.* Thus what was at the centre can wander off to the periphery, like in a Copernican turnaround of the Ptolemaic world view. The centre of behavioral development is not fixed in itself, but rather changes with time. Rather than coming to a standstill in either the centre of an environment or outside of this in a world, it moves between the two. It does not stand still. A thrust of behavioral excentering away from the body (*Körperleib* understood as the unity of *Körper* and the lived body) creates an imbalance and promotes a thrust of behavioral recentering back to the body. This oscillating in its self-movement pervades all characteristic human behavioral rhythms, whether it be learning to walk upright or to cycle or walk the tightrope, or whether it be the expressionistic countermovement to the impressionistic challenge of modern painting.

Entities such as human beings, who position themselves excentrically in comparison to other living beings, are subject to a constitutive ambivalence in their behavioral development. These living beings require a counterbalance for the hiatus between the excentring of their behavior away from the *Körperleib* and the recentring of their behavior back to the *Körperleib.* Plessner described this ambivalence in behavior in various aspects, with respect to the vertical and horizontal comparative arrays, as "natural artificiality," "mediated immediacy," and "immanent transcendence."[61] Today for instance, in archeological finds, we can still distinguish human remains from the remnants of other primate groups, according to empirical criteria for such behavioral ambivalences. Do the results of the DNA analysis (for the centric organizational form of homo sapiens) match with the technical artefacts (natural artificiality), the cultural symbols for an excentric expressivity, in e.g. cave paintings (mediated immediacy), and the religious symbols for a personal distancing which go beyond the immanent world to a locus which is not of this world and not of this time (immanent transcendence)? Through such questions on the connection of bio-anthropology with social and cultural anthropology at the interface of specifically human plasticity, the quick-fix reduction of the world to the environment (and within this to an organism type or even a genome type) is fended off and the presuppositions of the investigation are appropriately retained in recognizable form.

c) The Individualization of Playing *in* and Play-acting *with* Socio-cultural Personal Roles

If we assume the distinction between the *Körper* and the living body for the personal world, the question emerges how this connection can be made at least rudimentarily understandable. The concept of personhood is refined through the concept of the roles of persons, which the human progeny are assumed to take on in all cultures and societies, and historically modify in their practical execution.

Elementarily viewed, such a *role* links a certain language in which one can take up certain perspectives (as opposed to other perspectives of possible behavior) with a filmic series of habitus images according to which the socio-cultural body and the living body are interlocked into behavioral unities. This process of combining a certain language with the moving pictures of a certain habitus comprises three aspects.

Firstly, in the form of *acting*, the sociocultural embodiment dominates the living body, whose proprioception (vegetative, muscular, skeletal, and balance senses) should proceed during the action as unobtrusively as possible. Exemplary for acting is upright standing, which enhances one's range of movement within space. From this position, one can act within the eye-hand field through the coordination of the distance-sense of seeing and the tactile close-senses, particularly that of the multifunctional hand. Secondly, in *expression*, the lived embodiment outweighs the having-a-body. In the coordination of interactions, the simultaneous proprioception of one's own corporeality as the living body proceeds continually, sometimes more and sometimes less extensively. Body schemas/body images emerge in the living body's response to this backflow of interactions towards the living body.[62] In the interaction field, the *Körperleiber* express themselves to one another through a transformation of facial expression for the gaze of the others and in the development of the voice orbit, i.e., in the articulation and hearing of one's own and others' voices. Thirdly, speaking combines expression and action to form functional behavioral units. In the turn-taking between speakers, the articulated speech moves from expression to action and from action to expression until the behavioral relativity of the individual sense-modes is habitualized not only in the external conversation but also in the internal one. Speaking integrates the different sense modes, according to themes whose horizon is indicated by syntagmata defining what and whom it is perspectively about and by schemata on why something is to be done.[63] The basic narrative form of speech between personal beings can be developed through the personal pronouns in the singular and plural, and in the script it can be consolidated beyond the circle of those present. The written language can again, according to the socio-cultural purposes, be institutionally specialized and limited to certain types of discourse, including that of literature or the empirical sciences.

In contrast to the playing behavior of the mammal, which remains limited to the childhood phase and essentially consists in participation, but also in contrast to other primates who are capable of aping such and such a behavioral unity, without however being able to detach complete roles from their actual incumbent (e.g. alpha males), the specification of human behavioral development requires a dramaturgical model. The model of exhibited play[64] references lifelong imitation and variation of complete personal roles in perspectival difference to other personal roles and their respective individual bearers.

Human children, through identification with concrete reference persons, play-act themselves out of their own body (*Körperleib*) into the interactive roles of the latter. From these personal roles, their first excentric positionings, they establish the interlocked proportions of the *Körper* and the living body within themselves, i.e., returning to their own body. The execution of the behavior diverges – for good or bad – from the expectations of the role. These departures cumulate into an individual variation of the role or into its continually being exceeded or fallen short of, which then leads to conflicts. Other reference persons and their roles may be more suitable. But even in the case of a successful individual variation of the role in identification with its reference person, the continuation of the success requires dramaturgical precautionary measures against occasional or longer failures in its execution of a future here and now. Also one who identifies with the role must sooner or later play not only *in* it but also *with* it, all the more so when there is a distance to the role rather than an identification with it. Whether in front of others as opposed to one's own self or in front of other selves identified with one's own self, the evaluation must be conducted in front of others *and* one's own self. The differentiation between one's own self and others' selves requires a doubling up of the person in front of others and for oneself: into the person who is to be kept private and the person who is to be presented to the public. Thereby it oscillates between the need for admiration (boisterousness) and shame (reticence), which can develop into a fervor to exceed the established roles or into an addiction to falling short of them.[65]

The public-private doppelganger mode (*Doppelgängertum*)[66] allows the individualization of the person, i.e., their self-differentiation between the bearer, whose living body has fused with the role, and the player of personal roles, who plays these as if they were mere masks. The individualization allows a retrospective change of roles. There can be no play-acting between a minimum of two people who can change their roles, without a doubling up of each person into the one who socio-culturally embodies the role and the one who bears it as a living body. This indicated acting approach can be elaborated on the basis of personal pronouns (I, you, he/she/it, we, you, they). Here the third person singular and plural take on referee roles. The dramaturgical model can also be developed along the lines of Mead's differentiation. *Play*, in which the perspective of particular and concrete others is acquired during childhood, is followed in one's youth by *games* in and with the personalized roles of generalized others depending on the given community, until from early adulthood onwards *games* begin in and with societal roles, with the discourse universes functioning as court of appeal.[67]

d) The Limits of Human Behavioral Development in the Non-play-acted Laughing and Crying

Human behavioral plasticity has limits which are experienced in laughing and crying that is not acted. One who, play-acting, disregards the seriousness of laughing and crying risks both wounding the dignity of those concerned as well as launching a process that can degenerate into dehumanization. Generally, in human cultures, before these limits are reached, there are playable forms of laughing and crying. They demarcate the borders appellatively. And where possible, the non play-acted forms which have fallen from the sphere of self-controlled behavior should be reclaimed for the playable.

In the non-play-acted laughing and crying the personal interlockedness between having a body and being a body is lost. The hiatus of the excentric positionality, its break between the excentering and the recentering, becomes phenomenally apparent in the loss of self-control. These phenomena "make their appearance as uncontrolled and unformed eruptions of the body, which acts, as it were, autonomously. Man falls into their power; he breaks-out laughing, and lets himself break into tears. He responds to something by laughing and crying, but not with a form of expression which could be appropriately compared with verbal utterance, expressive movement, gesture or action. He responds – with his body as body as if from the impossibility of being able to find an answer himself. And in the loss of control over himself and his body, he reveals himself at the same time as a more than bodily being who lives in a state of tension with regard to his physical existence, yet is wholly and completely bound to it."[68] In the non-play-acted laughing, too many mutually-defeating possibilities of physical embodiments fly outside away from the living body which is then, so to speak, left to its own devices. In the non-play-acted crying, the potential for physical embodiments slumps inwards into nothing but a living body and a loss in meaning of the whole. If, in the excentering direction of laughter, the *Körper* leaps out into polysemous worlds without the living body being able to follow, in the recentering direction of crying, the world horizon dissolves into a diffuse lived embodiment, which in the end is unable to differentiate itself from its environment. Both series of phenomena reverse the normal conditions that confer meaning, but in different directions: "Openness, immediacy, eruptivity characterize laughter; closure, mediacy, gradualness characterize crying. These characteristics are not accidental. The laughing person is open to the world. In consciousness of our withdrawal and disengagement which can frequently be combined with a feeling of superiority, we seek to know that we are one with others. Laughter succeeds completely only in company with those who laugh with us."[69] In contrast to crying where, "In the act of inner capitulation which has a significance for crying at once evocative and constitutive, the individual becomes detached, in the sense of being isolated, from the situation of normal behavior. Deeply moved, he implicates himself by this act in the anonymous 'answer' of his body. Thus in weeping he cuts himself off from the world."[70]

Such border experiences show what is existentially important for the individuality of humans for the conduct of life in its totality. In a mediated way, concerning the generational succession, this can also be said of cultures and communities in view of their collective history, where they learned the limits of their self-determination and self-fulfillment. In the cultural comparison, Western modernization suffers from a misunderstanding of human sovereignty. Sovereignty is often falsely identified with absolute self-determination and self-fulfillment on both an individual and a collective basis. The opposite of such ideologies of limitless self-empowerment is really the case. Human sovereignty begins in the affirmation of the limits – which are beyond people's influence – of their self-determination in the cognitive sense and of their self-fulfillment in the volitional sense. Awareness of this is certainly present in all religions, but need not be exclusively religious. It also derives from life-experience, literature and art, and belongs to medical and philosophical practices insofar as they devote themselves to these border experiences and questions. This awareness includes doing everything humanly possible in the here and now to improve the shifting of the border. But it excludes all ideologies which imply that humans can take possession of the Absolute without distorting it into inhuman barbarity. Finite determinations and conditions can be changed in a reproducible manner, as above all the empirical sciences successfully teach us in their standard contexts of observation and experiment. But it would be a serious category mistake to simply wish to transfer this welcome improvement of the conditional and determined *Körper* aspects onto the Absolute, i.e. onto the *un*conditional, *un*determined and *in*finite. We will never be able to dispense of the unfathomability of the totality of human conduct of life in any reproducible laboratory context, unless it be at the price of their – human – freedom (including that of the laboratory scientist). Not only God, but also man in the absolute sense is unfathomable. What the *deus absconditus* grants as orientation for the conduct of life as a whole in religious worlds is made possible in secular worlds by the *homo absconditus*.

The fact that the question about personhood of human beings is ultimately open encourages a continuation of all research directed at facilitating and improving the conduct of life. These investigations have a future for the very reason that their questions are actually answerable in aspects, but not conclusively for the totality of this life form. In helping to solve problematic lived aspects, it is vital to determine the corresponding *Körper* correlate. But one will not be able to provide such help if one separates the body correlates from the living body (as experienced distinctly from the *Körper*) and from the personal dimension of those engaged in the task of conducting their lives. But this is the consequence of today's ever-increasing expansion of reductive naturalism and economism. Both of these could win through if individuals are fixed to specific personal roles, without there being an initiative for an appropriate change in roles with the individuation of persons.

By contrast, in the personal realm of the distinction between having a body and being a body, "the true crux of lived-body character" remains its "interlockedness in the *Körper*."[71] Therein we find the mutual task of all life-scientific research.[72]

e) Natural Philosophy:
Excentering in Nature as the Third of the *Natura Abscondita*

The joint research also requires a new natural philosophy, a deficit which contemporary philosophy suffers from. It is particularly in dealings with the life sciences that the inner-philosophical problems should not be concealed. By "natural philosophy" I do not mean a separate and overspecialized field, which could create the impression that its methods and objects had already been fixed before philosophy began. And especially I do not mean a theory of natural sciences insofar as this – in a pre-decision for the dualism of either nature or spirit – occludes the therapeutic aspect of natural science practices. Rather, under natural philosophy I understand the question of how the so-called first empirical, scientific-technologically definable nature is historically and mentally linked to the so-called second – socio-cultural – nature, in which we human life forms have always habitually participated. Thus, I am concerned with a differentiation in philosophizing, which poses anew the border question in the total context of human life conduct, rather than fragmenting itself into a division of labor amongst academic spin-off industries, such as are to be found in social and cultural philosophy, morality and ethics, or maintenance of traditions.

The empirical scientific-technological practices themselves are of a socio-cultural nature. This happens to appear, in particularly challenging ways, in medical sciences, in the ethos of doctors and in the legal situation of medical practices which is addressed in fierce political disputes. If the socio-cultural nature of empirical scientific and technological practices is overlooked, hermeneutical pre-projections from these onto the natural objects tend to be declared as natural fallacies, as if such results were not dependent on the methods. A culture which also imagines its hermeneutical prejudices as an irreversible naturalism of positivities falls victim to its most dangerous learning block. The hermeneutical confusion turned naturalistic fallacy can appear in certain politically and economically deformed utilization structures, but hinders the empirical scientific-technological practices themselves. Their research character is referred back to the method-dependency of the outcomes and artefacts produced. To the extent that their reproduction succeeds under standard conditions, not only is a surplus of the first nature produced going beyond the previously well attuned second nature. The research horizon encompassing these positively determined entities expands out into another indeterminacy. The distinction between understanding and explaining opens up anew in the research practice and remains historically disputed.[73]

Thus research does not lead away from philosophy, but rather towards philosophical border questions such as: What is in need of explanation? What provides an explanation? What is explainable at all? It amounts to an invitation to philosophize not only in respect to its relation of indeterminacy, but also concerning the reproducibility of its positive determinations. How was it possible to successfully reproduce the first nature, without falling victim to a false transfer of this positive determination to the Absolute and thus becoming incapable of learning?

An Immanuel Kant, in view of the success of great paradigms of empirical sciences (such as the disputed one of natural and social evolution), would pose the enabling question anew ("quasi-transcendentally") and thereby reset philosophy, thus keeping it alive. When today philosophy takes part in proxy wars waged upon empirical scientific research, wars in which the problem of the public or private utilization structures of these investigations disappears, this is a declaration of bankruptcy on the part of the philosophies concerned. Normativity is inherent in empirical scientific research practices. Philosophy can take up their therapeutic, understanding, and explanatory tasks and also elaborate the problems that researchers represented within these research practices have as persons, particularly as the citizens (*citoyens*). To this extent, the objection raised against normativity coming from outside must appear trivial or strategic in an all too familiar *Weltanschauung* dispute amongst experts. What would not be normative as far as humans are concerned? Behind this triviality, the conflict between different normativities and their facts begins. Or is, in fact, only the conservation of one particular normativity, that of the respective philosophy, intended? For morality, if one were to take its requirements seriously, conservation would be a bad game. Morality is not helped by any form of cognitive blindness which pushes it back into the helplessness of an ethics of conviction. It should rather be capable of creating a sense of responsibility for the future consequences of today's action and non-action in a plural society. Experiments in public learning processes are required for this and not their premature privatization.

I believe it is possible to understand historically how, in the aftermath of the Second World War with its racist genocide, the great "denaturalizing" strategies were able to take hold in philosophies, such as those of Derrida or Habermas. This proceeded in different, but also similar ways, with both being influenced by the devastating political consequences of the preceding false naturalisms. I can also see – from a systematic perspective – the uncircumventable nature of not just any language, but of the self-referential ones. But thanks to this (illocutionary-propositional) self-reference we do not have a language prison, but rather the opening up of an external reference to it from a world vantage point, and this even more so through writing, in particular the *Ur-schrift*. Language could have freed one from the prison of self-consciousness, without moving philosophy to another prison, if only the "primordial" Christian fear of life had not taken refuge in it: Insofar as we can say in the language what we are doing in it, it sets free that which is distinguished from it, which in turn also imposes obligations upon us. It is as if it wanted (if you like: in the repetition of the same in the other) to be renewed. At one end, it slips without question into the sedimented second nature of a bygone present. At the other end, it questions today what might be answerable in a future turned present through action. Between these language borders – opened up and imposed by the discursive language-use itself – of the habitualized second and the problematic first nature, language emerges doubly as a quasi-transcendental enabling amidst an evolutionary dowry of behavioral disposition. It does not follow from the justified battle against false naturalisms that there is no nature going beyond human consciousness which is linguistically anticipated on the basis of phenomena and linguistically resorted to in the reconstruction of the phenomena. Human living beings take part in nature which goes beyond consciousness to the extent that this (willy-nilly, and for better or worse) participation has become problematic. And they fall out of it in such a way that they must answer this questionability culturally, *in order to keep hold of themselves in the questionability of their nature.* Nature cannot be dissolved into sociocultural and personal attributions ("agency") even if these are understood as the up and coming future order of things (possibly to be distributed more justly through aporias).

Why must the idea of decentering, which is correct and worth preserving, be situated exclusively outside of living nature (in argumentative discourses, in script reconstructed as antecedent) rather than being accommodated within it, namely in its being suspended? In the meantime human living beings, in consequence of the socio-cultural evolution of primate brains, are viewed as mammals who have been suspended in language behavior. At the periphery of a galaxy, in the representative methods of their written language, they concern themselves with black holes and antimatter in another place and another time, whilst their closest relatives, the chimpanzees lack this "sense for the negative,"[74] which is again why the latter are known as the "happier humans." I am not convinced by the false either-or alternative in which nature is usually thought. Yes, according to the canonical legend, it can be understood either in a Rousseauian or in a Hobbesian manner. But why should nature, in an aspectual sense, not be both the *Körper* and the living body simultaneously while in the totality not being absorbed into the one or the other? Doesn't every new thrust of technology drag us into the indissoluble distinction of human nature, its living body dimension as unjustifiable in the life-world and its *Körper* dimension, which is empirically justifiable in a scientific and technological mode. And do we not, to answer this questionability, also avail of nature, especially as a third entity, in the conduct of our lives? This third of the life process with its un- and in-predicates of absoluteness (unconditionality, undeterminedness, infinity, in short: unfathomability) cannot be determined any longer by those concerned as positive, either rationally or emotionally.[75] "Language, an expression in second potency, is therefore the true proof of existence of those situated in the middle of their own life form and thus beyond it, in the locationless, timeless position of human beings. In the strange nature of the meanings of expressions, the basic structure of mediated immediacy is cleansed of anything material and appears sublimated in its own element."[76]

With Plessner, performativity can be understood as a behavioral disposition towards one's own *Körper*/living body distinction, but as a personal disposition from no location and from no time, thus from the third of an excentric positionality, which in its exection does not dissolve into any physical or living body dimension. Why cannot the correct transcendental question on the conditions of the possibility of experience be shifted into the task of human beings to specify themselves in their suspension of living nature? This suspension can neither be overcome (in a god-like manner) nor continued (for mammalian primates), but can indeed for its own part be categorically suspended as if it could *all by itself* be lived in the subjunctive (the phantasms) of life conduct. This subjunctive is categorical for the dignity of persons. I am speaking of the suspension in view of the modernistic mania for self-empowerment through self-positing (since Fichte), in whose answer the questionability of the being-questioned (in contrast to self-questioning) disappears. And why should living nature in its suspension not retain a remaining dimension which eludes our judgment of "feeling at home in it or remaining a stranger in it." "Being-human is being the other of oneself. It is only through his transparency in another realm that his public unfathomability is attested. (...) Neither of the two is the earlier. They do not mutually posit each other and do not logically induce each other. They do not support each other and are not ontologically derived from each other. They are not one and the same only seen from different sides. Between them there is emptiness.

Their connection is and-connection and also-connection."[77] Ultimately nature remains for us *natura abscondita*.

NOTES

1. Cf. Thomas Lemke, *Biopolitik zu Einführung* (Hamburg: Junius Verlag, 2007); Roberto Esposito, *Bios: Biopolitics and Philosophy*, trans. Timothy Campbell (Minneapolis: University of Minnesota Press, 2008).
2. Andreas Kuhlmann, *Politik des Lebens − Politik des Sterbens. Biomedizin in der liberalen Demokratie* (Berlin: Fest, 2001).
3. Cf. Anthony Giddens, *Modernity and Self-Identity* (Cambridge: Polity Press, 1991), chap. 3.
4. Ulrich Beck (ed.), *Perspektiven der Weltgesellschaft* (Frankfurt am Main: Suhrkamp, 1998).
5. Ulrich Beck, *Risk Society: Towards a New Modernity*, trans. Mark Ritter (London: Sage, 1992).
6. Ulrich Beck, *The Reinvention of Politics: Rethinking Modernity in the Global Social Order*, trans. Mark Ritter (Cambridge: Polity Press, 1997).
7. Cf. Anthony Giddens, *Beyond Left and Right: The Future of Radical Politics* (Cambridge: Polity Press, 1994).
8. See Hans-Peter Krüger, *Zwischen Lachen und Weinen: Der dritte Weg Philosophischer Anthropologie und die Geschlechterfrage*, vol. 2 (Berlin: Akademie Verlag, 2001), especially part 2; *Philosophische Anthropologie als Lebenspolitik. Deutsch-jüdische und pragmatistische Moderne-Kritik* (Berlin: Akademie Verlag, 2009).
9. Giddens, *Beyond Left and Right*, p. 253.
10. *Ibid.*, p. 219.
11. Giorgio Agamben, *The Coming Community*, trans. Michael Hardt (Minneapolis: University of Minnesota Press, 1993), p. 62.
12. *Ibid.*, p. 64.
13. *Ibid.*, p. 89.
14. *Ibid.*, p. 81.
15. *Ibid.*, p. 85ff.
16. Giorgio Agamben, *Homo Sacer: Sovereign Power and Bare Life*, trans. Daniel Heller-Roazen (Stanford: Stanford University Press, 1998).
17. Agamben, *The Coming Community*, pp. 96–100.
18. Bruno Latour, *We Have Never Been Modern*, trans. Catherine Porter (Cambridge: Harvard University Press, 1993), pp. 10ff., 13ff.
19. Bruno Latour, *Politics of Nature: How to Bring the Sciences into Democracy*, trans. Catherine Porter (Cambridge: Harvard University Press, 2004), pp. 47–9.
20. Cf. *Ibid.*, pp. 180ff., 194–209.
21. Gesa Lindemann, "'Allons enfants et faits de la patrie…' Über Latours Sozial- und Gesellschaftstheorie sowie seinen Beitrag zur Rettung der Welt", *Bruno Latours Kollektive. Kontroversen zur Entgrenzung des Sozialen*, eds. Georg Kneer, Markus Schroer, Erhard Schüttpelz (Frankfurt am Main: Suhrkamp, 2008), pp. 339–60.
22. Latour, *Politics of Nature*, pp. 121–7, 259, 265, 270, 281.
23. See *Ibid.*, pp. 262ff., 281.
24. Richard Shusterman, *Body Consciousness: A Philosophy of Mindfulness and Somaesthetics* (Cambridge: Cambridge University Press, 2008).

25. For more detail cf. Hans-Peter Krüger, "De-Zentrierungen und Ex-Zentrierungen. Die quasi-transzendentalen Unternehmungen von Heidegger und Plessner heute," *Dezentrierungen. Zur Konfrontation von Philosophischer Anthropologie, Strukturalismus und Poststrukturalismus*, eds. Thomas Ebke und Matthias Schloßberger (Berlin: Akademie Verlag, 2012), pp. 17–48.

26. Esposito, *Bios*, p. 48. For more detail cf. Roberto Esposito, *Immunitas: The Protection and Negation of Life*, trans. Zakiya Hanafi (Cambridge: Polity Press, 2011), pp. 94–111.

27. On the history of philosophical anthropology cf. Michael Landmann, *Philosophical Anthropology*, trans. David J. Parent (Philadelphia: Westminster Press, 1974).

28. Cf. Herbert Schnädelbach, *Philosophie in Deutschland 1831–1933* (Frankfurt am Main: Suhrkamp, 1983), pp. 269–72; Joachim Fischer, *Philosophische Anthropologie. Eine Denkrichtung des 20. Jahrhunderts* (Freiburg – München: Verlag Karl Alber, 2008), p. 14ff.

29. Helmuth Plessner, "Die Aufgabe der Philosophischen Anthropologie," *Gesammelte Schriften: Conditio Humana*, vol. 8, eds. Günter Dux, Odo Marquard, and Elisabeth Ströker (Frankfurt am Main: Suhrkamp, 1983), pp. 36–9; "Immer noch Philosophische Anthropologie?" *ibid.*, pp. 242–5.

30. Krüger, *Zwischen Lachen und Weinen*, vol. 2.

31. Helmuth Plessner, *Die Stufen des Organischen und der Mensch: Einleitung in die philosophische Anthropologie* (Berlin-New York: De Gruyter, 1975), p. 32.

32. Max Scheler, *The Human Place in the Cosmos*, trans. Manfred S. Frings (Evanston: Northwestern University Press, 2009), p. 25.

33. Helmuth Plessner, *Gesammelte Schriften: Macht und menschliche Natur*, vol. 5, eds. Günter Dux, Odo Marquard, and Elisabeth Ströker (Frankfurt am Main: Suhrkamp, 1981), pp. 139–44.

34. Plesssner, *Die Stufen des Organischen und der Mensch*, pp. 302–8.

35. *Ibid.*, p. 292ff.

36. Cf. *Ibid.*, pp. 309ff., 341ff.

37. On the natural and historico-philosophical founding, cf. Olivia Mitscherlich, *Natur und Geschichte: Helmuth Plessners in sich gebrochene Lebensphilosophie* (Berlin: Akademie Veralg, 2007).

38. Plessner, *Macht und menschliche Natur*, p.160ff., 181, 292, 222ff.

39. Cf. Hans-Peter Krüger, *Zwischen Lachen und Weinen: Das Spektrum menschlicher Phänomene*, vol. 1 (Berlin: Akademie Verlag, 1999).

40. See Plessner, *Macht und menschliche Natur*, p. 226ff.

41. Scheler, *The Human Place in the Cosmos*, p. 12ff., 27ff, 29ff

42. See Plessner, *Die Stufen des Organischen und der Mensch,* pp. 28–37.

43. Cf. Helmuth Plessner, *The Limits of Community: A Critique of Social Radicalism*, trans. Andrew Wallace (New York: Prometheus Books, 1999), pp. 87–90.

44. See *ibid.*, pp. 109–24.

45. Cf. *ibid.*, pp. 174ff., 192ff.

46. See Plessner, *Macht und menschliche Natur*, pp. 161–4, 185ff., 201–4.

47. See *ibid.*, pp. 192–200.

48. Helmuth Plessner, *Die verspätete Nation: Über die politische Verführbarkeit bürgerlichen Geistes* (Frankfurt am Main: Suhrkamp, 1974), pp.120ff., 131ff., 137.

49. *Ibid.*, pp. 101, 147, 149.

50. Plessner, "Die Aufgabe der Philosophischen Anthropologie," p. 50.

51. Plessner, *Die verspätete Nation*, pp. 83, 88, 120ff., 131.

52. Plessner, "Die Aufgabe der Philosophischen Anthropologie," p. 45.

53. Cf. Georges Canguilhem, *The Normal and the Pathological*, trans. Carolyn R. Fawcett (New York: Zone Books, 1991); Andreas Heinz, *Der Begriff psychischer Krankheit* (Berlin: Suhrkamp, 2014, forthcoming).

54. Cf. Hans-Peter Krüger, Gesa Lindemann (eds.), *Philosophische Anthropologie im 21. Jahrhundert* (Berlin: Akademie Verlag, 2006).

55. Helmuth Plessner, *Laughing and Crying: A Study of the Limits of Human Behaviour*, trans. James S. Churchill and Marjorie Grene (Evanston: Northwestern University Press, 1970), p. 34.

56. *Ibid.*, p. 36ff.

57. Cf. Plessner, *Die Stufen des Organischen und der Mensch*, pp. 300–4.

58. Helmuth Plessner, "Die Frage nach der Conditio humana," *Gesammelte Schriften: Conditio Humana*, vol. 8, p. 166.

59. Cf. Daniel J. Povinelli, *Folk Physics for Apes: The Chimpanzee's Theory of How the World Works* (Oxford: Oxford University Press, 2000).

60. Cf. Michael Tomasello, *Constructing a Language: A Usage-Based Theory of Language Acquisition* (Cambridge: Cambridge University Press, 2003).

61. Cf. Plessner, *Die Stufen des Organischen und der Mensch*, pp. 309–42.

62. Helmuth Plessner, *Gesammelte Schriften: Anthropologie der Sinne*, eds. Günter Dux, Odo Marquard, and Elisabeth Ströker (Frankfurt am Main: Suhrkamp, 1980), p. 369.

63. Cf. Helmuth Plessner, "Die Einheit der Sinne. Grundlinien einer Ästhesiologie des Geistes," *Gesammelte Schriften: Anthropologie der Sinne*, pp. 187–92.

64. Plessner, *Gesammelte Schriften: Anthropologie der Sinne*, p. 391.

65. Cf. Krüger, *Zwischen Lachen und Weinen*, vol. 1, chap. 4.

66. Plessner, "Die Frage nach der Conditio humana," p. 201.

67. Cf. George Herbert Mead, *Mind, Self and Society: From the Standpoint of a Social Behaviourist* (Chicago: Chicago University Press, 1934).

68. Plessner, *Laughing and Crying: A Study of the Limits of Human Behaviour,* p. 31.

69. *Ibid.*, p. 146.

70. *Ibid.*, p. 147.

71. *Ibid.* p. 146.

72. Cf. Gesa Lindemann, *Die Grenzen des Sozialen. Zur sozio-technischen Konstruktion von Leben und Tod in der Intensivmedizin* (München: Fink, 2002); Hans-Peter Krüger, *Gehirn, Verhalten und Zeit: Philosophische Anthropologie als Forschungsrahmen* (Berlin: Akademie Verlag, 2010).

73. Research investigations are genuine historical undertakings which change the relationship between questions and answers. On the critique of the geographical model of exploration, cf. Nicholas Rescher, *Rationalität, Wissenschaft und Praxis* (Würzburg: Königshausen and Neumann, 2002), p. 67ff.

74. Plessner, *Die Stufen des Organischen und der Mensch*, p. 270. This lack has also been confirmed in the language experiments with chimpanzees in the last decade. They do not go beyond the level which human children reach in their third year. As a follow up to Michael Tomasello cf. Krüger, *Gehirn, Verhalten und Zeit*, chap. 3.

75. For more details cf. Hans-Peter Krüger, "Die Antwortlichkeit in der exzentrischen Positionalität: Die Drittheit, das Dritte und die dritte Person als philosophische Minima," *Philosophische Anthropologie im 21. Jahrhundert*, pp. 164–83.

76. Plessner, *Die Stufen des Organischen und der Mensch,* p. 340.

77. Plessner, "Macht und menschliche Natur," p. 225.

ABOUT THE CONTRIBUTORS

Rosa M. Calcaterra lectures in Theoretical Philosophy and Philosophy of Knowledge at Roma Tre University. She is President of Associazione Pragma, Director of the Interuniversity Research Center "Pragmatism, Knowledge Construction and Education," and General Editor of the *European Journal of Pragmatism and American Philosophy*. She has edited collections of international studies including *New Perspectives on Pragmatism and Analytic Philosophy* (2011) and published a number of books and articles among others: *Idee concrete. Percorsi nella filosofia di John Dewey* (*Concrete Ideas: Paths in John Dewey's Philosophy*, 2011), *Pragmatismo: i valori dell'esperienza. Letture di Peirce, James e Mead* (*Pragmatism: The Values of Experience. Reading Peirce, James and Mead*, 2003), *Introduzione al pragmatismo americano* (*Introduction to American Pragmatim*, 1997), *Interpretare l'esperienza. Scienza, etica, metafisica nel pensiero di Ch. S. Peirce* (*Interpreting Experience: Science, Ethics and Metaphysics in Ch. S. Peirce's Thought*, 1989).

Adam J. Chmielewski is a scholar writer, translator, social activist and political columnist for Polish and international media. He studied in Wrocław, Oxford, New York and Edinburgh. He is Professor of Philosophy in the Institute of Philosophy at the University of Wrocław, Poland. In 2010–2012 he was the director of the Institution of culture Wroclaw 2016 and the author of the successful bid of the city of Wroclaw for the title of the European Capital of Culture 2016. He is the Editor-in-Chief of the quarterly *Studia Philosophica Wratislaviensia*. He has published several books in Polish, among them *Niewspółmierność, nieprzekładalność, konflikt* (*Incommensurability, Untranslatability, Conflict*, 1997, 2014) *Społeczeństwo otwarte czy wspólnota* (*Open Society or Community?* 2001), *Dwie koncepcje jedności* (*Two Concept of Unity*, 1996), and *Psychopatologia życia politycznego* (*Psychopathology of Political Life*, 2009)

Robert Dobrowolski is Adjunct Professor at the University School of Physical Education, Wroclaw. His current research focuses on the body in modern and post-modern culture. He has published on contemporary aesthetics and somaesthetics, with a particular focus on psychoanalytical and phenomenological perspectives. He is the author of a number of articles on aesthetics and contemporary culture, including "Sampling No(body)" (in *Shusterman's Pragmatism. Between Literature and Somaesthetics*, 2012).

Leszek Koczanowicz is Professor of Philosophy and Political Science at Wroclaw Faculty of the University of Social Sciences and Humanities. He specializes in political philosophy, social theory, philosophical psychology, and cultural aspects of politics. His previous appointments include Wroclaw

University, SUNY/Buffalo (1998–1999 and 2000–2001), Columbia University (2004–2005), and SUNY/Geneseo (2013). He is the author and editor of eight books and numerous articles in Polish and English, including *Politics of Time: Dynamics of Identity in Post-Communist Poland* (2008), and *Nowoczesny lęk. Eseje o demokracji i jej adwersarzach* (*Modern Fear: Essays on Democracy and its Adversaries*, 2011).

Hans-Peter Krüger is the Chair for Political Philosophy and Philosophical Anthropology and the Director of the Philosophy Department at the University of Potsdam, Germany. After Fellowships at the University of California at Berkeley (1989), the Wissenschaftskolleg zu Berlin (Institute for Advanced Study, 1990–91), and the University of Pittsburgh, PA (1992–93), he was Visiting Professor at the Jagiellonian University, Kraków, Poland (2002–03), the University of Vienna, Austria (2003), and Ernst Cassirer Professor at the Swedish Collegium for Advanced Studies in Uppsala, Sweden (2005–06). His research includes philosophical anthropology, classical pragmatism and neo-pragmatism, and social philosophy. He is one of the Editors of the *German Journal of Philosophy*. His most recent publications include monographs: *Philosophische Anthropologie als Lebenspolitik. Deutsch-jüdische und pragmatistische Moderne-Kritik* (*Philosophical Anthropology as Life Politics: German-Jewish and Pragmatist Critiques of Modernity*, 2009), *Gehirn, Verhalten und Zeit. Philosophische Anthropologie als Forschungsrahmen* (*Brain, Behaviour, and Time: The Research Framework of Philosophical Anthropology*, 2010), and *Heroismus und Arbeit in der Entstehung der Hegelschen Philosophie* (*Heroism and Labour in the Origin of Hegel's Philosophy*, 2014).

Katarzyna Liszka studied philosophy and cultural studies at the University of Wrocław, from which she received a Ph.D. with a dissertation on the consequences and meaning of the Shoah for ethics and anthropology. She has published on contemporary ethics and philosophy, focusing particularly on the Holocaust and the Jewish philosophy. She is the author of numerous articles and translations, and co-editor of two books *Lektury postrukturalistyczne* (*The Postructuralist Readings*, 2007), and *Kultura demokracji* (*The Culture of Democracy*, 2009). Her most recent work is *Etyka i pamięć po Zagładzie* (*Ethics and Memory after the Shoah*, 2014, forthcoming).

Sami Pihlström is Professor of Practical Philosophy at the University of Jyväskylä, Finland, and the Director of the Helsinki Collegium for Advanced Studies at the University of Helsinki (2009–2014). He is the author of several books and numerous articles on pragmatism, metaphysics, ethics, the philosophy of religion, and transcendental philosophy. His recent monographs include *Pragmatist Metaphysics* (2009), *Transcendental Guilt* (2011), and *Pragmatic Pluralism and the Problem of God* (2013).

Michael Rings is a Ph.D. candidate in the Department of Philosophy at Indiana University, Bloomington. His research focuses on aesthetic cosmopolitanism, the ethics of authenticity, and the philosophy of popular music. He is currently working on a dissertation addressing the ethical, political, and aesthetic issues that arise in contexts of cross-cultural art appreciation, media consumption, and aesthetic self-cultivation. He explores these issues through the theoretical lens of philosophical cosmopolitanism, considering how they would be successfully negotiated by the virtuous "aesthetic cosmopolitan." His most recent work is "Doing It Their Way: Rock Covers, Genre, and Appreciation," published in *The Journal of Aesthetics and Art Criticism* (2013).

John Ryder is Professor of Philosophy and Provost at the American University of Ras Al Khaimah, United Arab Emirates. He is the editor of *American Philosophic Naturalism in the 20th Century* (1994), co-editor, with Armen T. Marsoobian, of *The Blackwell Guide to American Philosophy* (2002), and co-editor, with Scott Pratt, of *The Philosophical Writings of Cadwallader Colden* (2002). He is also the co-founder and co-chair, with Emil Višňovský, of the Central European Pragmatist Forum (CEPF), and co-editor of five volumes of selected papers from CEPF conferences. He is the author of *The Things in Heaven and Earth: An Essay in Pragmatic Naturalism* (2013) and *Interpreting America: Russian and Soviet Studies of the History of American Thought* (1999).

David Schauffler studied at Oberlin College, New York University and Nicholas Copernicus University in Toruń, Poland, from which he received a Ph.D. in philosophy with a dissertation on the writings of Herbert Marcuse. He works in the Institute of English Language Cultures and Literatures at the University of Silesia, Katowice, Poland, and has published numerous articles in the fields of social philosophy, cultural theory, and American literature.

Richard Shusterman is the Dorothy F. Schmidt Eminent Scholar in the Humanities at Florida Atlantic University (Boca Raton) and Director of its Center for Body, Mind, and Culture. A graduate of the Hebrew University of Jerusalem (B.A. and M.A.) and Oxford University (D. Phil.), he has held academic appointments in France, Germany, Israel, Japan, Italy, and China, and has been awarded research grants from the National Endowment for the Humanities, the Fulbright Commission, the American Council for Learned Societies, the Humboldt Foundation, and UNESCO. His research in somaesthetics is nourished by his work as a certified somatic educator in the Feldenkrais Method. The author of *Body Consciousness* (2008) and *Thinking through the Body: Essays in Somaesthetics* (2012), he has also written *Surface and Depth* (2002), *Performing Live* (2000), *Practicing Philosophy* (1997), and *Pragmatist Aesthetics* (1992, 2000, translated into fourteen languages) as well as other books.

Emil Višňovský is Professor of Philosophy at Comenius University and Senior Research Fellow at the Slovak Academy of Sciences in Bratislava, Slovakia. He is the co-Chair of the Central-European Pragmatist Forum (since 2000), the Editor-in-chief of international postdisciplinary journal *Human Affairs* (since 2002, published in English by Springer) and the editor of the book series *Central European Value Studies* published by the international publisher Rodopi (since 2006). He has published on the pragmatist art of living. His latest books include *Štúdie o pragmatizme & neopragmatizme* (*Studies in Pragmatism and Neopragmatism,* 2009), *Človek ako Homoagens* (*Human Being as Homo Agens*, 2009), *Človek by mal žiť v záhrade* (*Human Being Should Live in the Garden*, 2010). He is the co-author and editor of several other books and numerous articles on philosophy published in Slovak, English, and other languages (Czech, Polish, Italian, Turkish, Russian).

INDEX

VIBS

The **Value Inquiry Book Series** is co-sponsored by:

Titles Published